TEMPLES OF SOUTH INDIA

About the Author

J. Ramanaiah is a teacher of long standing and is connected with various educational and cultural organisations. He visited almost all the important temples in India from Kanyakumari to Kashmir. He got his M.A degree in History from the Osmania University, Hyderabad in 1963. In the midst of his teaching career, he joined as a research scholar in the Central University of Hyderabad under Faculty Improvement programme of the University Grants Commission, Government of India, New Delhi. He was awarded M. Phil. degree with distinction in 1983 and obtained his Ph.D. degree in History from the University in 1988. At present he is working as a senior Lecturer in History at S.K.N.R. Government Degree College Jagtial, district Karimnagar, Andhra Pradesh.

TEMPLES OF SOUTH INDIA

(A Study of Hindu, Jain and Buddhist Monuments of the Deccan)

J. Ramanaiah

CONCEPT PUBLISHING COMPANY PVT. LTD.
NEW DELHI-110059

ISBN : 978-81-7022-223-1

Edition 2020

Published and Printed by

Concept
Since 1974

Concept Publishing Company Pvt. Ltd.
A/15-16, Commercial Block, Mohan Garden,
New Delhi-110059 (INDIA)
T : +91 11 25351460, +91 11 25351794
E : publishing@conceptpub.com, *W* : www.conceptpub.com

By grace of
Lord Raja Rajesvara of Vemulavada
dedicated to
my beloved parents
Jaisetty Shivanandam, Gangu Bai.

Foreword

I have great pleasure in introducing the present work to the world of scholars. It incorporates a comprehensive study of the temples of Karimnagar district in Andhra Pradesh. The district of Karimnagar, though very rich in archaeological sites, discovery of artifacts and architectural monuments bearing sculptural beauty and elegance, hitherto remained ignored for any scholarly study. The work of Dr. J. Ramanaiah fulfils this vacuum and throws extensive light and projections on varied unexplored areas of historical and cultural significance. It bears the stamp of his originality and scholarship in dealing with the subject matter. The work based on a multiple of original and secondary sources, is the first of its kind in survey, subject-matter, treatment and interpretation.

The author did vigorous field work to identify the Hindu, Buddhist and Jain monuments as well as in discovering the relevant epigraphs of the area under study, during his tenure as a research scholar in the university of Hyderabad under the Faculty Improvement Programme of the University Grants Commission, Government of India, New Delhi.

The first two chapters are introductory, while the third one vividly describes the sites of the temples and thus forms the nucleus of the study. The rest of the chapters deal with the architectural and sculptural features of the monuments, the role played by the different religious sects in the growth and development of these monuments and bring out the role of the temple as a socio-cultural institution as well as the concomitant economic functions of the temple. A lively picture of the polity, society and economy of the period has been drawn on the basis of a deeper analysis of the data. Thus the present work has attempted to provide a total pageantry of the period under study.

The work, while bringing out the countrywide similarity in most of the sculptural pieces and architecture, has also projected the regional distinctiveness in the art forms and styles of architecture. Thus it provides the readers with an encyclopaedic information on all aspects of the temples in Karimnagar district.

I congratulate Dr. J. Ramanaiah for this distinction in research and have no doubt to state that none else could do justice to such a comprehensive study.

Dr. Tej Ram Sharma
Professor of History
School of Social Sciences
University of Hyderabad
Hyderabad - 500134

Hyderabad
Dated: 16.6.1988

Acknowledgements

It gives me immense pleasure to express my profound gratitude to Professor Tej Ram Sharma, Department of History, University of Hyderabad for writing the foreword to this book. Professor Sharma took all pains to visit the temples at Dharmapuri, a remote place in the Karimnagar district of Andhra Pradesh and made a primary study of the historical potentiality of this region. After getting convinced of the fact that this region would yield some tangible results, he initiated me to take-up the present work, which is prepared under his affectionate care, valuable instruction and thorough guidance from time to time.

I am highly indebted to the Director of Higher Education, Government of Andhra Pradesh, Hyderabad and the University Grants Commission of Government of India, New Delhi for providing me an opportunity to do my Ph. D. in the Central University of Hyderabad under Teacher Fellowship and Faculty Improvement Programme.

It is my pleasant duty to express my gratefulness to all those friends, who accompanied me in my toilsome tours to the temple sites and some times walked with me for half a day or more along the inconvenient and inaccessible tracks both in cold and hot seasons. They have been very helpful in taking the photographs and measurements of the temples.

I visited all the temples and many of them three to four times to make a thorough study. Wherever I went I was received well by my old students, colleagues, friends and the temple priests. Hundreds of villagers and townsmen of Karimnagar district have placed me in their debt. I should not forget the friendliness, exhuberant welcome and spontaneous help and hospitality, I received from them during my itineraries.

In the course of writing this book, I have consulted several books and articles, written by many scholars on art and architecture. I acknowledge with gratitude that I have liberally used their material with the idea that the knowledge is for propagation. All these books and articles have been enumerated in the bibliography at the end of the book.

Finally I would like to record that my wife Varalakshmi has always been spiritual support to me. She kept me free from all household botherations. Without her sustained and intimate collaboration and assistance of immense value, my humble endeavour could not have achieved a concrete shape. I express my deepest appreciation to my daughters Revathi and Uma Rani, Sons-in-law A. Ashok and J. Ramu and Sons Raja Shekhar and Rajender, who helped me in many ways in the preparation of the present work.

I take the opportunity to express my sincere thanks to all those, who extended me their unstinted co-operation and help in making this project a success.

Finally I would like to thank Shri Naurang Rai Ji and his son Shri Ashok Kumar of Concept Publishing Company, New Delhi for publishing it with the beautiful getup.

Dr. J. Ramanaiah

H. No. 2-5-24
Shiva Veedhi
Jagtial - 505327
Dist. Karimnagar (A.P.)

Contents

LIST OF PLATES

Preface

The present work incorporates a full length and comprehensive study of the temples in Karimnagar district (Andhra Pradesh), built during the reign of the Chalukyas of Vemulavada, the Western Chalukyas of Kalyani and the Kakatiyas of Warangal.

The Karimnagar district, by virtue of its proximity to the river Godavari, has been the cradle of culture through centuries, dating back to the early dim phases of the dawn of history. The recent archaeological operations at Dhulikatta. Peddabankur and Kotilingala have thrown ample light on the history of the Satavahanas in the district. Yet the district has not been sufficiently explored from the research point of view by any scholar for the study of the temples, which are of great architectural and artistic value. This region is historically potential and the present work is an attempt at a thorough and expository study mainly based on the epigraphs and an on-the-spot investigation of all the Buddhist, Jain and Hindu religious edifices in various aspects viz., historical, structural, sculptural, religious, social, economic and cultural. The results of my continuous study and researches are precisely presented in the present work, which, I am sure, will help in understanding the temple monuments in their true perspective.

Curiously enough Karimnagar District is studded with numerous magnificent temples, big and small, rich in variety and splendour. So far no authentic work has been done on these temples, hence the need for the present work.

As a teacher, I had the privilege of taking the students on educational tours a number of times from Cape Camorin to Kashmir and the whole of the Himalayan region including Nepal. The inspiration drawn from the great temples of various places, prompted me to study the temples of my own region with a specific area of Karimnagar district, which is as important as any other part of the country.

About eighty inscriptions in all were copied in the Karimnagar district and they were compiled and published in a book in the year 1974, by the Department of Archaeology and Museums, Hyderabad. Most of them are found in Sanskrit, Kannada and Telugu languages. All these epigraphs noticed in and around the temple monuments have still remained as bare historical facts and no historian has so far attempted to give them due interpretation. The epigraphic evidences cannot speak themselves, unless a historian makes them speak. In the words of E.H. Carr "History is nothing but a continuous process of interaction between the historian and his facts, an unending dialogue between the present and past".

It is desirable to mention that the texts of all these epigraphs speak of the glorious past of the district, which was ruled successively by various dynasties namely the Chalukyas of Vemulavada, the Western Chalukyas of Kalyani and the Kakatiyas of Warangal besides the local rulers known as the Polavasa Chiefs. The beginning of the temple building activity in the district may be traced back to the period of the Chalukyas of Vemulavada (A.D.750-973), who ushered in the practice of building with lasting materials especially in dressed stone and brick. The architecture of Karimnagar district was essentially a product of the soil and whatever touched it in its long course of development practically grew into it, giving it new form and vigour in each successive phase. It was in religious architecture that the genius of the builders of this region played an important role in creating, developing and perfecting number of significant forms.

The important sculptural panels which form inseparable part of various existing monuments have been often discussed to make the study more comprehensive. At the same time the parallels and comparisons have been drawn from other early art producing centres of the country so as to present a coherent story of the full development of the sculpture in this region.

During the course of my visits to the temple sites two unpublished inscriptions of the Kakatiya period have been noticed one at Nagunuru and the other at Raikal which have been noted in the Appendix. An additional list of the other minor temples is also given in the Appendix for favour of information. I felt the need of glossary because a few Telugu terms found in the epigraphs have been occasionally used. I would like to mention humbly that the dia-critical marks have not been followed in the present work.

The book consists of eight chapters. The first chapter is an introduction while the second chapter gives the historical background of the district. The third chapter is most important in the sense that it forms the nucleus of this work by providing us a detailed description of the temples on various sites. The ground plans and elevations of a few early temples are also exhibited in this chapter. The fourth and the fifth chapters deal with the significant features of architecture and sculpture respectively, while the sixth and seventh chapters throw fresh light on the temple as a religious and socio-cultural institution with its multifarious activities catering to the needs of the people. The last chapter deals with the economic role of the temple, its feudal character, sources of income, development of agriculture, remission of taxes to the temple, method of taxation, trade around the temple, coins, weights and measures, which were in vogue during the period and several other important aspects.

Thus a sincere and humble attempt is made to focus the predominant role of the temple in the day to day life of the common man during the early medieval period.

Jagtial
Date 17-6-1988

J. RAMANAIAH

Abbreviations

APGKD	:	Andhra Pradesh Gazetteer, Karimnagar District.
ARDAM	:	Annual Report of the Department of Archaeology and Museums A.P.
ARE	:	Annual Report on Epigraphy.
ASI	:	Archaeological Survey of India.
CORPUS	:	Corpus of Inscriptions in Telingana Districts.
EA	:	Epigraphia Andhrica.
EHD	:	Early History of the Deccan, Vol. I & II Ed. Dr. G. Yazdani
EHI	:	Elements of Hindu Iconography, by T.A. Gopinatha Rao.
HAS	:	Hyderabad Archaeological Series.
HSI	:	History of South India, by K.A. Nilakanta Sastry.
IAPKD	:	Inscriptions of Andhra Pradesh, Karimnagar District.
IAPWD	:	Inscription of Andhra Pradesh, Warangal District.
JAHRS	:	Journal of Andhra Historical Research Society.
RE	:	Report on Epigraphy.
SII.	:	South Indian Inscriptions.

ONE

Introduction

Karimnagar district, selected for the study of the temples, was once a thriving centre of cultural and religious activity containing several structural temples of exceptional beauty and outstanding merit. These temples form a magnificent group exhibiting the influence of both the Chalukyas and Kakatiyas in their architectural features. The Chalukyas of Vemulavada, the Western Chalukyas of Kalyani and Kakatiyas of Warangal who ruled over this district from mid-eighth century A.D. to the early fourteenth century A.D. were fond of architecture and their buildings are characterized by a breadth of vision and loftiness of spirit on the one hand and superior craftsmanship on the other. The majority of these temples are dedicated to Siva, but some belong to the Vaishnavite cult, while the numbers of fanes built by Jains is not inconsiderable.

Name and Location of the District:

The district derived its name from Karimnagar, its headquarters town, founded by Syed Karimuddin, the quiladar of Elgandal fort which was controlled by the Asaf Jahis of Hyderabad.[1]

Karimnagar district is located between 17°-50' and 19°-5' of the northern latitudes and 78°-29' and 80°-22' of the eastern longitudes.[2] The district is bounded on the north by Adilabad district, on the west by Nizamabad district, on the south by Medak and Warangal districts, on the east by Bastar district of Madhya Pradesh and on the north-east by Chanda district of Maharashtra State. The district covers an area of 4582 square miles.[3] Karimnagar town is connected by fairly good roads to Hyderabad, Warangal and Nizamabad. The state highway from Hyderabad to Balharshah passes through Karimnagar and Peddapalli taluks touching the district headquarters. The Kazipet-Balharshah railway line passes through the district though it does not connect the district headquarters town.

Karimnagar district forms the northern part of Telingana in Andhra Pradesh State and lies to the south of river Godavari. By virtue of its proximity to the mighty river Godavari, the district has been the cradle of culture and civilization through centuries dating back to the early dim phases of the dawn of history.

The Changes in the component parts of the district:

Karimnagar district was originally known as Elgandal district with headquarters at Elgandal, a place about six kilometers from Karimnagar. In A.D. 1897[4] it constituted nine taluks viz. Chinnur, Jagtial, Jammikunta, Karimnagar, Lakshettipet, Mahadevpuram, Siddipet, Sircilla, and Sultanabad. During the reorganisation of the districts in the erstwhile Hyderabad State in 1905, the district headquarters was shifted from Elgandal to Karimnagar and three taluks namely Lakshettipet, Chinnur and Siddipet were transferred from this district to the neighbouring districts of Adilabad and Medak. But Parkal taluk was added to this district from Warangal district thereby constituting in all seven taluks. No important changes were effected till 1913, when the headquarters of the taluk was shifted from Jammikunta to Huzurabad.[5] In 1950 when the Jagirs were integrated, Metpalli, independent sub-taluk was constituted raising the total number of taluks to eight. Again in 1953 at the time of the formation of Khammam district, Parkal taluk was transferred back to Warangal district leaving only seven taluks for Karimnagar district namely Metpalli, Jagtial, Sircilla, Karimnagar, Huzurabad, Sultanabad and Manthani. Since then the district has not undergone any changes until 1979, when the Government of Andhra Pradesh accorded the status of a taluk to each Panchayat Samithi in the state. Thus all the fourteen Panchayat Samithis in the district are converted into taluks namely Metpalli, Jagtial, Mallial, Vemulavada, Sircilla, Gangadhara, Karimnagar, Husunabad, Bhimdeverpalli, Huzurabad, Sultanabad, Peddapalli, Manthani and Mahadevpur.

These taluks were grouped under three revenue divisions namely Karimnagar, Jagtial and Peddapalli. The Karimnagar revenue division contains five taluks namely Karimnagar, Gangadhara, Husunabad, Bhimdeverpalli, and Huzurabad. The Jagtial revenue division also contains five taluks namely Jagtial, Metpalli, Mallial, Vemulavada and Sircilla, whereas Peddapalli, revenue division has only foui taluks namely Peddapalli, Sultanabad, Manthani and Mahadevpur.

The Physical features of the district:

The history of the area is in large measure influenced by its geography. The hills, forests and rivers play an important role in shaping and moulding the culture and character of the people. There are indeed no mountains except three important hill ranges in the district. The first range of hills commencing at Gurrapalli in Metpalli taluk runs in a north-easterly direction as far as Jagtial and then proceeds to Vemalkurthi near the Godavari. A second range of hills popularly known as the Sanigaram range proceeds from Sanigaram and Mallangur parallel to the former range at a distance of about 50 kilometres. The third range in the south-west corner of the district starts from the maner river valley, runs in a north-easterly direction and passes beyond Ramagiri intersecting the Sanigaram range. This range ends near the river Godavari.[6]

Besides the above hill ranges, there are many isolated hills throughout the district which were used for the construction of forts ad temples during the medieval period. Some prominent hills in the district afforded in historical times excellent natural strongholds and some, therefore, have been converted into hill-forts. Elgandal, Mallangur, Ramagiri and Pratapagiri are the best examples of medieval hill forts in the district. The hills and hillocks were also source of inspiration for the people to construct temples on their tops. The important temples that stand on the hills are at Bejjenki, Ramagiri, Kothagattu, Kothakonda, Nampalli, Nallagonda, Beerpur, Mallapur, Valgonda, Vellulla and Dumpeta. The Tribhuvanatilaka Jaina basadi of tenth century A.D. also existed on a hillock called Bommalagutta near Kurkiyala village.[7]

Rivers:

River Godavari, the largest in peninsular India, rises in the western Ghats at Triambak near Nasik in Maharashtra state and enters Andhra Pradesh near Basar in Adilabad district. The gigantic river enters Karimnagar district near Kandukurti in Metpalli taluk and forms the northern and eastern boundaries of the district separating it from Adilabad district. It flows for about 283 kilometres in the district and separates Chanda in Maharashtra state and Bastar area in Madhya Pradesh from Karimnagar district.[8] The Godavari flowing inside the deep river banks was not useful for the purpose of irrigation. It appears that this river was never a barrier to the movement of the prehistoric and early historic people of this area as similar stone age tools and common cultures of megalithic and early historical period are found on either side of this river.[9] Like all the rivers in India, the Godavari is also deemed as the most sacred river in this area and beautiful temples were erected all along its southern bank in the district. The holy temples that stand on the banks of Godavari are at Valgonda, Vempalli, Dharmapuri, Thimmapur, Kotilingala, Jangaon, Sundella, Kasipeta, Manthani and Kalesvaram.

The river Maner, a tributary to the Godavari originating near Kalkur, traverses through Karimnagar district from west to east as far as Karlagunta in Manthani taluk, then flows towards the north and joins the Godavari near Venkatapur and Damarlakunta villages in Manthani taluk.[10] It flows for about 230 kilometres in the district and forms an important source of irrigation. Moyatummedavagu, Nagunuruvagu, and Vemulavadavagu are the rivulets that join the Maner. The temples that stand on its banks are at Neerakulla in Sultanabad taluk, Chandravelli and Adavi Somanapalli in Manthani taluk.

Peddavagu, Chinnavagu and Bokkalavagu are the other direct tributaries that flow in this district and join the Godavari. These rivulets also sustained ancient cultures in this region from times immemorial.[11] The streams, rivulets, lakes and tanks afforded the most beautiful and sacred spots for temple building in this area.

Geology and Minerals:

Human culture is closely related to geology. Architecture, which is one of the principal expressions of man's culture, is greatly determined by the Physiography of the place. The history of architecture in Karimnagar district by no means is an exception. Geologically this district can be divided into two parts. The western part consisting of the peninsular granite complex with minor bands of Dharwarian rocks and the eastern portion comprising the purana sedimentaries The Dharwars occur in a narrow belt of 10 to 32 kilometres wide in parts of Karimnagar, Peddapalli and Jagtial taluks.[12] The major portion of the district is composed of the peninsular granite, the colour of which depended upon the felspars contained in them.[13] It is considered that the grey granites are older than the pink. Numerous dykes of dolerite cluster in parts of Peddapalli, Jagtial, Sircilla and Karimnagar taluks. The Puranas cover the portions of Peddapalli and Manthani taluks. In the area of north-east of Ramagundam the Sullavais rest directly on the granites. The Gondwana rocks cover the eastern parts of the district including Manthani and certain portions of Peddapalli taluk.[14]

The granites, dolerites, quartzites and sandstones occuring in the district can be used for the purposes of construction.[15] The temple architecture in Karimnagar district is closely related to the rocks of this area because the temples were constructed mostly with the stone quarried locally. It was also economical to use the local stone. The temples of Nagunuru were constructed with local red sandstone during the period of Kakatiyas. The sandstone of Nagunuru is so fine and qualitative that the large blocks of stone, quarried from the local hills, are now being exported to the countries like Korea and Japan. Generally speaking the material wrought by the Chalukyas and Kakatiyas is soft rock such as sandstone, trap or similar material. Such soft material could be easily quarried in large blocks, and the same could be worked to some extent on the quarry site itself. The roughly finished product could be transported over long distances for final erection and finish. Secondly it contributed to the destiny and lavishness of sculpture and decoration.

An interesting aspect of Hindu religious architecture in Karimnagar district is the existence of rock cut cave temples at Adavisomanapalli in Manthani taluk. These shrines are hewn out of the living sandstone rock on the right bank of river Maner. The existing huge soft rock was properly used by the architects of these shrines, earlier to the advent of the Western Chalukyas in this region. Outwardly these caves look like the caves of Undavalli, near Vijayawada.[16] Dr. N.S. Ramachandra Murthy assigned these caves to 7th - 8th centuries A.D. on stylistic grounds owing to their resemblance with the Akkanna-Madanna caves near Vijayawada.[17]

The Artists have made use of the faces of some of the boulders existing on the hills and carved on them the figures of Hindu and Jain faiths. The nude Jain figures are found at Nagunuru, Sanigaram, Nampalli, and Bommalagutta. A Bhairava image is carved on a huge boulder on the hills of Bejjenki. These boulders were also used for carving inscriptions. The label inscriptions in Brahmi characters are found on Munulagutta facing the Godavari near Kapparraopet. A lengthy inscription[18] of tenth century AD. is incised on a huge boulder of Bommalagutta near Kurkiyala village in Gangadhara taluk.

In certain cases the large rock surfaces are used for the temple construction as they need no foundation. Such temples are found at Thimmapur, Pothgal, Neerakulla and Elkaturti. There are many occurances of magnetic quartz rocks in Jagtial taluk. The iron content of those rocks is 35 to 40 per cent. The iron ore was collected and smelted at Rangapet and Konapur in Jagtial taluk. The iron ores turned into fine steel known as wootz at the famous steel producing centres like Elgandal, Ibrahimpatnam and Rangapet in Karimnagar district and Konasamudram in Armur taluk of Nizamabad district attracted the traders from Rome, Damascus and Persia during the early historical period.[19] Lime stone is also abundantly available at Basantnagar near Ramagundam and Nerella near Jagtial.

Prehistory of the District:

The district of Karimnagar abounds in several prehistoric sites. The unique situation of the district to the south of the Godavari helped its people to play their part in shaping and unifying the people of different cultures in and around the Godavari valley from prehistoric to modern times. Early and middle stone age artefacts like hand-axes and flake-scrapers were reported by L. Munn from Allur and Jangoan villages in Peddapalli taluk.[20] In recent years Thakur Rajaram Singh of Sultanabad had explored many Early,

Middle and Late stone age sites in the district.[21] Late stone age or upper palaeolithic sites are noticed at Bugga around a spring at the foothills of Takkellapalli range, Devunipalli, Rachapalli, Vemnur, Buchayyapalli, Narsampalli and Sabbitam village facing the Gourigundam water falls.[22]

Neolithic Sites:

As in other parts of India, Karimnagar district was also a favourite haunt of the Neolithic man. The physiographical and geological features have considerably contributed to the establishment of Neolithic settlements in Karimnagar district. Some of the rock-shelters noticed at Regonda, Budigapalli and Kadambapur in the vicinity of the Neolithic settlements, must have been utilised by them. Occasionally Neolithic axes were collected around late stone age sites and sometimes in the vicinity of megalithic burials, but permanent settlements are very few. The recently discovered settlements are at Thogarrai and Kadambapur both on the northern bank of river Maner in Sultanabad taluk, Peddabankur in Peddapalli taluk and Budigapalli in Husunabad taluk. A Neolithic factory site was also discovered at Thogarrai over a granitic out crop. The Collection included a large number of unfinished tools besides a good number of finished adzes and axes.[23] Many Neolithic stone axes were collected from Peddabankur. Apparently the tools must have been imported from places like Kadambapur and Thogarrai which are at a distance of about 8 kms. from here. Peddabankur is an example where the Neolithic man, instead of selecting a hilly region, settled over the plains possibly to serve his farming needs.[24] At Budigapalli, the granite hills, the rock shelters and nullah emanating from the hills and now crossbunded for supplying water to a huge lake, were suited for a Neolithic settlement. Explorations over the early historical mound, girdled by a medieval mud rampart at the foothills of Valasagattu, yielded Neolithic stone axes besides early historical pottery.[25] Flakes, cores and artefacts belonging to Neolithic culture, were also noticed at Gunjapadige in Manthani taluk, Parlapalli and Koheda in Husunabad taluk, Sanigaram in Huzurabad taluk and Vemulavada in Vemulavada taluk.[26] Neolithic artefacts, polished stone axes are also found at Jangoan and Allur in Peddapalli taluk.[27]

Megalithic Culture:

The existence of Megalithic culture was revealed by the discovery of burials found in stone circles with a cist in the middle at Singapur, Thummanapalli, Chilpur and Sirisipalli in Huzurabad taluk, Budigapalli in Husunabad taluk, Kadambapur in Sultanabad taluk, Nampalli in Vemulavada taluk and Wastapur in Jagtial taluk and many more similar sites may be found in other parts of th district. The location and type of the Megalithic burials depended upon the geological and geographical conditions. They are usually found in the neighbourhood of hillocks and over rocky high grounds unfit for cultivation. Singapur situated at a distance of 6 kilometres from Huzurabad contains about 50 stone circles by roadside at the foot of the hillock. Budigapalli, a small village about 6 kms. from Husunabad is surrounded by a ring of hills locally known as Valasagattu, Sanjivarayanigattu and Venkayagattu. At the base of Sanjivarayanigattu is a huge megalithic burial complex consisting only of cist burials, most of which are damaged.[28] At Kadamobapur a huge burial complex consisting of more than 500 burials perched on the western and eastern slopes of the hills is found. The river Maner is abutting the burial complex to the south. Five burials were excavated by the Andhra Pradesh Department of Archaeology and Museums.[29] There are six burials intact at Thummanapalli and about fifty at Sirisipalli in Huzurabad taluk.

The Magalithic burials yielded a large variety of antiquities such as pottery, iron objects, ornaments like beads of terracotta, semi-precious stones, gold, copper etc. The pottery consisted mainly of the black and red, the black polished, red polished and coarse red wares. It is interesting to note that rock paintings consisting of horses with riders are noticed at Budigapalli and Regonda in Husunabad taluk.

Early Historical Culture:

As in the other parts of the country, the early historical period succeeded the Megalithic period in this district. The Department of Archaeology and Museums of the State of Andhra Pradesh conducted large scale excavations at Peddabankur near Peddapalli during the years 1968-1974. Later another important early historical site near Dhulikatta was excavated. At present the site at Kotilingala is being excavated. Dr. V.V. Krishna Sastry under whose supervision the sites were excavated opines that the Karimnagar region is marked by a number of early historical sites almost in every alternate village.[30] It is really puzzling to find why they are mainly concentrated in this area. It is likely that the political nucleus of the whole or the part of Deccan might have been situated in this region; secondly the population during the Satavahana period must have increased manifold; thirdly it might be a commercially important region traversed by the ancient trade routes; and lastly agriculture being the main occupation, they found the black soil plain congenial.[31]

The mounds with early historical pottery such as red polished, black and red, coarse red and large number of brickbats are also noticed at Chinnabankur, Vemnur, Kachapur, Bodagutta, Bompalli, Rachapalli, Paidichintalapalli, Khadeemkanagarti and several other places.

The excavations conducted at Peddabankur near Peddapalli revealed many brick structures, cisterns and wells besides an array of antiquities such as pottery, iron, copper and terracotta objects. Numerous Satavahana coins were collected.[32] A terracotta seal inscribed as "VIJAYAPURA HARA KASA RATHASA" and a Roman silver coin are also found.[33]

Dhulikatta, a corrupt form of Dhuli Kota, which literally means a mud fort revealed in excavations a palace complex and the residential quarters. Lime plaster is used for walls while the floors had lime concrete and occasionally brick layings. There is a mud rampart of 5 mt. height around the palace complex. A beautiful ivory button seal inscribed with Brahmi characters datable to 2nd century A.D. is recovered from excavations. It reads as "AJANISIRIYA GAME KUMARIYA".[34]

The site at Kotilingala is under excavation. As at Dhulikatta, the mound at Kotilingala is also encompassed by a mud fort with several gates. The visitors can notice the Satavahana bricks, mostly used by the local villagers for the construction of their houses. On the way to Munulagutta from Kotilingala a few label inscriptions in Brahmi

Characters of 2nd century B.C. are noticed.[35] On a sand stone pillar now lying in the fields contains a label inscription incised as "NAGAGOPINIKAYA" datable to 1st century A.D.

The early historical settlers in the Karimnagar region had attained a very high degree of civilization having fortified towns, palatial buildings, sewage, well-laid out roads and good water supply. Most of the towns and villages were raised in the middle of arable lands. Peddabankur was a Satavahana village, but Dhulikatta promised to be a walled town of Andhras.

Early religious Architecture and Objects :-

None of the sites excavated or explored in the district gave an evidence of the temples of Brahmanical origin. A single brick cell, appeared like a temple without giving us any knowledge as to what deity it was dedicated to. The brick temple[36] measured 5.30 x 4.50 mt. The evidence is, however, not clear in the absence of a deity. The religious beliefs still centred round the local primitive forms of worship and rituals. The early inhabitants believed in village gods and goddesses, tree and serpent cults and probably practised the worship of spirits. The worship of serpent (Naga cult) is attested by a figure of a snake made of iron from Peddabankur.[37] A terracotta sealing of Gajalakshmi datable to around 1st century B.C. is noticed in the excavations at Peddabankur. The goddess is shown standing naked in a Lotus pool and being bathed by two elephants with pails in the trunks.[38]

The excavations have yielded the archaic terracotta female figurines of Mother Goddess. The cult of Mother Goddess of great antiquity is represented by a nude Goddess sitting with legs apart; the figurines are reported from Yelesvaram, Nagarjunakonda and Kondapur. It had great popularity among the urban as well as rural populace.[39]

The Mother Goddesses of Peddabankur are hand made with protruded and pointed breasts and the hands depicted like pointed masses.[40] One figurine is shown with out-stretched hands and arms lifted. The second type holds a bunch of fruits in her right hand and a parrot perching on her left arm is nudging the breast of Goddess with its beak. In the third type the Goddess holds her prominent breasts with her hands from below.

A bronze sculpture[41] of Mother Goddess, found in the early levels of Dhulikatta, assignable to 2-3rd century B.C. is holding a baby in the left hand while her right hand is resting on her knees. She is seated on a pedestal. The figure of a mother and the child is of the *ankadhatri* type and represents the fertility cult. It is evident from the above objects that people had faith in the fertility cult in the early historical times.

The Buddhist Architecture:

The excavations at Dhulikatta revealed a Buddhist *Stupa*. The *stupa* consisted of a brick drum of 2 mt. height over a single layer of rubble basement. The anda or the dome rises over the garbha to a height of 5 mt. crowned with a *harmika* and *chatra*. A square enclosure around the drum filled up with bricks is raised to strengthen and also it served as a *pradakshinapatha*. During the second phase of constructional activity the drum was enlarged which is 36 mt. in diametre. It is built with bricks entirely. The remnants of *harmika* and *chatravali* were found in the excavations.

The *garbha* of the *stupa* was decorated with 47 carved Ayaka slabs which are now seen mostly in tact on the spot. A few of them are brought recently to Karimnagar and they are now placed in the local museum. Sculptural representations on the slabs include five hooded Muchilinda Naga, Bodhi tree, Mahabhinishkramana etc.

Muchilinda Naga is believed to have sheltered Buddha for a week from a terrible storm. But nowhere else he has been so glorified as on the stupas of Andhradesa particularly at Amaravati and Nagarjuna Konda.[42] Similar glorification of Muchilinda Naga is noticed on the ayaka slabs of Dhulikatta, the figures of which are quite similar to those of Amaravati and Nagarjunakonda.[43]

On one of the slabs at Dhulikatta, the Muchilinda Naga, a five hooded cobra, protecting Lord Buddha, symbolically represented by his feet, is exquisitely delineated. It contains a label Brahmi inscription[44] datable to 2nd century B.C. It reads as

"GAHAPATHINO PATHALASA MATHUYA DANAM".

Another slab contains the figures of ladies standing with floral offerings. The ladies are profusely decorated with cubical ear ornaments stamped with beautiful lotus medallions, the profuse hair made into side knots, broad necklaces, waist belts and beaded wristlets.

As there is no anthropomorphic representation of Buddha, the stupa may belong to the Hinayana sect. The Brahmi characters of label inscriptions suggest that this stupa had its nucleus in early 2nd century B.C.

The Stupa at Pashigoan:

There is another small *stupa* on a hillock at Pashigoan, a small village near Stambhampalli on the right side of the road leading from Karimnagar to Lakshettipet. This stupa is about 3 kms. from the Godavari. The glittering casing slabs on the hillock attract the attention of the visitors from a long distance. It contains only six slabs standing erect one beside the other. One of the slabs is found broken into pieces. The slabs contain the designs of pilasters, vases and full blown lotuses. To the south of the stupa exist the remains of a big hall in a rectangular shape, perhaps a monastery intended for the monks. The visible layers contain the Satavahana bricks. Generally the dwelling houses of the monks form an important adjunct of Buddhist establishment.[15]

The Epigraphs of the District:

The epigraphic material, which forms the main authentic source for the reconstruction of the political, cultural and social history of this district, is of immense value. No other material has so faithfully preserved the glimpse of contemporary life of those days as these lithic and copper plate documents. The majority of them are the gift inscriptions found either in the temples or in their vicinity. These inscriptions are the important source to know about the patrons and the period to which the temples belonged to. The temple played an important role in the society as gleaned from these inscriptions. The epigraphic evidences show that a number of local chiefs have constructed the temples and endowed them with grants of various types. They reveal about the several taxes gifted to the deities for the performance of *anga-ranga-vibhoga* and for the daily offerings of the gods. There are instances where in feeding houses were also maintained by the tax remissions gifted to the deities.[46]

After the study of the early historical culture from 2nd century B.C. to 3rd A.D. as gleaned from the recent excavations, the history of Karimnagar district is indeed in darkness in the absence of clear archaeological or epigraphic evidence. The known history of the district begins from about A.D. 750 with the advent of the Chalukyas of Vemulavada, who flourished as subordinates of considerable prominence under the Rashtrakutas. The earliest inscriptions[47] found in the district belong to Arikesari II of Vemulavada, who ruled between A.D. 930-955. This region, according to the inscriptions, is known as Sapadalaksha or Kosavala which corresponds to the present day districts of Karimnagar and Nizamabad.[48] About half a dozen stone inscriptions of Vemulavada rulers are noticed in the district.

The Western Chalukyan Kings of Kalyani are represented by nearly twenty epigraphs, of which the inscription of Choppadandi is the earliest. It is dated A.D. 992 and belongs to Ahavamalladeva.[49] The Chalukyan inscriptions are in Kannada script while the inscriptions of the Kakatiyas are in Telugu. About fifteen inscriptions of the Kakatiyas are noticed in the district, besides many other miscellaneous inscriptions including those of Polavasa chiefs and Velama chiefs. A single inscription of Vijayanagara Devaraya is noticed at Kalesvaram. Besides these Lithic records, one copper plate record[50] pertaining to Chamanpalli village over a canal dispute is also published. These plates are dated A.D. 1246 and belong to Kakati Ganapatideva.

The Department of Archaeology and Museums, Government of Andhra Pradesh, started a village wise survey of the districts for copying all the extant epigraphs. In this direction, Warangal and Karimnagar districts were taken up for the proposed exhaustive epigraphic survey and the two volumes on these districts have been published. All the available epigraphs numbering about eighty ranging from tenth century A.D. to modern times were copied and the same are published in the Volume of Karimnagar district in 1974.

The Temple Monuments:

Little is known about the temples built during the early period except the rock cut temples of Adavi Somanapalli. The practice of constructing temples in the district owes its origin practically to the times of the Chalukyas of Vemulavada. The earliest extant Hindu temples noticed in the area are at Vemulavada. The most active period of temple construction in this region was under the Western Chalukyas of Kalyani and the Kakatiyas of Warangal.

The temples of the present study, were constructed under the rule of the various dynasties, of whose territory, Karimnagar district formed only a part. The Chalukyas became the pioneers in the field of temple architecture as evinced from the fact, that the traditions set up by them, were followed by the Kakatiyas who were their successors. A comparative study of the architectural features of the various temples, built in a different epoch, in this region will clearly reveal that the temples constructed by the Kakatiyas are indeed marvellous specimens and they are superb in their architectural qualities. They are lofty in conception and in no way inferior in grandeur to the temples built by them at Hanumakonda,, Palampet, Pillalamarri and other parts of their Kingdom.

For a student of architecture, the entire area of Karimnagar district appears to be prolific for studying the salient features of the Chalukyan and Kakatiyan temples. At present Karimnagar district consists of 1053 inhabited villages. In connection with the study of the temples an extensive and exhaustive survey is made in all the fourteen taluks of the district, withstanding the vigors and rigors of nature, and the traces of ancient structural temples are noticed in about a hundred villages. Some of the temples are in a dilapidated condition, but most of them are still in tact and attract the attention of the visitor. About fifty sites with the temples of structural beauty and sculptural elegance are chosen for the present study which so far have not received the due attention of the scholars.

REFERENCES

1. *APGKD*, 1974, p.61
2. *Census of India, Administrative Atlas, A.P..*, 1971, p. 453.
3. *Census of Hand Book, Karimnagar District*, 1961, p.1
4. *APGKD*, 1974, p.2.
5. *Ibid.*
6. *Census Hand Book, Karimnagar District*, 1961, p.1.
7. *EA*, Vol.II, p.21.
8. *APGKD*, 1974, p.3.
9. V.V. Krishna Sastry, *The Proto and Early Historical Cultures of A.P.*, pp.11-14.
10. *Ibid.*, p.1.
11. *Ibid.*
12. *APGKD*, 1974, p.4.
13. V.V. Krishna Sastry, *Op. Cit.*, p.4.
14. *APGKD*, 1974, pp.3-7.
15. *Ibid.*, p.9.
16. C. Sivaramamurti, *Early Andhra Art and Iconography*, Fig.45.
17. N.S. Ramachandra Murthy, "Art and Architecture of Karimnagar District" in *Proceedings of A.P. History Congress*, Section II, pp.1-8, Warangal, 1983.
18. *EA.*, Vol.II, p.21.
19. V.V. Krishna Sastry, *OP. Cit.*, p.5 & 152.
20. Munn, L., *Annual Report of the Archaeological Department of H.E.H. the Nizam's Dominions*, 1925-26, pp.19-20.
21. V.V. Krishna Sastry, *Op. Cit.*, p.12.
22. *Ibid.*, p.15.
23. *Ibid.*, p.25.
24. *Ibid.*, p.26.
25. *ARDAM*, 1976-77, p.35.
26. *APGKD*, 1974, p.33
27. *JAHRS*, Vol.XXXII (I-IV Parts), p.48.
28. *ARDAM*, 1976-77, p.35.
29. V.V. Krishna Sastry, *Op. Cit.*, p.83.
30. *Ibid.*, p.123.
31. *Ibid.*
32. M. Rama Rao, *Satavahana Coins in A.P..*, Govt. Museum, p.9.
33. *JAHRS*, Vol.XXV. p.314.
34. *ARDAM*, 1976-77. p.14
35. *ARDAM*, 1977-78, p.2
36. V.V. Krishna Sastry, *Op. Cit..*, p.143.
37. *Ibid.*, Plate No.76.
38. *Ibid.*, Plate No. 104
39. B. Rajendra Prasad, *Art of South India - Andhra Pradesh*, p.55.
40. V.V. Krishna Sastry, *Op. Cit.*, Plates No.93,94,95.
41. *Ibid.*, Plate No.82.
42. C. Sivaramamurti, *Op. Cit.*, p.5.
43. *Ibid.*, Plates No. 14 and 22.
44. V.V. Krishna Sastry, *Op. Cit.*, p.145.
45. B. Rajendra Prasad, *Op Cit.*, p.26.
46. *Telengana Sasanamulu* (Telugu), Lakshmanaraya Parishodhaka Mandali. Hyderabad, 1935, Nos.19 & 21.
47. P. Sreenivasachar, *The Archaeological Bulletin No.II,* p.48.

48. B. Rajendra Prasad, *Temple Sculpture of Andhra Pradesh,* p.42.
49. *IAPKD*, No.8.
50. *JAHRS*, Vol.XXXV, PP.183-86.

TWO

History of Karimnagar District

1. Early History

Among the popular sixteen Mahajanapadas of sixth century B.C. Asmaka or Assaka (Prakrit form) was one in the Deccan which had its capital at a place styled Potali, Potana, Podana or Paudanya. The form Podana which occurs in certain old manuscripts of the Mahabharata, reminds one of modern Bodhan which lies south of the confluence of the Godavari and the Manjira in Nizamabad district. This Asmaka possibly corresponds to the Asmagi of Pliny.[1] There is possibility to presume that Karimnagar region once formed a part of Asmaka in view of its antiquarian ties and close contiguity with the area of Bodhan.

The Nandas:- The history of Karimnagar district can be traced from the time of the Nandas, who extended their rule over the Deccan. The existence of a city called 'Nav Nanda Dehra' modern Nander on the bank of the Godavari also suggests that the Nanda empire included a large portion of the Deccan of which this district formed a part.

The Mauryas:- When the Nandas were overthrown in 323 BC by Chandragupta Maurya, a large part of India was brought under his control. According to Jain tradition, Chandragupta is believed to have spent his last days at Sravanabelagola in the present Karnataka state. Some parts of the Deccan appear to have been taken by force of arms during the reign of his son and successor Bindusara (299-272

BC). The extension of the Mauryan empire into the south touching river Pennar in Andhradesa, perhaps during Bindusara period fostered close political as well as cultural ties with the north. Bindusara seems to have conquered the Deccan and became the master of all territory between the eastern and western sea.[2] The minor rock edicts found at Maski and Kopbal in the Raichur doab and the rock edicts brought to light at Yerragudi[3] in Kurnool district may be accepted as proof that a large part of the Deccan was ruled by Ashoka. In the first quarter of the twentieth century A.D. 418 punch marked silver coins were discovered from an unrecorded place in Karimnagar district, which are now exhibited in the State Museum of Hyderabad. Srinivas classified these coins and assigned them to the pre-Mauryan and Mauryan periods.[4] After Ashoka the vast Mauryan empire disintegrated and the Satavahanas or the Andhra Kingdom of Dakshinapatha asserted its hegemony over this region.

The Satavahanas:- After the fall of the Mauryas, Karimnagar area passed under the sway of the Satavahanas which is revealed by their numerous coins and fortified towns. In A.D. 1952 a hoard of 8 silver coins and 39 silver Roman coins came from Nustulapur situated about 15 kms. from Karimnagar.[5] The Nustulapur hoard is of great importance because of its association with Roman coins belonging to Augustus (27 B.C. to 14 A.D.) and Nero (A.D. 14-37). This is a clear proof to show that the Karimnagar area had trade ties with the Roman empire during the Satavahana period from the first century B.C. The Romans paid for the Indian goods in gold coins, which have been found in hoards all over the peninsula. It is no wonder that Pliny, the Roman historian complains of the luxury trade with India draining the Roman treasury.[6] The excavations at Peddabankur yielded two hoards of silver punch marked coins one consisting of 168 and the other of 30.[7]

Some of the coins collected recently from the Kapparraopet area in Peddapalli taluk belong to CHIMUKA or SIMUKA, the founder of the Satavahana dynasty, which proves beyond doubt that the early Satavahanas had their early settlement in the Karimnagar region which was the nucleus of their political activity.[8] There is also a large collection of copper coins 284 full and 116 broken belonging to Satavahana rulers from Karimnagar district.[9] The coins obtained from Peddabankur belong to Satavaha, Satakarni I, Gautamiputra

Satakarni, Vasistiputra Pulumavi, Sivasiri Pulumavi, Yajna Satakarni and Rudra Satakarni.[10]

Besides a large number of coins, the recent excavations revealed fortified towns at Dhulikatta and Kotilingala, while Peddabankur is noticed only as a Satavahana village site with several brick structures and brick wells. According to Megasthenes, the Andhras possessed numerous villages and 30 fortified towns.[11] Karimnagar district is marked by a large number of Satavahana sites and probably Dhulikatta and Kotilingala might be among those 30 fortified towns taken into account by Megasthenes as the excavations revealed a very high degree of civilization with palatial buildings, sewage, well-laid out roads and good water supply.

The existence of a Buddhist stupa at Dhulikatta with beautifully sculptured Ayaka slabs is a testimony to the development of early religious architecture in Karimnagar district. Unfortunately no Brahmanical structure is found surviving this day and it may be surmised that the Buddhist religion was rather more organised than the Brahmanical among the common folk and mercantile groups. There are favourable references to the Setthi-gahapatis and the merchants in Buddhist literature, who rendered financial assistance to the stupas and monasteries.[12] One such instance of assistance by a gahapati is noticed on one of the ayaka slabs at Dhulikatta with the Brahmi label inscription "GAHAPATHINO PATHALASA MATHUYA DANAM".

2.The Chalukyas of Badami

The Imperial Chalukyas of Badami usually known as the Early Western Chalukyas rose to power in A.D. 543 and ruled fro two centuries till A.D. 753 when they were over thrown by Rashtrakuta Dantidurga. Pulakesin-II (A.D. 610-642) extended his rule from shore to shore across the Deccan and installed his brother Kubja Vishnuvardhana as the ruler of Vengi in A.D. 624, who started a new line called the Eastern Chalukyas. However the greater part of Telingana which included Karimnagar district too, remained under the Badami Chalukyan empire.

The Chalukyas of Badami made valuable contribution for the

evolution of art and architecture which had an influence on the temples of Karimnagar in later times. The temple building movement in the Deccan originated at Aihole about the beginning of the fifth century A.D. and flourished for about three centuries.[13] The Ladkhan temple[14] dated to A.D. 425-450 is considered the oldest early Chalukyan temple at Aihole, which was one of the cradles of Indian temple architecture. In the later half of the seventh century A.D. as the surviving monuments show, the temple structure in its medieval aspect was beginning to assume a prescribed form in the Badami region.[15] A good number of temples were built at Aihole, Badami and Pattadakal by the early kings of this dynasty. The influence of this early Chalukyan art and architectural tradition travelled from its epicentre to the far distant areas in Andhra Pradesh like Alampur, Mahanandi and Satyavolu which stand as living testimony to the genius of the great builders, who followed the course of this great art tradition, which continued in Karimnagar region also during later times.

James Fergusson opines that the temples of Badami Chalukyas do not belong to the style of their own and their sikharas or towers either show the curvilinear outline of the northern style or the storeyed pyramids of the Dravidian.[16] According to him the Chalukyan curvilinear Sikharas are copied from the northern Indo-Aryan or Orissan style. But it is not totally true. No doubt the Sikharas of both the Chalukyan and Orissan styles appear to be similar with an *amalaka* and *kalasa* at the top, but there is a marked difference which distinguishes one from the other in their architectonic qualities. The Orissan structures generally go high with elongated narrow towers and are very akin to those of the Gupta structures in the north, whereas the towers of the early Chalukyan temples are slightly curvilinear and pyramidal.[17] A comparative study of the temples of Bhuvaneshwar and Alampur will prominently reveal this notable contrast. Unless one has a critical acumen to notice the significant differences, it is not possible for one to drive away the wrong notion that the builders of the early Chalukyan temples borrowed the art tradition of the Gupta school of northern India. It is evident from the variation in style that the early Chalukyas followed the architectural tradition of their own and evolved new idioms to embellish their monuments. They became the pioneers in the field of temple architecture as evinced from the fact that the traditions set up by them were followed by the successive dynasties which came in their wake.[18]

Karimnagar district, which was successively ruled by various dynasties of the Chalukyan lineage such as the Chalukyas of Badami, Chalukyas of Vemulavada and the Chalukyas of Kalyani from the beginning of the seventh century A.D. to mid-twelth century A.D. had naturally imbibed the traits and trends of this early Chalukyan style, which had an impact on the temples constructed here during the later Chalukyan period. The temples of Valgonda, Raikal and Dharmapuri in Karimnagar district contain curvilinear Sikharas which are more akin to the Chalukyan tradition than the Orissan. The curvature of these Sikharas starts at the base like those of the Chalukyan and whereas it begins only at the top in the Orissan tradition. Moreover these Sikharas have the Sukanasa projecting-forth from their base above the roof of the antarala, which is an early Chalukyan feature acquired from the Nava Brahma temples of 7th-8th century A.D. at Alampur in Mahboobnagar district.

Several loose images of Ganesa endowed with two arms and a natural elephant head with the absence of a crown are found in the archaic form at various places like Vemulavada, Dharmapuri, Potlapalli, Nagunuru, Road-side Hanuman temple at Rajaram and Gandhinagar in proper Jagtial. These images are believed to have belonged to the early Chalukyan period and may be securely dated to 7th and 8th centuries A.D. if not to the earlier times in view of the fact that a similar image of Ganesa is found beside the holy tank of the temples of Mahakut near Badami dated to A.D. 600.[19]

3. The Chalukyas of Vemulavad

The next phase in the historical period of the region begins with the reign of the Chalukya collateral branch called the Vemulavada Chalukyas, who continued their rule contemporaneous with the Rashtrakutas and got extinct also with them in A.D. 973. The Vemulavada rulers flourished as the subordinates of considerable prominence under the Rashtrakutas. There are five stone inscriptions, two at Vemulavada, one at the local museum of Karimnagar and other two at Kurkiyala and Repaka which reveal about the history and genealogy of this branch. Besides these incriptions, the

Parbhani copper plates[20] of Arikesari III dated A.D. 966, the great works like *Vikramarjuna Vijaya*[21] of Pampa and *Yasastilaka champu*[22] of Somadeva Suri throw a flood of light on the history of this family. The Chalukyas of Vemulavada made wonderful contribution to the growth of temple architecture and Vemulavada preserves to this day excellent examples of Hindu temples known to be the earliest in the district. They also patronised Jainism and built temples to Jain Tirthankarás at several places like Vemulavada, Sanigaram, Nagunuru, Repaka, Koratla and Bommalagutta near Kurkiyala village.

Vinayaditya Yuddhamalla, the founder of this dynasty and a subordinate of Rashtrakuta Dantidurga is said to have ruled over the country sapadalaksha or Kosavalam Savalakhe, that is consisting of one and one-fourth lakh villages with Podana (Bodhan) as his capital. Sapadalaksha constituted the present districts of Nizamabad and Karimnagar which included Asmanta, Sabbinadu one thousand and other regions of the early period. Yuddhamalla is said to have caused his elephants bathed in a reservoir filled with oil at Podana. He extended his rule from Podana to Chennur in Adilabad district along the river Godavari. He assisted his overlord Dantidurga in his military expeditions.

The Vemulavada[24] inscription of Arikesari II, the Parbhani copper plates of Arikesari III and the famous Kannada literary work *Vikramarjuna Vijaya* of Pampa form the main source material and on the basis of which the following genealogy is formulated for the Vemulavada rulers.[25]

Genealogy of the Chalukyas of Vemulavada

Vinayaditya Yuddhamalla I (A.D. 750-775)

Arikesari I (A.D. 775-800) V(B)iragriha

Narasimha I (AD. 800-825) Bhadradeva
Yuddhamalla II (AD. 825-850)
Baddega AD.(850-85)
Yuddhamalla III (AD. 895-915)
Narasimha II (AD.915-930) (wife Jakavve)
Arikesari II (AD. 930-955)(Wives Revakanirumadi & Lokambika)

Vagaraja (AD. 955-965 **Bhadradeva or Baddaga II**

Arikesari III AD 966-973

Vinayaditya Yuddhamalla was succeeded by his son Arikesari I who helped Rashtrakuta Nirupama Dhruva (A.D.780-793) in the civil war against his brother Govinda II. He is known to have captured the entire Vengi country together with Trikalinga by the strength of his arm. He fought on behalf of his overlord Dhruva and he was duly rewarded with certain portions of newly conquered territory. It is believed that Vemulavada became the headquarters of this Chalukya family at an early stage probably under Arikesari I.[26]

Arikesari I was succeeded by his son Narasimha I and the latter was followed by his son Yuddhamalla II who were mere shadowy rulers of less prominence. Baddega, the son and successor of Yuddhamalla II was a distinguished hero of forty two battles and bore the title Solada-ganda[27] (the unvanquished hero). However he faced the defeat at the hands of Gunaga Vijayaditya III (A.D.849-892) of Vengi in a disastrous war conducted against his overlord Rashtrakuta Krishna II.[28] Neither Baddega nor his master Krishna II forgave the Eastern Chalukyas. *Pampa-Bharata* says that Baddega defeated Chalukya Bhima I of Vengi and captured him as a prisoner as if one might capture a ferocious crocodile in its own water.

The Vemulavada inscription mentions the names of four temples Rajesvara, Adityagriha, Baddegesvara and Nagaresvara to which gifts were made by King Arikesari II. The very name of the temple Baddegesvara states that it might have been built by King Baddega (A.D. 850-895). The stone inscription which stands to the left of the sanctum of the Bhimesvara temple, refers to it as the old Baddegesvara temple.[29] Most probably Baddega, the hero of forty two battles might have raised this monument in honour of his victories during the last years of his reign. The above epigraph mentions that Adityagriha alone was built by Peddana, the tantrapala of Arikesari II, but it does not mention that the rest of the three temples were built by either Peddana or his ruler Arikesari II. It can be presumed that these three temples existed already by the time the gifts were made. If Baddegesvara were to be believed as the present Bhimesvara, this temple may be dated back to the last quarter of the ninth century A.D. which can be further confirmed by its early Chalukyan architectural style.

Baddega was succeeded by Yuddhamalla III who appears to have taken little or no interest in warfare. Narasimha II, his son and successor, was a person of different calibre. He was a powerful warrior and participated in all the military exploits of his overlord Rashtrakuta Indra III. He conquered the Latas and Malavas. He took a prominent part in inflicting a crushing defeat on Mahipala the King of Gurjara-pratiharas and set up a pillar of victory at Kalapriya. It is said that Mahipala fled as if struck by thunderbolts. While pursuing him Narasimha II bathed his horses in the Ganges.[30]

Narasimha II was undoubtedly a great military general and led the armies of Indra III successfully in the Kanauj expedition. He is said to have married Jakavve, probably a sister of Indra III and mother of Arikesari II. The period of Indra III is known for the carvings of the Jain Chaumukhas. Such few Chaumukhas are noticed in the Verandah of Bhimesvara temple at Vemulavada.

Narasimha II was succeeded by his son Arikesari II (A.D. 930-955) who was the most remarkable personage of his family. Not only he was the son of Rashtrakuta princess Jakavve but also he married Revakanirumadi, the daughter of Indra III and Lokambika another princess of the same royal family. *Vikramarjuna Vijaya*of Pampa eulogised the most illustrious and eventful career of this ruler. He is said to have given asylum to Bijja or Vijayaditya V, one of the claimants to the Vengi throne. He defeated in battle a mahasamanta sent by Gojjiga or Rashtrakuta Govinda IV against him at the head of an army. He assisted Rashtrakuta Baddega Amoghavarsha III (A.D.935-939) and installed him on Rashtrakuta throne in A.D. 936 by removing Govinda IV, the wicked and vicious ruler.[31]

The Vemulavada inscription[32] states Gunamkusa as Mahasandhi-Vigrahi (The minister of war and peace) and Peddanarya as tantrapala (minister of army) under Arikesari II. Peddanarya built a temple to the god Aditya (The Sun) but it is now no more extant. At his request on the holy occasion of Uttarayana-Sankranti, King Arikesari II granted in the north-east corner of his capital Lembulavataka (Vemulavada) one hundred nivartanas of bhu-kshetra or land for the maintenance of a choultry or feeding house attached to it.

Pampa, the author of *Adipurana* and *Vikramarjuna Vijaya,*

adorned the court of Arikesari II. The Kurkiyala inscription[33] gives the genealogy and a detailed account of Pampa and his brother Jinavallabha. It states that they were the sons of Bhimapayya, a Kamme-Brahmana of Vangiparra of Venginadu, while their mother Vabbanabbe was the daughter of great astrologer Singha of Anngere in Belvola. Pampa was born in A.D. 902 and composed *Adipurana* in A.D. 941 at the age of thirty nine. It tells in beautiful language the story of Rishabha, the first Tirthankara. *Vikramarjuna Vijaya* is universally regarded as a masterpiece of art. It has set the norm for epic poetry in Kannada. Graceful and dignified in its diction, the work has a charm rarely met with elsewhere in Kannada literature. As a model of sweet mellifluous and elegant verse, it remained unrivalled. The poet identified his patron Arikesari II with the epic hero Arjuna and thereby contrived to interweave several incidents of contemporary history into his narrative of the epic story, besides giving a reasonably accurate account of his patron's ancestors in the introduction to his work.[34] The King having been pleased with *Vikramarjuna Vijaya,* gave Pampa the village Dharmavura (Dharmapuri in Jagtial taluk) an abode of the Brahmanas as agrahara. Pampa is also known as Subhanandi and he is believed to have spent his last days at Bodhan, where his Samadhi is noticed recently.[35]

Jinavallabha, who was also a staunch Jain like his elder brother Pampa, constructed a Jain basadi called Tribhuvanatilaka on Vrishabhadri, now known as Bommalagutta near Kurkiyala village during the period of Arikesari II.

Arikesari II held his sway over the region extending from Bodhan to Chennur along the river Godavari which can be attested by the Chennur epigraph[36] dated A.D. 940 in Adilabad district. It states that Baddega son of Gonagarasa, a prince of another Chalukyan lineage and a feudatory of Arikesari II made some grants in his Chennur agrahara included in Podana-nadu.

Arikesari II had two sons named Vegaraja by Revakanirmadi and Bhadradeva or Baddege II by Lokambika. He was succeeded by Vagaraja (A.D. 955-965) who died without an issue. The next ruler Baddega II appears to have ruled for a short period and built Subhadhama Jinalaya for the favour of Somadeva Suri, the head of the Gauda-Sangha and a renowned theologian of the Jaina order. *Yasas-*

tilaka Champu, Nitivakyamrita and Syadvadopanishad are the famous works of Somadeva. He states that he composed his most famous work *Yasastilaka Champu* in the Saka year 881 or A.D. 959 at Gangadhara, a place characterized as overflowing with wealth under the rulers of Vemulavada.[37] The village Gangadhara, which is very close to the Jain basadi Tribhuvanatilaka of Jinavallabha on Bommalagutta must have been a great Jain centre in those days. Pampa and Somadeva, both Jains, two of the greatest names in medieval Indian literature shed their lustre on the court of the Chalukyas of Vemulavada.

Arikesari III, who succeeded his father Baddega II, was the last ruler of this dynasty. He issued the Parbhani plates in A.D. 966 registering a gift of the village in the midst of Repaka twelve (Sircilla taluk) in the Sabbi thousand to Somadeva Suri for the white washing and repairs of Subhadhama Jinalaya built by his father. The Repaka epigraph[38] dated A.D. 968 states that Arikesari III also built a Jina temple at Repaka and endowed it with gifts of lands. The rule of Arikesari III ended by A.D. 973 when the Rashtrakuta power was overthrown by Taila II, the founder of the Western Chalukyas of Kalyani.

The reign of the Chalukyas of Vemulavada is considered a glorious epoch in the history of Karimnagar district witnessing a remarkable progress in the fields of art and architecture, language and literature, religion and philosophy.

4. The Western Chalukyas of Kalyani

The power of the Rashtrakutas waned towards the end of the tenth century A.D. and the main line of the Early Western Chalukyas of Badami emerged from the obscurity of two centuries as the later Western Chalukyas of Kalyani. They rose to prominence again in A.D. 973 and ruled for a further period of two hundred years. They were great builders and one dominate style of Indian architecture known as the later Chalukyan style derives its name from them.[39] This dynasty is represented by nearly twenty epigraphs in Karimnagar district alone.

Taila II(A.D. 973-997):- Taila II, the founder of the dynasty, who assumed the title Ahavamalla, ruled from his capital Manyakheta or Malkhed. He is represented by four[40] epigraphs in the district. An undated inscription on a broken stone lying at the tank in Vemulavada introduces Ahavamalla as the conqueror of the Chola armies. One of his subordinates made some gift to Mahesvara Sakti-Pandita for feeding the ascetics. The second incomplete record on a stone dated A.D. 992, now placed in Karimnagar Museum states that certain Commander of Ahavamalla visited along with his army the temple of Mallikarjunadeva and endowed it with some wet land and flower garden. The third epigraph of this King is from Choppadandi village. It is dated A.D. 992 and records the construction of the tank Achebbe-Samudra named after Achebbe, the daughter of Anunga Duggaraya, the follower of the prince Irvabedanga. It also registers that Divakabbe the *dadi*(female nurse) of prince Irvabedanga Satyasraya made gift of lands and seventy drammas to the god Martandadeva of Choppadandi village. The last inscription of Ahavamalla dated A.D. 995 at Jammikunta[41] village states that a subordinate of the king named Nagiyagavunda made gift of lands and two ratanas to the god Aditya of Jammikunta to commemorate his master's northern conquest over utpala or utpala also known as Munja, the paramara king of Malwa. All the four epigraphs found in different corners of the district confirm that the whole Karimnagar region passed directly under the sway of the Western Chalukyas of Kalyani after the fall of the Chalukyas of Vemulavada which synchronized with the fall of the Rashtrakuta empire in A.D. 973.

Satyasraya (A.D. 997-1008):- Taila II was succeeded by his son Satyasraya, who assumed the title Irvabedanga, which means a wonderful man among those, who pierce in attack. There are three[42] records, which mention him as the reigning king. The fragmentary record dated A.D. 1005 at Kadparti village and another undated epigraph on a stone lying on the tank bund at Husunabad village register certain gifts of land perhaps to the local deities. The much abraded inscription of Choppadandi village dated A.D. 1008 standing in the Siva Temple records some gift of lands to the god Divakesvara, set up by Divakabbe the *dadi*(female nurse) of Irvabedanga. As the name of Divakabbe appears in both the records dated A.D. 992 and A.D. 1008 at the same Choppadandi village, it can be deduced that she lived there for more than sixteen years and constructed the temple of Divakesvara after her name. The temple is still extant outside the village which is locally known as Shamhuni gudi.

Vikramaditya V (A.D. 1008-1015):- Satyasraya was succeeded in A.D. 1008 by his nephew Vikramaditya V who had short reign of only a few years. His records do not appear in Karimnagar district.

Jagadekamalla Jayasimha II (A.D. 1015-1042)- The next ruler was Jagadekamalla Jayasimha II who is represented by only one epigraph at Vemulavada[43] dated A.D. 1033. This is a pillar inscription carved on four sides and set up in front of the temple of Kedaresvara. It states that for worship and offerings of the god Rajesvaradeva, installed by Chikaraja, a gift of land was made by certain chief.

The Name of Rajesvaradeva which figures often in the inscriptions of Vemulavada is indeed confusing as the names of the temples have undergone change in the course of time. A detailed study is required to identify them. At present there are four important old temples at Vemulavada which are in good state of preservation. They are known locally as Bhimesvara, Nagaresvara, Kedaresvara and Raja Rajesvara.

An undated inscription[44] of Arikesari II (A.D. 930-955) mentions the names of the four temples of Rajesvara, Adityagriha, Baddegesvara and Nagaresvara. The name of Rajesvara figures for the first time in this inscription. Among the four, the Adityagriha (Sun temple) built by Peddanarya the tantrapala of Arikesari II is now no more extant. The Nagaresvara temple referred to in the inscription is in tact today in the middle of the village and probably it was the shrine of the mercantile community.[45] As already stated the old Baddegesvara temple is referred to as the present Bhimesvara by Dr. N. Venkataramanayya. Now the question of Rajesvara mentioned in this epigraph remains unsettled and it cannot be identified with the present temples of either Kedaresvara or Raja Rajesvara because they contain the separate stone inscriptions erected within their courtyards stating the names of their builders. As such the Rajesvara temple mentioned in the epigraph of Arikesari II may be deemed as no more extant. A further survey of the ruins may bring to light some other structures, which owe their existence to the period of the Chalukyas of Vemulavada. An inscription[46] of the reign of Vikramaditya VI dated A.D. 1083, set up within the premises of the present Raja Rajesvara temple states that Mahamandalesvara Rajaditya installed Rajadityesvaradeva, after his name and built a lofty temple for the same. This temple stands at an elevated place beside the holy tank and now it is popularly known as the temple of Raja Rajesvara Swamy. The name Rajadityesvara appears to have changed into Raja Rajesvara in the course of time.

The name of the present Kedaresvara temple does not figure anywhere among the half a dozen inscriptions of Vemulavada, although this temple, by its architectural style, belongs, more or less to the same period. The inscription of the reign of Jayasimha II dated A.D. 1033, which is now under study, stands within a stone-walled compound of the temple of Kedaresvara. It states that the god Rajesvaradeva was installed by Chikaraja. If the location of the inscription is to be taken as the criterion, as it is considered elsewhere, this Rajesvaradeva installed by Chikaraja in A.D. 1033, may be identified with the present Kedaresvaradeva. It may be presumed that Rajesvaradeva of Chikaraja has assumed the name of Kedaresvaradeva in recent times.

Somesvara I (A.D. 1042-1068):- Jayasimha II was succeeded by his son Somesvara I, who is known with the title of Trailokyamalladeva. It was during the reign of Somesvara I that the capital was shifted to kalyani. Bilhana the great poet in his *Vikramankadeva Charita* credits Somesvara with having adopted Kalyani as the capital of his empire.[47] It was during Somesvara's reign that the foundation of the Kakatiya empire was laid. In recognition of the meritorious service rendered by Prola I, Somesvara I bestowed Anumakonda Vishaya on him in perpetuity.

Somesvara I is represented by four[48] lithic records in the district, two at Sanigaram, one at Potlapalli and the other at Koratla. His first epigraph dated A.D. 1051, found at Sanigaram introduces Mahasamanta Kakatiya Betarasa, (Beta I) whose pergade or minister named Narnayya son of Vaijaraja is said to have renovated the Duddhamalla-Jinalaya of the village Sanagara and endowed it with a ratana after obtaining the consent of the local elderly gamundas named Muppadayya and Punnaraddi on the occasion of the Uttarayana-Sankranti. The Jain temple Duddhamalla-Jinalaya to which the ratana (water drawing device from a well) was gifted, might be a Jinalaya built by Yu(Du)ddhamalla, probably one of the kings of that name belonging to the line of the Chalukyas of Vemulavada.[49] The present hillock, where some Jain images are located might have been the place where the said Duddhamalla Jinalaya flourished in those days.

Another record dated A.D. 1053 at the same village states that the King's subordinate, Mahasamanta Kakatiya Prolarasa (Prola I) made a gift of twelve sites for residential purpose on the occasion of the solar eclipse, with the approval of the local gamundas. He also made gifts of lands with the consent of Kateraddi and others of Bejavanke village to the god Madhupesvara of Khandi Sanagara, installed by pergade Madhuvappayya. The name mentioned in the record as Khandi-Sanagara must be the village Sanigaram itself or a particular locality of the village where Madhupesvara temple was set up. Bejavanke is obviously the present neighbouring village Bejjenki.

The Potlapalli record dated A.D. 1066 registers a gift of ratana to a temple by Mahasamanta Chamdayyarasar of Remgomda village on the occasion of solar eclipse. The name Remgomda mentioned in the record is the present neighbouring village Regonda. An undated epigraph of the reign of Somesvara I at Koratla records a gift of some land for the worship, offerings, renovation etc. to the Rattamartanda-Jinalaya probably by a Rashtrakuta Chief, who was a subordinate of the king. The name of the donor is not found as the edge of the stone is broken and the letters are missing in each line.

Somesvara II (A.D.1068-1076): Somesvara I was succeeded by his son Bhuvanaikamalla Somesvara II. His records do not appear in the district. He was deposed and succeeded on the throne by his younger brother Vikramaditya VI.

Vikramaditya VI (A.D. 1076-1126):- Tribhuvanamalla Vikramaditya VI was the most powerful ruler of this dynasty and he extended his dominions widely upto Sitabaldi (Nagpur) in the north and beyond the river Krishna in the south. As a mark of his victories over his neighbouring kingdoms, he ventured to found an era bearing his name known as the Chalukya Vikrama era which never came into general use. However it was regularly employed for 51 years through out his reign in all his dominions. There are two such epigraphs of his reign at Vemulavada which are recorded in Chalukya-Vikrama era. Pottalakere (modern Patancheru near Hyderabad) and Kollipakke (Kulpak or Kolanupaka in Nalgonda district) were the important centres for his military camps. Earlier also they were the capital cities of the Chalukyan empire for some time before the city of Kalyani was built.[50] Vemulavada is nearer to Kollipake than Pottalakere. It appears that there was a straight military route from Kolanupaka to Vemulavada via the old historical towns of Cherial, Duddeda, Siddipet and Potuganti (Pothgal in Sircilla taluk).

Karimnagar district contains three[51] inscriptions at Vemulavada and one[52] at Sanigaram belonging to the reign of Tribhuvanamalla Vikramaditya VI. The earliest inscription of his reign dated in Chalukya-Vikrama era C.V. 8 corresponding to A.D. 1083 is found in the Raja Rajesvara temple at Vemulavada. It records that Mahamandalesvara Rajaditya of Chabbi-Twenty one thousand included in Kosavala, one and a quarter lakh country, installed Rajadityesvaradeva, probably after his name in the capital town Lembulavade (Vemulavada) and built a lofty temple for it. With the permission of his overlord Tribhuvanamalla of Kalyanapura, he made some gifts of land and the village Sankayapalli in Vennisale-seventy and the tax talavritti of Lembulavade for the maintenance and worship of the god and also for feeding the ascetics, students and their teachers working in the educational institution attached to the temple. The same Rajadityesvara deity is now known as Raja Rajesvara.

The second inscription of his reign dated in Chalukya-Vikrama era 29 corresponding to A.D. 1106 records the gift of a flower garden to the south of Lembulavada agrahara included in the venisale-seventy of Sabbi-one thousand for the offerings and worship of the god Arikesvaradeva by Kumara Somesvara. It also mentions certain Machiganga, the garland maker of that garden. The third inscription dated A.D. 1108 at the same place records the gift of a village Illimdikumta (Illentakunta) for the offerings of Harikesvaradeva and feeding of ascetics by Mahamandalesvara Jagaddevarasar of Pravarakula. The gift was made into the hands of Brahmesvara-

Pandita of Simgha parise. This Jagaddeva is none other than the Paramara prince, who ruled for some time from Kollipake, the subsidiary capital of the Western Chalukyas. There is now no more temple extant at Vemulavada with the name of either Arikesvara or Harikesvara, mentioned in the above epigraphs.

The Sanigaram epigraph dated A.D. 1107 of the reign of Tribhuvanamalla mentions Mahamandalesvara Kakatiya Betarasar (Beta-II) and states that the dandanayaka of Mahamandalesvara Jagaddevarasar (Parama Jagaddeva) named Kondamayya made a gift of ratana and some lands to the god Bhimesvara of Baliya Sanagara included in Pulgunur-Seventy on the occasion of the lunar eclipse. Like Khandi-Sanagara, Baliya-Sanagara must be a particular locality in the village Sanigaram itself.

An important event of the reign of Vikramaditya VI is that Vaija-dandadhisa took his master Beta II to the court of the emperor at Kalyani and made the latter to confer on Beta the Sabbi-one thousand probably comprising the southern portions of Karimnagar district.

Somesvara III (A.D. 1126-1138):- Vikramaditya VI was succeeded by his son Somesvara III who was also known as Bhulokamalla. Somesvara III is the author of *Manasollasa* which deals with the science of administration, justice, medicine, astrology etc. There are two epigraphs of his reign one at Sanigaram[53] and the other at Gangapuram[54] in Manthani taluk. His Sanigaram epigraph dated A.D. 1128 states that the King's subordinate (Padapadmopajivin) Mahamandalesvara Kakatiya Prolarasar's (Prola II) officer of Sabbi-Sahasram region named Repola Kuruvaraju made a gift of one ratana, oil mill and some lands for the worship and offerings to the god Kommesvaradeva of Khandi-Sanigara and for feeding and clothing of the ascetics. The gift included eight *mattars* of land in Bejavanka which is identifiable with Bejjenki village near Sanigaram. The word *Mattar* or *Martur* is a land measure, the exact value of which is yet to be known. Another undated epigraph of Gangapuram states that a subordinate of the king Bhulokamalla, named Gundaraja made a gift to the god Suresvaradeva. This Gunda can be identified with Manthenya Gunda, who was the younger brother of Medaraja II of Polavasa in Jagtial taluk.

Jagadekamalla II (A.D. 1138-1151):- Somesvara III was succeeded by Jagadekamalla II whose Sanigaram[55] inscription dated A.D. 1149 mentions Kakatiya Prolarasar (Prola II) still as his subordinate. His officer Repola Kuruvarasar's dandanayaka (Commander) Mamdaparasar of Atreya gotra made the gift of a ratana, some lands and an oil mill for the offerings and perpetual lamp to the god Parthesvaradeva at Sanigaram and for feeding and clothing of the ascetics. The epigraphic evidences show that Prola II was a loyal subordinate of the three Kings Vikramaditya VI, Somesvara III and Jagadekamalla II.

The village Sanigaram (Husunabad taluk) which has yielded five inscriptions ranging from A.D. 1051 to A.D. 1149, appears to have been a place of prominence for about a century during the reign of Western Chalukyas of Kalyani. It might have been a strategic centre from the military point of view as it exists almost on equal distance to all the three important fiefs of the region namely Kolanupaka in the south, Anumakonda in the east and Vemulavada in the north. The existence of a big tank formed naturally amidst the hillocks of Sanigaram might have been very useful for the military camps of the Western Chalukyas. The epigraphs of Sanigaram are important to build up the history of the four early members of the Kakatiya dynasty namely Beta I, Prola I, Beta II and Prola II, who started consolidating their power slowly as the loyal subordinates of the Western Chalukyan rulers. It is evident from the epigraphs that Sanigaram, included in Sabbinadu-one thousand was a stronghold of the early Kakatiya chiefs for more than a century.

Taila III and Somesvara IV:- Jagadekamalla II was succeeded by his brother Taila or Tailapa III (A.D. 1151-1163) who was over-thrown by Kalachuri Bijjala in A.D. 1163. The Kalachuris continued their rule upto A.D 1183. The last Chalukya ruler Somesvara IV regained his power and retained it upto A.D. 1189.

As regards religion under the Chalukyas of Kalyani, Saivism and Vaishnavism were the major creeds in Brahmanical Hinduism, the former occupying a more important place. The worship of Aditya (sun), Sakti, Vighnesa and Kumara is also noticed from their epigraphs. For the rest Jainism was more widespread than Buddhism.

The brief tenure of Bijjala was marked by the rise of Lingayat sect or Virasaiva sect under his minister Basava. The members of this sect worship Siva in his phallic (Lingam) form, reject the authority of the Vedas, disbelieve in the doctrine of rebirth, object to the child marriage and approve of the remarriage of widows. This revolutionary sect to a great deal had an impact on the common folk. The sect, when established, displayed bitter hostility to Jainism.[56]

Genealogy of the Western Chalukyas of Kalyani

Ahavamalla Taila II (A.D. 973-997)

Satyasraya Irvabedanga (A.D. 977-1008) — Dasavarman or Yasovarman

Vikramaditya V (A.D. 1008-1015) — Jagadekamalla Jayasimha II (A.D. 1015-1042)

Trailokyamalla Somesvara I (A.D. 1042-1068)

Bhuvanaikamalla Somesvara II (A.D. 1068-1076) — Tribhuvanamalla Vikramaditya VI (A.D. 1076-1126)

Bhulokamalla Somesvara III (A.D. 1126-1138)

Jagadekamalla II (A.D. 1138-1151 — Taila or Tailapa III (A.D. 1151-1163)

Kalachuris (A.D. 1163-1183)

Somesvara IV (A.D. 1184-89)

5. The Polavasa Chiefs:

Polavasa is the modern Polas village lying at a distance of 6 kms. from Jagtial on Jagtial-Dharmapuri Road. About a dozen epigraphs from the fiefs of Polavasadesa and Anumakonda-Vishaya refer to the Polavasa Chiefs. This family with its feudal principality in the region extending from Polavasa to Narsampet along the river Godavari and abutting the dominions of Anumakonda, is closely associated with the history of the early Kakatiyas particularly Prola II and his son Rudradeva.

The Govindapuram[57] epigraph in Narsampet taluk of Warangal district dated A.D. 1122 furnishes the genealogy of the Polavasa chiefs. Apart from their mythical ancestor Madhava-Chakravartin or Madhavavarman and Durgaraja, who is otherwise unknown, this family of four members Meda I, Jaggadeva I, Meda II and Gunda, as gleaned from their records, appear to have flourished during the period between A.D. 1075 and A.D. 1160. The Chronology of these chiefs is formulated on the basis of their epigraphic records and their relations with the early Kakatiyas.[58]

Family of Madhava-Chakravartin or Madhavavarman

Durgaraja upto A.D. 1080

Medaraja I (A.D. 1080-1110)

Jaggadeva I (A.D. 1110-1116)

Medaraja II of Polavasa (A.D. 1116-1159)	Gundaraja of Mantrakuta (A.D. 1116-1138)
Jaggadeva II	

Medaraja I, (A.D. 1080-1110):- The earliest epigraph which refers to Medaraja I is from Banajipet[59] in Narsampet taluk. It records the gift of some land by Mahamandalesvara Betarasar (Beta II) to Virakamala Jinalaya, built by Mahamandalesvara Medarasa (Meda I) of Ugravadi, subordinate (Padapadmopajivi) of the Western Chalukya King Tribhuvanamalla Vikramaditya VI. It states that Medaraja belonged to Venugontakula of the lineage of Madhavavarman. It is evident from the epigraph that both Meda I and Beta II were the subordinates of the Western Chalukyas. Beta II of Anumakonda might have visited this temple on friendly terms.

Another pillar inscription dated A.D. 1108, set up in the Pulastyesvara temple of Polavasa[60] refers to Mahamandalesvara Meda-Kshamapati, who bears the titles of Lattaluru-Puravaradhisvara and Suvarna-garuda-dhvaja, which indicate his Rashtrakuta affiliation. He is said to be the lord of the town Polavasa which was his capital. It was set up by the Virabalanja merchant community stating some gifts to the god Pulastyesvara.

Both the families of the Polavasa chiefs and Kakatiyas belonged to the same stock of Rashtrakuta generals of rank and settled in the regions of Karimnagar and Warangal districts respectively. Subsequent to the fall of the Rashtrakuta power, the Chalukyas of Kalyani allowed them to continue as Mahamandalesvaras with their respective fiefs of Polavasa and Anumakonda adjacent to each other.

Jaggadeva (A.D. 1110-1116):- The single epigraph of the period of Jaggadeva dated A.D. 1112 from Medapalli[61] village in Narsampet taluk records the construction of the temples of Achesvara and Vishnudeva by Achiraja Peggade at the command of his master Jaggadeva son of Medaraja, Lord of Maninagapura and a descendant of Madhavavarman. It also states that Jaggadeva was a great warrior and a hero of twenty one battles, but the details of his heroic battles are not mentioned.

The epigraphs of Jaggadeva and his father reveal that they were the patrons of Jainism and Saivism. The worship of Aditya and Vishnu was also in vogue. Jaggadeva ruled only for a short period as the next inscription of Padmakshi temple[62] at Hanumakonda dated A.D. 1117 refers to his son Meda II as Mahamandalesvara of Polavasa. Jaggadeva had two sons named Medaraja and Gundaraja. After his death Medaraja ruled from the capital Polavasa, while his younger brother Gundaraja ruled from Manthenya or Mantrakuta now known as Manthani.

There is possibility to presume that the town Jagadalaya, Jagatyala or Jagtial might have derived its name from Jaggadeva, who might have founded this village after his name, in the neighbourhood of his capital Polavasa to perpetuate his victories.

Medaraja II (A.D. 1116-1159):- Meda II continued his rule at Polavasa totally contemporaneous with the rule of Prola II (A.D. 1116-1157) at Anumakonda. There are half a dozen inscriptions which refer to Meda II. He figures for the first time in the epigraph of Padmakshi temple at Hanumakonda dated A.D. 1117. It records the construction of a Jain temple called Kadalalaya basadi on the top of the hill and gift of lands by Mailama, the wife of Pergede Beta, who was the minister of Kakati Prola II, the Lord of Anumakonda and ruler of Sabbi-one thousand, which included the southern portions of Karimnagar district. It also records a subsidiary gift of lands by Mahamandalesvara Medarasa of the line of Madhavavarman. It is evident from this epigraph that there were friendly relations between Meda II and Prola II during the early years of their reign.

The Govindapuram epigraph in Narsampet taluk dated A.D. 1122 states that both the brothers Meda and Gunda made gifts of lands to the temple of Parsvanatha constructed by their minister Nagaraja. The gifts were made for the merit of their father Jaggadeva. It also registers the gifts made by Nagaraja and several other devotees of the Vaisya community to Parsvanatha Jinadeva.

The Polavasa chiefs disregarded their Chalukyan overlord and discontinued to mention his name in their epigraphs of Polavasa, Medapalli and Govindapuram. As a contrast the Kakatiyas never failed to mention their overlord in their inscriptions. This obviously shows that the Polavasa chiefs tried to flout the authority of the Chalukya King, which necessarily resulted in the latter's taking steps to subdue them.

An undated inscription of Rudra's minister Vellaki Gangadhara is found broken into pieces, of which the two upper portions[63] are now preserved in Raja Rajanarendra Library of Hanumakonda, while the bottom portion[64] of the same stone pillar containing the subjoined fragmentary record, is recently unearthed on the tank bund near the new bus-stand at Hanumakonda and preserved in the local post-graduate centre. One of the upper portions of this epigraph (big piece) reveals that Prola II conquered Polavasa and subjugated the Kingdom of Medaraja. The bottom portion records the exploits of Prola II who put to flight Edaraja in the presence of King Jagadekamalla II. This Edaraja is identified as the ruler of Ramagundam area in Karimnagar district. His undated epigraph of Ramagundam[65] mentions his titles which are similar to those of Medaraja recorded in the Polavasa epigraph. The similarity of titles like Lattaluru-Puravaradhisvara, Suvarna-garuda-dhvaja and of the names like Eda and Meda suggest that both these chiefs must have belonged to the same stock of Rashtrakuta family of generals. Eda might have joined the confederacy of Meda and Gunda, who rose in revolt against King Jagadekamalla II.

The Thousand pillar temples[66] inscription of Rudradeva at Hanumakonda dated A.D. 1163 recording the victories of Prola II states that he defeated and beheaded Gundaraja, the Lord of Mantrakuta and made Edaraja flee from the battle field in the presence of the king. But the conquest of Polavasa by Prola II, which is recorded in Gangadhara's fragmentary epigraph, does not figure in this inscription.

After a critical study of the above epigraphs, it can be deduced that the Western Chalukya king Jagadekamalla II (A.D. 1138-1151) personally visited the Karimnagar region to put down the revolts of Meda, Gunda and and Eda who disregarded his sovereignty. When the King visited this area, the Kakatiya chief Prola II as a loyal subordinate stood by the side of the king and suppressed the revolts of the disloyal subordinates. Prola II defeated Gundaraja of Mantrakuta and beheaded him after having his head shaved and chest marked with the symbol of Varaha (boar) as a mark of humiliation. He put Edaraja to flight in the presence of the King. He conquered Polavasa and subjugated the kingdom of Medaraja. The suppression of these revolts might have taken place between A.D. 1138 and A.D. 1140 soon after Jagadekamalla's accession to the throne. With the defeat of Gundaraja, Manthena on the Godavari and its dependent territory must have passed into the hands of Prola II. Meda II was a powerful chief. Though he is said to have suffered a defeat in the hands of Prola II and to have lost his kingdom as a consequence of this, he appears to have recovered it again for he figures in the Anumakonda inscription among the enemies later subdued by Rudradeva.[67]

After a lapse of about two decades Medaraja appears again in the battle field together with Dommaraja and Mailigideva. Dommaraja was the Mahamandalesvara of Nagunuru, a village near Karimnagar. Pandaraja probably his predecessor appears in an epigraph on a stone set up near Birannagudi at Nagunuru[68] which is dated A.D. 1112. It records that Mahamandalesvara Pandaraja constructed the temple of Ravvisvara and endowed it with some lands irrigated under tank. Dommaraja of Nagunuru, Medaraja II of Polavasa and Mailigideva of Kalachuri Bijjala of Kalyani formed into a confederacy against Kakati Rudradeva, the son and successor of Prola II. In order to bring back Rudradeva to submission to the authority of Kalyani, Kalachuri Bijjala might have despatched an army with Mailigi at its head. Dommaraja, Meda II and his son Jaggadeva at its head. Dommaraja, Meda II and his son Jaggadeva II who were already hostile to Rudra, took this opportunity to take vengeance against Kakati Rudra and stood by the side of Mailigideva. This confederacy was indeed formidable for Rudra. They attacked Rudra and got initial success, which can be noticed from four label inscriptions[69] found on hero stones at Nagunuru. They refer to Dommaraja and record the victories of his warriors. One of these label inscriptions dated in Chalukya Vikrama era is rather unintelligible. But the year Pramadhin mentioned in the epigraph corresponds to A.D. 1159. It records that Medaraja II and his son Jaggadeva got victory with an army of eighty thousand over some enemy not mentioned by name. It is not unlikely that this unnamed enemy was Rudradeva himself and the record refers in all probability to an early phase of struggle in which he was involved with these chiefs.[70]

Rudradeva, who was a valiant fighter, shattered the hopes of confederacy and ultimately became victorious. The beautiful Sanskrit verses recorded in the Thousand pillar temple inscription eulogise his victories over the above chiefs. The defeat of this confederacy can be assigned to A.D. 1159. This conflict appears to have taken place on the banks of river Maner and in the surroundings of Nagunuru village with heavy loss of life and property. The Nagunuru epigraphs of Dommaraja indicate the death of several warriors and generals like Jaggadeva, probably the son of Meda II. Rudra put to flight Dommaraja, famous as a rider and cavalry commander by hundreds of his shining arrows as Arjuna did to Karna and occupied the city of Nagunuru having all excellences. In fact Dommaraja himself might have been killed by Rudra as Karna by Arjuna. Rudra humbled the pride of Mailigideva, who retreated to Kalyani being pursued by the Kakatiya armies. He worsted Medaraja in battle and drove him into the woods. Instead of offering his daughter and making peace with Rudra, Meda lost his wealth, pride and family reputation.[71] A graphic description of the event, how Meda was defeated and how his town Polavasa was burnt is recorded in the fragmentary epigraph of minister Gangadhara. Gangadhara sacked the city of Polavasa, acquired wealth and built a temple to the god Prasanna Kesava at Anumakonda. Once for all Polavasadesa was annexed to the Kingdom of Rudra. Thus it was an end of the family of the Polavasa Chiefs who once played a pre-dominant role in the tracts lying along the river Godavari.

Gundaraja (A.D. 1116-1138):- Gundaraja, the younger brother of Medaraja II ruled from Manthenya or Mantrakuta, which formed the eastern part of Polavasadesa. An undated inscription of Gangapuram[72] in Manthani taluk mentions Bhulokamalla of Kalyani as the overlord of Gundaraja, who made a gift to the god Suresvaradeva. Another inscription from Venkatapur[73] village in Mulug taluk states that Gundaraja made some gifts to the god Mallikarjunadeva. This epigraph ignores the name of Chalukya overlord and states an independent rule of Gunda over the areas of Mulug and Narsampet in Warangal district. The Palampet inscription dated A.D. 1213 states that certain Kama son of Kataya, the ancestor of general Recherla Rudra led the armies of Prola II against Manthenya Gunda and defeated him. Perhaps this was the same battle in which Gunda was caught and beheaded by Prola II as stated in the Thousand pillar temple inscription.

Edaraja of Ramagundam:- The undated fragmentary epigraph of Ramagundam in Peddapalli taluk mentions Edaraja as Mahamandalesvara bearing the titles similar to those of Medaraja of Polavasa. It can be inferred that Edaraja was connected with the family of the Polavasa chiefs. He ruled from Ramagundam area which lies in between the territories of Polavasa and Mantrakuta. As stated earlier Prola II made Edaraja flee from the battle field like a boy in the presence of the King Jagadekamalla II. Then onwards he is heard no more.

The Polavasa Chiefs and their ministers built several Jain and Siva temples and endowed them with gifts of lands. The tradition of erecting trikuta temples in Chalukyan Style was already in vogue in Polavasadesa. A fine specimen of trikuta temple built by Medaraja is still extant at Nandi Mydaram village in Sultanabad taluk. The capital Polavasa contains the ruins of several temples. Among them the temples of Pulastyesvara and Venugopala are found in good state of preservation.

6. **The Kakatiyas of Warangal:**

The Kakatiyas of Warangal, who ruled over Karimnagar district, built a good number of majestic temples, dedicated to Siva and Vishnu. The grand galaxy of Siva temples at Nagunuru, Kothapalli and Thotapalli in Karimnagar taluk, Godisala, Katkuru and Mutharam in Bhimdeverpalli taluk, Manthani and Chandravelli hamlet of Khammampalli in Manthani taluk exhibit the grandeur of the Kakatiya art and architecture in Karimnagar district. The profusely carved ceilings, lintels, gateways, glistening pillars and the sculptural decor of the temples bespeak of the heightened glory of the Kakatiya art.

Curiously enough, Karimnagar district has yielded recently a hoard of 52 gold coins[74] at Suddala village in Vemulavada taluk. These coins are ascribed to the Kakatiyas, as they contain the legend Daya-gaja-Kesari, a title borne by the Kakatiya rulers.

The Early Chiefs:- The Kakatiyas rose to prominence during the rule of the Western Chalukyas of Kalyani. The epigraphs of Sanigaram in Husunabad taluk have revealed that all the four early members of this family namely Beta I, Prola I, Beta II and Prola II, were the loyal subordinates of the Western Chalukyas. Beta I (A.D. 1000-1052) started his career as a petty chief of Anumakonda. His son Prola I (A.D. 1052-1076) remained firmly loyal and won the affection and favour of his overlord. Delighted by the military ability and unswerving loyalty of Prola I, the emperor Ahavamalla Somesvara I granted him Anumakonda Vishaya as a permanent fief. Prola I thus became the founder of the Kakatiya principality, which under his ambitious successors grew into a mighty and glorious empire embracing the whole of the Andhra country.

Prola I was succeeded by his son Beta II (A.D. 1076-1108) who visited the court of the emperor Tribhuvanamalla Vikramaditya VI at Kalyani, offered his submission and secured for him Sabbi-one thousand territory in addition to Anumakonda-Vishaya as stated in the Padmakshi temple inscription of Anumakonda. As a matter of fact the territory bestowed on Beta II was only a part of Sabbi-nadu, which formed the southern portions of Karimnagar district including Sanigaram village, because the northern portions of the same were governed by Mahamandalesvara Rajaditya and then by Kumara Somesvara as evidenced from the epigraphs dated A.D. 1083 and A.D. 1106 respectively at Vemulavada, the most important town of Sabbi-nadu.

Beta II was followed by his sons Durganripati (A.D. 1108-1116) and Prola II (A.D. 1116-1157) in succession. As stated earlier Prola II defeated Meda II of Polavasa, beheaded Gundaraja of Mantrakuta and made Edaraja flee from the battle field like a boy in the presence of the King Jagadekamalla II. Manthena on the Godavari with its dependent territory appears to have been annexed to Anumakonda Vishaya between A.D. 1138 and 1140. Though Medaraja was defeated, he recovered his territory again and remained a powerful chief in the north-west portions of Karimnagar district with his capital at Polavasa.

Rudradeva (A.D. 1158-1195):- Prola II was succeeded by his son Rudradeva. He defeated the confederacy of Dommaraja of Nagunuru, Meda II of Polavasa and Mailigideva the representative of Kalachuri Bijjala of Kalyani. Polavasa was sacked, its wealth and elephants were acquired and its territory was annexed to the Kakatiya Kingdom in A.D. 1159. With this the whole Karimnagar district passed under the sway of the Kakatiyas for the first time and Rudradeva, who proclaimed himself independent at Anumakonda became the ruler of this district also since A.D. 1159. There are two epigraphs[75] of the reign of Rudradeva in this district.

A pillar inscription dated A.D. 1171 belonging to Nagunuru village, was shifted to Karimnagar and now it stands within the compound of the district collector's residence. It records that Rudradeva appointed his able general and minister Gangadhara as the governor of the entire Sabbi-nadu. It gives a lengthy account of the career of Gangadhara who belonged to a Brahmana family of Vellaki village in Vengidesa. He is said to have built temples at Anumakonda, Nagunuru, Kalesvaram and several other places. He also granted Dimdomta village as an *agrahara* to the Brahmanas. Another fragmentary epigraph of Nandi Mydaram village in Sultanabad taluk refers to the name of Rudradeva, but the details of the gifts are lost.

Mahadeva (A.D. 1195-1198):- Rudradeva was succeeded by his younger brother Mahadeva, whose epigraph dated A.D. 1197 is found in the village Sundella of Manthani taluk. But the contents are not clear.

Ganapatideva (A.D. 1199-1261):- Mahadeva was succeeded by his younger brother Ganapatideva, the most important personage of the Kakatiya dynasty. His long reign of more than sixty years was a brilliant epoch and the Kakatiya empire reached its zenith under him. There are seven[76] epigraphs of the reign of Ganapatideva, which are found at Manthani, Katkuru, Godisala, Dharmapuri, Kalesvaram, Nandi Mydaram and Khammampalli in Karimnagar district. Besides the above stone epigraphs, two copper plates[77] of Ganapatideva dated A.D. 1246 have been noticed recently, which record a decree issued by the King over a canal dispute of Chamanpalli village in Karimnagar taluk. The document is in Nagari script and states certain subordinate Maharaja Akshayachandradeva as the ruler of Karimnagar region.

Rudramadevi (A.D. 1261-1295):- Ganapatideva was succeeded by his daughter Rudramadevi. Though feminine in gender, she was quite masculine in spirit and assumed herself the name as Rudradeva Maharaja, whose undated inscription is found on a stone lying in a field near the tank at Husunabad, recording certain gifts to the god Rudresvara.

Pratapanudradeva A.D. 1295-1323):- Rudramadevi was succeeded by her grand son Prataparudradeva, who was the last ruler of the dynasty. He is represented by three[78] epigraphs at Yelgedu in Sultanabad taluk, Chittapur in Metpalli taluk and Regonda in Husunabad taluk. The Yelgedu epigraph dated A.D. 1301 records gift of some local taxes to the god Ramanathadeva by Lakmadevi, stated as the queen of Prataparudradeva Maharaja. His Chittapur inscription states that certain Bairisetti built a trikuta temple and a tank at Chittapur. The King is said to have visited this temple and made some gifts. But this temple is now no more extant except a few traces of its ruins. The epigraph of Regonda records land gifts to the god Somanathadeva. An unpublished inscription is noticed at the trikuta temple of Raikal village in Jagtial taluk. It is dated A.D. 1305 and found broken into two pieces which recorded certain gifts to the local deities.

Prataparudra expected the danger of Muslim invasions from Delhi and organised an army of 100 elephants, 20,000 horses and 9,00,000 (Nine lakhs) of archers. This preparedness enabled him to meet the Muslim expeditions no less than seven times on the battle field, though he had to make treaties of peace paying enormous tributes in shape of jewels, money, horses and elephants.[79] The earliest expedition of the commander of Allauddin Khalji took place in A.D. 1303 near Upparapalli village in Huzurabad taluk of Karimnagar district. The Velama Chiefs Venna and Potuganti Maili, the two commanders of the Kakatiya armies, according to the chronicle *Velugotivati-Vamsavali* claim to have destroyed the pride of the Turushkas of Delhi in a battle near Upparapalli where the temples of Godisala exist. Potuganti Maili, by his name appears to have belonged to the village Potuganti (Pothgal) in Sircilla taluk of Karimnagar district. On one occasion Potuganti Maili and Telinga Bijjana, who visited the imperial court of Delhi to convey the tribute, are said to have fought an exhibition duel in the presence of the imperial court, perhaps in order to display before the Sultan and his courtiers, the skill in swordsmanship for which the Deccani Hindu soldiers had long been famous.[80]

During the series of Muslim expeditions, certain temples of Karimnagar region appear to have been spoiled and several beautiful sculptures were mutilated. There is hardly any temple which escaped the vandalism of mutilation.

In the final battle of A.D. 1323, Prataparudra was defeated and was taken prisoner by Ulugh Khan, later known as Mohammad bin Tughlaq. Prataparudra, however, died on his way to Delhi and with this ended the rule of the Kakatiyas. The whole Kingdom passed into the hands of Muslim conquerors of Delhi belonging to a different race and religion.

7. The Muslim Rulers:

As a dependent territory, the history of Karimnagar district is associated with the history of Warangal during the 14th and 15th centuries A.D. After the fall of the Kakatiyas in A.D. 1323, the

Musunuri Chiefs, Prolayanayaka and Kapayanayaka rose in revolt against the Muslim armies. Kapayanayaka drove away Malik Maqubul and re-established Hindu rule at Warangal in about A.D. 1336. When he ruled for about two decades, he was killed by the Recherla Velama Chiefs of Rachakonda, a village in Nalgonda district. The Recherla Velama chief Anapotanayaka occupied Warangal and became the ruler of Telingana comprising the tract between the Godavari in the north and Krishna in the south which included Karimnagar district.

KAKATIYAS

Beta I (A.D. 1000-1052)

Prola I (A.D. 1052-1076)

Beta II (A.D. 1076-1108)

Durganripati (A.D. 1108-1116) | Prola II (A.D. 1116-1157)

Rudradeva (A.D. 1158-1195) | Mahadeva (A.D. 1195-1198)

Ganapati Deva (A.D. 1199-1261)

Rudramadevi (.A.D. 1261-1295)

Prataparudradeva (A.D. 1295-1323)

When the Velama chiefs entered into an alliance with the Bahmani Sultan, the traditional foe of the Vijayanagara Rayas, Harihara II despatched his son Devaraya with armies against Telingana. Devaraya subdued the Velama chiefs and erected a victory pillar dated A.D. 1397 at Kalesvaram[81] on the banks of Godavari in Karimnagar district. It records his victories and *Tulapurushadana,* one among the sixteen *mahadanas,* to the god Muktisvara. Karimnagar district was under the sway of the Vijayanagara rulers for a brief period which is further evidenced by a hoard of 31 gold coins of Vijayanagara dynasty, discovered at Gutturajepalli village of Jagtial taluk in A.D. 1976.[82]

After the departure of the Vijayanagara armies, the Velama chiefs appeared again on the scene and joined their hands with the Rayas of Vijayanagara against the Bahmanis. Ahmed Shah I (A.D. 1422-1436) who shifted his capital from Gulbarga to Bidar invaded Warangal twice in A.D. 1424 and A.D. 1433. He devastated the town, destroyed the temples and humbled the Velama chiefs.[83]

When Lingamanedu, the Velama chief of Warangal was attacked by Humayun Shah (A.D. 1458-1461) he appealed for help to Kapilesvara Gajapati of Orissa, who sent his son Hamvira and cousin Raghudeva to Warangal with a large army. They freed the forts of Warangal and Devarakonda from the control of the Muslims in A.D. 1460.[84] After the death of Kapilesvara Gajapati in A.D. 1470, Hamvira sought the help of Mohammad Shah III, defeated his brother Purushothama and became Gajapati. He ceded Telingana to Bahamani Sultan for the help he rendered in his war of succession. With this the Gajapatis and the Velamas were no more seen on the stage of Telingana politics.

When Warangal was under the sway of the Velama chiefs for more than a century, a large number of Velama subordinates of different ranks appear to have settled in Karimnagar district as the Velama population appears more in this district than in the other parts of Telingana. Though they lost their power, they wielded influence as petty local chiefs. They patronised temples and endowed them with lands as evidenced by their epigraphs[85] found at Anantagiri (A.D. 1517) in Sircilla taluk, Vellulla (A.D. 1613) in Metpalli taluk, Dharmapuri (A.D. 1644) and Mallannapet (A.D. 1753) in Jagtial taluk. Till recent times they were the Jagirdars, Makhtedars and Watandars under the Asaf Jahi rulers.

The last political phase in the history of Warangal refers to the exploits of Shitapkhan alias Sitapati of Bhogi-kula and son of Manaya and Gauramba. The word khan affixed at the end of his name, is only a title received from Muslims, when he was under their service. His inscription dated A.D. 1504 states that he occupied the fort of Warangal, restored Hindu Dharma and re-installed the images of gods removed by the Turushkas.[86] With Sitapati alias Shitapkhan the rule of Hindus ended at Warangal and then onwards the history of Karimnagar centred round its forts.

The strong hill-forts of Elgandal, Molangor and Ramgir, which were once under the control of the Kakatiyas, later became the centres of political activity in Karimnagar district under the Bahamanis, Qutubshahis, Mughals and Asafjahis.

Sultan Quli, the founder of the Qutub Shahi dynasty, became independent in A.D. 1518. A rebel named Qiwamul-Mulk occupied the forts of Elgandal and Molangor in Karimnagar district. Sultan marched against him and a battle reged in and around Elgandal fort. Having been defeated, Qiwamul-Mulk fled to Berar and returned soon with the forces of Daraya Imadul-Mulk, which were also defeated by Sultan Quli near Ramgir fort.[87] With this all the important forts of Karimnagar district were brought under the control of the Qutubshahis. Sultan Quli was succeeded by Jamshid (A.D. 1543-1550) whose copper coins, now preserved in State Museum, were recovered from Karimnagar district.[88]

During the reign of Ibrahim Qutubshah (A.D. 1550-80) Jagadeva Rao, a Hindu Commander revolted against Sultan and made Elgandal his centre of activity. He went to Berar and secured the help of Daraya Imadul-Mulk (A.D. 1529-1572). When Jagadeva Rao returned, Sultan sent his forces against him. A fierce battle took place at Elgandal which resulted in heavy losses on both sides. However Jagadeva Rao faced defeat and fled to Vijayanagar. An immense booty fell into the hands of Qutubshahi soldiers.[89] Sultan Abdullah Qutubshah (A.D. 1626-1672) offered the fort of Ramgir and the adjoining district to the Mughals as dowry for the marriage of his second daughter with prince Muhammad Sultan son of Aurangzeb in A.D. 1656.[90]

The rule of Qutub-Shahis ended in A.D. 1687 when Aurangzeb occupied the fort of Golconda and annexed it to the Mughal empire. Elgandal Sarkar (Karimnagar district) remained under the Mughals for about 39 years. Two mosques in the Mahadevpur taluk, one at Kalesvaram and the other at Sonipet are said to have been built by Aurangzeb.[91] Consequent to the invasions of Khiljis, Tughlaqs, Bahamanis and Mughals, several temples of Karimnagar district, as elsewhere in the country, were spoiled and beautiful sculptures were mutilated. A few temples were also converted into mosques as evidenced by the mosque at Dharmapuri, which was originally a trikuta temple beside the temple of god Narasimha.

When the Mughal empire started declining, Nizamul-Mulk Asaf Jah became independent in A.D. 1724. The fort of Elgandal passed into the possession of Asaf Jahis. A hoard of 129 silver coins of Asaf Jahi dynasty were found at Jivella village in Sircilla taluk.[92] Nawab Salabat Jung appointed Mubarizul-Mulk Zafaruddaula Bahadur Ibrahim Khan Dhonsa as the Subedar of Elgandal. He reconstructed the fort of Elgandal and constructed a new fort at Jagtial in A.D. 1747 with the technical help of the French engineers. Similar fortifications of his period are also found at Nirmal. Elgandal was the headquarters of a Sarkar under Qutub Shahis and Asaf Jahis till 1905 when the district headquarters was shifted to the present Karimnagar Town.

The temple-building activity retarded and almost came to a stand-still as the district was ruled successively by the Bahamanis, Qutubshahis, Mughals and Asafjahis till A.D. 1948 when the Nizam dominions became a part of the Indian Union Government. However the liberal out-look and the spirit of toleration exhibited by some Muslim rulers enabled the local chiefs, merchants and rich people to raise temples of both small and medium size almost in every village for the daily worship. Many such temples of simple style and architecture, constructed during the late medieval period are visible in most of the villages of Karimnagar district.

REFERENCES

1. Hemchandra Raychaudhuri, "Geography of the Deccan", *EHD*, p.26.
2. K.A. Nilakanta Sastri & G. Sreenivasa Chary, *Advanced History of India*, p.8.
3. R. Subrahmanyam, *Ashokuni Yerragudi Sasanamulu* (Telugu) No. 1 to 13.
4. Parameshwarilal Gupta, *Punchmarked Coins in the A.P. Govt. Museum*, pp4,5.
5. *Ibid.*, p.27.
6. Romila Thapar, *The Past and Prejudice*, p.63.
7. V.V. Krishna Sastry, *Op. Cit.*, p.200.
8. *ARDAM*, 1977-78, p.26.
9. *Ibid.*, pp.39 & 43.
10. M. Rama Rao, *Satavahana Coins in the A.P. Govt. Museum*, p.9.
11. Gurty Venkat Rao, "Pre-Satavahanas and Early Satavahanas", *EHD*, p.69.
12. Romila Thapar, *Op.Cit.*, p.42.
13. M. Rama Rao, *Select Andhra Temples*, p.1.
14. Roy C. Craven, *a Concise History of Indian Art*, p.133.
15. Percy Brown, *Indian Architecture*, p.62.

16. James Fergusson, *History of Indian And Eastern Architecture*, p.421.
17. Abdul Waheed Khan, "Introduction", *Early Chalukyan Temples of Andhra Desa*, p.I.
18. *Ibid.*, p.II.
19. Stella Kramrisch, *The Art of India*, Plate 57.
20. N. Venkataramanayya, *Chalukyas of Vemulavada*, pp.92-94.
21. K.R. Srinivasa Iyengar, "Kannada Literature", Chapter-IX, *Bharatiya Vidya Bhavan*, Volume IV, p.224.
22. G.V. Devasthali, "Sanskrit Literature", Chapter-IX, *Bharatiya Vidya Bhavan*, Vol.IV, pp.188-189.
23. Kunduri Eashwara Dutt, *Prachinandhra Charitraka Bhugolamu* (Telugu), pp.316-317.
24. *RE*. 1966, No.170, pp.42-43.
25. N. Venkataramanayya, *Op.Cit.*, pp.9-12.
26. *EHD*. P.508.
27. N. Venkataramanayya, *Pallavulu-Chalukyulu* (Telugu), p.187.
28. D.C. Sircar, "The Eastern Chalukyas", Chapter VI, *Bharatiya Vidya Bhavan*, Vol.IV, p.135.
29. N. Venkataramanayya, *Chalukyas of Vemulavada*, pp.44, 45, 82.
30. R.C. Majumdar, "Rise and Fall of the Pratihara Empire", Chapter II, *Bharatiya Vidya Bhavan*, Vol.IV, p.36.
31. A.S. Altekar, "The Rashtrakutas", *EHD*., pp.290, 291.
32. *RE*., 1966, No.170, pp.42, 43.
33. *EA*., Vol.II, pp.21-28.
34. *EHD*., p.504.
35. *EA*., Vol.II, pp.31-35.
36. *ARE*., 1967, No.1, pp.22, 23.
37. *EHD*., p.511.
38. *IAPKD*., No.5, p.12.
39. Percy Brown, *Op.Cit.*, Chapter XXX.
40. *IAPKD*, nOS. 6, 7, 8, 9.
41. *EA*., vol.ii, pp.36, 37.
42. *IAPKD*., Nos. 10, 11, 12.
43. *Ibid.*, No.13.
44. *Telangana Sasanamulu* (Telugu), Vol.I, No.21, pp.173-77.
45. N. Venkataramanayya, *Op.Cit.*, p.45.
46. P. Sreenivasachar (ed), *Op.Cit.*, pp.48, 49.
47. K.A. Nilakanta Sastry, "The Chalukyas of Kalyani". *EHD*.. p.330.
48. *IAPKD*., Nos. 14, 15, 16, 17.
49. *EA*., Vol.IV, p.68.
50. Paul G. Hiebert, "A Brief History of Patancheru or Pottalakere", *JAHRS*, Vol.XXVI, (II-IV Parts), p.3.
51. *A Catalogue of Inscriptions Copied Upto 1964*, Nos. 187, 188, 189.
52. *EA*., Vol.IV, pp.74-78.
53. *Ibid.*, pp.81-84.
54. *IAPKD*, No.23, p.58.
55. *EA*., Vol.IV, pp.84-89.
56. Vincent A. Smith, *The Oxford History of India*, p.217.
57. *JAHRS*, XXXVI, Part I, pp.33-43.
58. P.V. Parabrahma Sastry, *The Kakatiyas*, pp.60-62.
59. *EA*., Vol.I, pp.111-113.
60. *IAPKD*., No.75, p.139.
61. *RE*., 1965, No.345, p.78.

62. *Ibid.* No.308, p.71.
63. *IAPWD.*, Nos. 44 & 45.
64. *JAHRS*, XXXVI, Part I, pp.58-62.
65. *Ibid.*, pp.63 & 64.
66. *Ibid.*, pp.1-24.
67. *EHD.*, p.582.
68. *IAPKD.*, No.77.
69. *Ibid.*, No.74.
70. *EHD.*, p. 586.
71. P.V. Parabrahma Sastry, *Kakatiya Sasana Sahityamu* (Telugu), pp.21, 22.
72. *IAPKD.*, No.23, p.58.
73. *IAPWD.*, No.31, p.87.
74. P.V. Parabrahma Sastry, *Kakatiya Coins and Measures*, pp.9, 10.
75. *IAPKD*, Nos. 25, 26.
76. *Ibid.*, Nos. 28 to 34.
77. *JAHRS*, XXXV, pp.183-188.
78. *IAPKD.*, Nos.37, 38, 39.
79. P.V. Parabrahma Sastry, *The Kakatiyas*, p.132.
80. *EHD.*, pp.644-647.
81. *RE.*, 1966, No.179, p.45.
82. *ARDAM*, 1976-77, pp.53, 61.
83. S.K. Sinha, *Medieval History of the Deccan*, Vol.I, pp.98, 99.
84. *IAPWD.*, Nos. 108, 109.
85. *IAPKD.*, Nos.46, 48, 49, 53.
86. *IAPWD.*, No.111, p.291.
87. H.K. Sherwani, *History of the Qutubshahi Dynasty*, pp.24, 25.
88. Abdul Waheed Khan, *Qutubshahi Coins in A.P. Museum*, p.17.
89. H.K. sherwani, *Op.Cit.*, pp.126, 127.
90. *Ibid.*, p.444.
91. *Census Handbook, Karimnagar District, 1961*, p.VI.
92. *ARDAM*, 1976-77, p.53

THREE

The Sites of Temples

1. Adavisomanapalli

The earliest specimens of Hindu religious architecture found in Karimnagar district are the rock cut temples at Adavisomanapalli which is about 22 kms. from Manthani. These cave temples can be reached through a thick forest of wild animals after covering a distance of about 4 kms. on foot from the Tadicherla bus-stop and they are totally inaccessible during the rainy season. The spot is picturesque on a hillock where four caves are scooped out of a huge sand-stone rock facing the west and overlooking the river Maner. These temples are dedicated to Siva and they are locally known as *NAINA GULLU.* Execution of these caves is not geometrical and quite irregular in measurements of length, depth and height. The caves consist of an inferior variety of sand-stone which is getting damaged due to the passage of time, vagaries of weather and the cold winds of the river Maner. These caves are simple and plain with a cell and a mandapa like a few rock-cut temples of the age of Vishnukundins located at Mogalrajapuram near Vijayawada. The pillars of these temples can be compared with those of the rock-cut temple No. 4 at Mogalrajapuram with octagonal middle part in between the parts with square sections.[1]

The Rock-cut Temple No. I

It consists of an open pillared mandapa with a shrine chamber at the back. The hall consists of two heavy pillars at the entrance with corresponding pilasters in the front. The pillars are of early type and their finishing is crude consisting of a base, shaft and bracket. The shaft consists of a square member, followed by an octagonal member of about 6" height, above which there is another square member surmounted by a bracket extending only two sides along the lintel. The mandapa measures 13'-10" x 12'-4" with the height of 7'-6". The walls of the hall are quite plain without any sculpture of niche. It is most interesting and astonishing to notice colour paintings on the ceiling, which appears to have been coated with a thin layer of lime. Unfortunately these paintings are peeled off completely leaving only faint traces in different colours such as pink, yellow, red, blue and black etc.. While no details can be made out from the panels, the existing portions reveal a few male and female figures dressed in an upper garment and an ardhoruka. The figures now seen wear Kiritamukutas, necklaces, Patrakundalas, armlets, Yajnopavita etc. A few dancing figures, battle scenes with archers and chariots drawn by horses and some palace scenes etc. can also be noticed in the remaining scattered paintings.

The mandapa leads into the shrine chamber through an offsetted doorway of 5'-6" height and 2'-3" width. The garbhagriha measures 10'-10" x 10'-1" with the height of 7'-3". There is a linga on a pedestal of 2'-5" height. The linga is in crude form with a height of 1'-7" and circumference of 4'-1". There is also a loose sculpture of Nandi with broken head.

The Rock-cut Temple No. II

This is comparatively a small cave consisting of small shrine chamber preceded by an open mandapa without pillars except two pilasters carved on either side in the front. The hall measures 8'-7" x 4'-7" with the height of 7' while the garbhagriha measures 5'-2" x 4'-3" with the height of 6'-10". The mandapa leads into garbhagriha through a doorway quite similar to that of Cave No. I. There is a small platform to the back wall of the cell. It contains a loose beheaded sculpture of Mahishasuramardini in black basalt. The devi is standing in dvibhanga with the right leg steady on the ground and the left kept on the neck of the demon, who is in buffalo form. Her upper left hand is broken and her upper right hand is piercing the trisula into the body of the asura. Her lower left hand holds the twisted tail of the animal while her lower right hand thrusts a Khadga into its body. She is adorned with graiveyakas, Keyuras, Katibandha, Yajnopavita, beaded wrist-lets and ear rings. She wears bangles and rings to all her fingers. The image shows the folds of drapery upto her ankles.

The Rock-cut Temple No. III

The third cave is only a hall with two pillars and corresponding pilasters in the front. It measures 12'-5" x 12'-2" with the height of 7'-6". In the centre of the hall stands a square pedestal consisting of Patta, Kumuda, Jagati and Vedi all in crude and mutilated form. There is a broken linga on the pedestal with the circumference of 4'. The pillars of this cave are similar to those of Cave No. I. In between the Cave II and Cave III there are two niches on the facade carved with the images of Ganapati and Dvarapala.

The Rock-cut Temple No. IV

It is an open mandapa with two pillars in the front. The pillars are crude in design and workmanship. The hall is vacant and appears to be an unfinished cave. It measures 14' x 8'-4" with the height of 7'. To the left of this cave on the facade are two niches, one with an indistinct image while the other is vacant.

On the facade of the caves, two label inscriptions[2] are noticed in the characters of 10th or 11th century A.D. in Telugu. The first inscription, which is incomplete, records the installation of a deity named Ramesvaradeva by certain Ekkate Vimuna and the work of stone-cutting by Kempena. The other epigraph records the gift of pannasa (land gift) for offerings, lamps and muggu (lime linings) to the god Ramesvaradeva by certain Penukanti Mucchi Reddy.

Outwardly these caves look like a few shrine models noticed on the hill range at Undavalli and elsewhere at Vijayawada. But these caves cannot be compared with the five storeyed rock temple known as Anantasayanagudi of Undavalli. On stylistic grounds, these caves can be assigned to 7th or 8th century A.D.[3]

2. Vemulavada

Vemulavada, is situated about 35 kms. to the west of Karimnagar. It was the capital of the Chalukyas of Vemulavada who ruled from A.D. 750 to A.D. 73. They appear to have been great builders as noticed from the extensive remains of temples and sculptures. There are seven published inscriptions,[4] which throw ample light on the past glory and grandeur of this place with a good number of temples. The place is referred to in the inscriptions as Lembulavataka, Lembulavade and Lembulavada. It became gradually corrupted into Lemulavada, Emulavada and Vemulavada.[5] The following are the principal temples in Vemulavada known as the earliest extant examples in Karimnagar district.

Bhimesvara Temple

Siva temples built of fine masonry, which evidence the growing popularity of the cult, first began to appear in southern India about the seventh century A.D.[6] Vemulavada preserves an excellent temple of ninth century A.D. known as Bhimesvara temple. This is said to have been the old Baddegesvara temple,[7] probably built by King Baddega (A.D. 850-895) during the last years of his reign. The temple stands inside a stone-walled compound. This is the most important temple in Vemulavada showing a vigorous style of architecture in which breadth of vision and loftiness of religious ideals are amply demonstrated.

The temple consists of a high platform with sopana on either side, a mukhamandapa, an antarala and a garbhagriha. Raised on a high upapitha, an uncommon feature in the prevailing times in various regions of Andhra, it has a Pratibandha type of Adhisthana showing plain Kumuda in the Karna sections and an astasra Kumuda in the Bhadra sections. The use of the astasra Kumuda is noticed in this period in the temples at Hemavati, Veldurti etc. In the Kanta Part of the Upapitha rich iconographic details of Siva, Dasavataras and the Panchatantra stories like the story of crocodile and monkey are carved. Atop the adhisthana, the Vedi moulding decorated with lion in frontal position is introduced recalling the similar convention noticed at Biccavolu. The Chandrasila at the foot of the sopana and the figures of Sankanidhi and Padmanidhi on the balustrade deserve notice. The wall is relieved with Brahmakanta type of pilasters, while the garbhagriha is plain. The gradation of the wall of garbhagriha is another feature. In the prastara portion the strongly projected uttara element, hamsamala and kapota are worthy of note.[8]

The gala part of the Adhisthana in the front platform is cut into numerous compartments by short pilasters. Curiously enough there are two panels depicting the images of primitive Mother Goodess with legs wide apart showing prominently the genital organ. Probably these figures represent the fertility cult. Even today the issueless ladies in Andhra worship these figures to beget children.[9] The spire of the temple seems to be a mixture of south Indian Dravida Vimana and Nagara Rekhaprasada with a considerable height.

The trisakha doorway leading into mukhamandapa is decorated with a makara torana at the lintel, Gajalakshmi on lalata and the dvarapalas at the base holding a club in one hand and keeping the other in abhaya. The dvarapala panels contain female figures with fly-whisk in one hand and the other resting on a thigh. They contain the hair-dress matted above the head. Inside the mukhamandapa the four central pillars are unusually tall and the other corresponding pillars four on each side are short, because slopy pent roof is adopted. The massive central pillars are fashioned in Chitrakhanda form of decoration. The base of the shaft contains shrine models in low relief on four sides and on the cube portions the hamsas, apsarasas, purnaghatas, elephants, and creeper pattern are carved. The ceiling is fashioned in the form of *Kadalikakarana process* (triangular slabs placed one above the other in two or three tiers cornerwise forming hallow in the middle) with a lotus medallion at the centre.

The mukhamandapa leads to antarala where the Vatayana or window houses the figure of Mahishasuramardini facing the north. The goddess is eight-armed and shown in the stance of combat, trampling the *asura*. The fluid movement of the combat is well captured by the grouping of arms, the arching body and the tilt of the head. The tight modelling of the slim figure and the smooth rendering of the surfaces characterize the art. Iconographically the form of this figure has close similarities to the Rashtrakuta examples at Ellora and Alampur.[10]

The door frame of the garbhagriha contains a projecting cornice over the lintel, above which the turrets are carved. Lalata contains Gajalakshmi motif. Beneath the sakhas there is a panel on either side with two female figures and a male figure holding trisula, naga, gada, in three hands while keeping one of the lower hands in abhaya. The garbhagriha contains four pillars inside and between them on a high pedestal stands the linga with 3' diametre. To have four pillars inside the garbhagriha is an early Chalukyan feature followed here, which can be noticed in the temples of Alampur,[11] Satyavolu[12] and Mahanandi.[13] The Chandrasila before the antarala is smooth with conches and floral design on either side.

Baddi Pochamma Temple

This is a very small old temple lying in front of the Nagaresvara temple. The garbhagriha contains Bhadrakali holding trident in upper right hand, damaru in upper left, head of an asura in lower left and a sword in lower right hand. There is an image of Baddi Pochamma, a female deity outside the temple. A nude Jain image of 2' height standing in Kayotsarga posture is noticed in the courtyard. The temple is now under total renovation.

Nagaresvara Temple

The Nagaresvara temple is one among the four temples mentioned in an undated inscription[14] of Arikesari II (A.D. 930-955). It was the shrine of the mercantile community,[15] built in the 10th century A.D. The temple is inside a walled compound facing the east.

The adhisthana, as visible contains upana, broad patta and Jagati. The bhitti which rises with pilasters is separated from the spire by a cornice in crude form. The Prastara portion contains Hamsamala and the spire is in the stepped pyramidal form.

The temple contains a four pillared porch which leads to the mandapa with four central pillars and corresponding pilasters bearing the lintels over which a flat roof is laid. The pillars in the porch and the mandapa are massive and crude in form. There is Ganapati on the right and Parvati on the left side of the ardhamandapa which leads to garbhagriha with Siva in the form of linga.

Kedaresvara Temple

This temple is also inside a walled compound. An inscription dated A.D. 1033 standing before the temple states that for the worship and offerings of the god Rajesvaradeva, installed by Chikaraja, a gift of land was made by certain chief. This Rajesvaradeva may be the present Kedaresvara. The temple contains a garbhagriha and a mukhamandapa connected with a passage in the shape of ardhamandapa.

This adhisthana of the temple contains upana, patta and a vedi containing several deities and floral devices. An image of primitive Mother goddess prominently showing her genital part can also be noticed. The wall contains pilasters and sala motifs. The first of the salas contains Ganapati seated in lotus, the second houses standing Brahma of 3' height. The third and fourth salas contain Siva and Vishnu respectively of similar height. Now and then there are huge elephant riders in between the pilasters.

The garbhagriha contains Linga between four pillars which enable to form a passage otherwise known as Pradakshinapatha around the deity within the garbhagriha between the pillars and walls. This peculiar feature is noticed in the temples of 10th and 11th centuries A.D. in this region.

Raja Rajesvara Temple

The Raja Rajesvara Temple is the most popular among all the temples in Vemulavada. There is a Sthalapurana known as *Sri Raja Rajesvara Kshetra Mahatmyam*. An inscription[16] dated A.D. 1083 of the reign of the Western Chalukyan King Vikramaditya VI states that Mahamandalesvara Rajaditya had installed Rajadityesvara and built a huge temple for it known as Raja Rajesvara temple. But the temple as it exists today contains several structural and sculptural additions of later times. The whole temple complex faces the east and it is inside, a very high stone-walled compound.

The adhisthana at present is partly buried in the ground and over the base, the wall rises with pilasters, their intervals filled with plain stone slabs. The method of making effective the wall content of the temples was based on that initiated by the earlier Chalukyan builders as at Pattadakal, in which the principle employed was that very sound one of spacing out the surface by means of pilasters.[17] But there are no niches here between the pilasters as noticed in the temples of Pattadakal. The cornice of the base and the portion above the cornice of the wall are decorated with the Chaitya window motifs. The figures of drummers, warriors with shields and swords, elephant riders, female figures and swans are carved in the prastara portion. The spire of the main shrine is totally reconstructed on a new pattern. Before the renovation it had a stepped pyramidal form. The mukhamandapa is also reconstructed over the old plan. The gopura, mukhamandapa with life size dvarapalas before it are present works.

The mukhamandapa contains three entrances on east, north and south, the west being the shrine containing Linga on a pedestal. In the mukhamandapa on right side is an idol of Lakshmi-Ganapati with goddess seated on his folded left leg. On left side is the image of Raja Rajesvari Devi with trident and damaru in upper hands, a sword and a bowl in lower hands.

The garbhagriha has a fine door frame of Kalyani Chalukyan type with Gajalakshmi motif on lalata. It has a projecting cornice over the lintel and the door jambs contain pilasters on either side flanked by floral designs. Below the jambs there is a panel on either side containing dvarapala flanked by female figures. The dvarapala holds trident and damaru in upper hands, gada in lower hand, while the lower rests on the lower right hand. The flanking female figures are of exceptional beauty and elegance. The grace of their limbs and the charm of their hair dress are admirably represented. A notable feature of the later Chalukyan temple is the artistic emphasis given to the doorways of garbhagriha. There is an architectural frame work consisting of a pilaster on either side with a moulded lintel and cornice above. Using this as his structural support, the craftsman has thrown over the whole a superb sculptured pattern of figures, foliage and decorative effects, replete with mythical imagery and carved with incredible detail and finish.[18] The garbhagriha contains linga on a pedestal.

The courtyard contains other temples of Ananta-Padmanabha

Swamy, Kodandarama and Kasi Visvesvara. There are number of sculptures in the precincts of this temple. The images of Bhairava, Murali Krishna, Vinayaka, Linga and Nandi are worth mentioning. At present there is also a tomb of a Muslim saint to the north-east of this temple. It is regarded sacred by both Muslims and Hindus.

To the north of the temple, there is a large tank fed by a rivulet. A special portion of the tank is called Dharmagundam which can be reached by numerous steps built on four sides. There are two pavilions in the holy tank each with four pillars containing a Linga at the centre. These pavilions remind the Linga pavilion constructed in Vishnu's Lotus pond at Mahakut near Badami datable to A.D. 600.[19]

Adityagriha:- Adityagriha is mentioned as one among the four temples in an inscription[20] of Arikesari II, but this temple is now no more extant. However there is a small image of Aditya or Surya placed near the present deepastambha in the Raja Rajesvara temple. He holds two lotuses in his two upraised hands. Similar image, broken at the feet, is noticed among the loose sculptures, now placed in Bhimesvara temple. This is a much worn out early sculpture with two hands each holding a lotus. According to *Amsumadbhedagama* and *Suprabhedagma* the hands are so held up as to cause the fists holding the lotuses reach the level of the shoulders.[21] He stands in samabhanga. His head is surrounded by Kantimandala or a halo.. He is adorned with mukuta, ear rings and a hara over his chest. Perhaps these two surya figures belong to Adityagriha built by Peddana the tantrapala of Arikesari II.

Subhadhama Jinalaya:- This temple is now no more extant. But the Parsvanatha figure of this Jinalaya was erected in the temple of Raja Rajesvara inside the prakara by the side of the gopura. When the temple is renovated in recent times, it is shifted and placed in the garden of Bhimesvara temple where a heap of marvellous sculptures is found neglected. The figure of parsvanatha is of red sand-stone with hoods of a serpent above his head. The coils of the serpent behind the lord are close packed. The figure is in Kayotsarga posture exhibiting youthful body, long arms extending upto knees, elongated ears and nudity. A small figure of a lady with her child is put in juxtaposition to this figure. Parsvanatha is believed to bless his devotees with progeny. A four lined inscription[22] on the pedestal of this image records the construction of Subhadhama Jinalaya by Baddega the son of Arikesari II for the favour of his guru Somadeva suri, the head of guada Sangha.

Epigraphic evidence confirms only one Jain temple, but one is surprised to notice today in Vemulavada as many as a dozen figures of Jain Tirthankaras scattered in all its temples. It is not probable that all these were housed in one and the same temple, for there are now in Vemulavada five Parsvanatha figures, three Vardhamanas, Gomatesvara and four other Tirthankaras not identifiable for want of their characteristic symbols below their seats or on their pedestals. The figures range from the early Rashtrakuta to the late Western Chalukyan period. The presence of Gomata figure at Vemulavada indicates the influence of Bodhan where these figures were made in profusion. His pose is determined, stately and severe. The face is equally impressive and hands add to the dignity of the resolve. The two red stone Jain figures, built into the walls of the Venugopalaswamy temple indicate that the installation of Jain icons was started at Vemulavada from the early period of the Rashtrakutas. The figures show the archaic features and they are reliefs like the Konakondla and Pedatumbulam types.[23]

Sculptures and Icons:- Several loose sculptures which once occupied the corridors of Raja Rajesvara temple, are now found placed in a verandah to the south-east of Bhimesvara temple. The sculptures have suffered having been exposed to the sun and rain.

1. *Saptamatrikas:-* This is a much worn out Saptamatrika slab with Vinayaka at one end. The slab contains Brahmi, Mahesvari, Kaumari, Vaishnavi, Varahi, Indrani, Chamundi and Vinayaka with their respective Vahanas swan, bull, peacock, garuda, mahisha, Airavata, fox and Mushika, carved below their seats as per the agamas. All the Saptamatrikas are carved with halos and adorned with mukutas. They are four handed and wear usual ornaments. This appears to be an early sculpture of 9th-10th century A.D..

2. There is another Saptamatrika slab flanked by Virabhadra and Vinayaka. All the figures are four handed with their cognizances carved below their seats. The Saptamatrika figures are adorned with mukutas, ear rings, graiveyakas, anklets and armlets.

3. *Surya:-* This is a small image broken at the feet holding lotus buds in his two upraised hands.

4. A Jain Chaumukh or Pratima Sarvatobhadrika contains seated Jain Tirthankaras carved on its four faces. It looks more tall than broad compared to the Danavulapadu one, and like that one, was used exclusively for the abhisheka festival being mounted on a Panavatta.[24]

5. Another Jain Chaumukh containing seated Jain Tirthankaras on its four sides with their hands in dhyanamudra.

6. The chauvisa Tirthankara modelled on the same lines as the Chaumukh, but is shaped as a miniature temple with two floors above the ground floor. It is of about 2' height with a Sikhara of south Indian type. On the three floors in their centres are found seated Jinas. The Jinas in the ground floor and first floor have each one of them two standing Jinas on either side. The seated ones have the triple umbrellas and chowry-bearers. At the rate of six on each face, there are twenty four Tirthankaras on the two floors of the Chauvisa temple. On the Sikhara there is an ornamental jina on each face surrounded by the spread of a creeper behind his head. The Chaumukhs and Chauvisas resemble the votive shrines of Siva set up at Elesvaram, Veldurti, Alampur and Mahanandi.[25] A similar Chaumukh from Danavulapadu in Cuddapah district, bears an inscription of Rashtrakuta Krishna III.[26] Hence the Chaumukhs and Chauvisas of Vemulavada can be dated to 10th century A.D.

7. A seated Jain Tirthankara with his hair in spiral ringlets and hands in dhyanamudra.

8. Another seated Jain image of black granite with his hands dhyanamudra.

9. *Vinayaka:-* A small image of Vinayaka endowed with two arms and a natural elephant head. The left hand holds a cup of modakas on which the tip of the trunk rests, while the right hand holds a tusk.

10. *Bhairava:-* The image is of 4' height. He holds damaru and trisula in his upper hands, Khadga and a bowl in his lower hands.

11. *Skanda:-* The figure is with six heads riding a peacock.

12. *Naga:-* A seven hooded Naga with coiled body interlocked in an artistic manner.

13. A worn out image of Chamundi.

14. A slab of two Nagas entwined with their hoods above

15. *Vinayaka:-* At the entrance of the Bhimesvara temple there is a round stone containing the image of Vinayaka in low relief. It is of 2' height endowed with two hands and a natural elephant head without a crown.

16. *Devi:-* A female figure is found with her left leg folded and rested on the seat and right leg bent up at the knee. She wears ear rings, broad necklace, armlets, anklets, nupuras, and a hara falling in between the breasts which are prominently carved. As the hands are broken and in the absence of attributes, it is difficult to identify the figure.

17. Another female figure similar to No. 16.

18. A medium size Nandi with chains of bells.

19. A seated jain Tirthankara in black granite with his hands in dhyanamudra. This image is in the garden of the Bhimesvara temple.

20. A Nandi of medium size in black granite with chains of bells at the above place.

The above sculptures reveal that Vemulavada was a centre of Siva, Jain and Surya worship during the period of the Chalukyas of Vemulavada and the Western Chalukyas of Kalyani.

3 Gangadhara

Gangadhara is situated about 25 kms. to the north of Karimnagar. Somadevasuri, the celebrated Jain scholar states that he composed his famous work *Yasastilaka Champu* at Gangadhara, the capital of Vagaraja,[27] the elder son of Arikesari II of Vemulavada. Vagaraja, the heir-apparent, might have been deputed by his father to rule over Gangadhara which is about 20 kms. to the east of Vemulavada. He succeeded his father at Vemulavada as a feudatory of Rashtrakuta Krishna III and accompanied him during his southern expeditions. Somadeva also states that he completed his work in A.D. 959 at Gangadhara when his patron Vagaraja was camping with the monarch at Melpadi in Chittoor district .[28] Baḍyaga or baddega II, the younger half-brother of Vagaraja also appears to have ruled over Gangadhara for some time which is characterized as overflowing with wealth.[29] As it was a big Jain centre during the mid-tenth century A.D., Somadeva a scholar of Jain order, stayed here to compose his work treating it as a place of pilgrimage.

Bommalagutta:

Bommalagutta, a hillock lying 2 kms. to the south of Gangadhara village was a famous Jain centre known as Vrishabhadri, when Arikesari II and his successors ruled over Vemulavada principality. The hillock can be reached after covering 2 kms. on foot either from Gangadhara or from Kurkiyala village, the latter lying on Karimnagar-Jagtial P.W.D. Road. The famous trilingual inscription of Jinavallabha, the brother of Pampa, is carved here in fine verses of Sanskrit, Kannada and Telugu. The last three verses in Telugu are in *Kanda* metre which are the earliest of their kind in the language. It is evident from this that the art of writing poetry in Telugu was known in north-western parts of Telingana at least a century before the composition of *Andhra Mahabharata* by Nannayyabhatta. At present the hillock is surrounded by fields. It is very difficult to climb up and reach the big flat faced rock, standing on the summit of the hillock, where the inscription and the Jain images are carved. This inscription can be dated round-about A.D. 945.[30] The inscription states that Jinavallabha was devoted to the construction of temples of Jina. He caused the images of his family deities the Adyanta (the first and the last) Jinas, Chakresvari and other Jina divinities carved on the Siddhasila (the rock of the Siddhas) and named the hill as Vrishabhadri because it contains the image of Vrishabha, the first Tirthankara. He constructed near it a Jain basadi (monastery) named Tribhuvanatilaka, dug a tank called Kavitagunarnava and laid a garden known as Madanavilasa.

The Jain images mentioned in the inscription are still visible on the face of the rock named as Siddha-sila. The image of Chakresvari, an excellent example of Jain sculpture, is flanked by the lady attendants. She is the Yakshini of Vrishabha. She wears mukuta, graiveyakas, Keyuras, Kankanas, and Katibandha. She is eight handed with her cognizance garuda below her seat. The number of hands of this Yakshini differ from place to place. The Mathura image has ten hands, the Deogarh image has sixteen arms, another image of the same place has eight arms and the Udayagiri image (Orissa) has twelve hands.[31] The image of Dilwara temple on Mount Abu in Rajasthan is highly decorative and stylised with eight hands as it is carved later in 13th century A.D. Chakresvari on Bommalagutta is seated with her right foot down and the left leg tucked up in front. But contrary to this, the image of Dilwara temple contains her left foot down and the right leg tucked up.[32] Her image is important due to her cult position as the Sasanadevi of the first Tirthankara. She is the Yakshini of Vrishabha with her cognizance garuda while Gomukha is his Yaksha with his cognizance bull.[33] By her name and symbols of disc and garuda etc., Chakresvari pertains to the nature of Vaishnavi, the wife of Vishnu, whose one name is Chakresvari. The Yakshinis as a rule combine in them influences from the Brahmanic goddesses as well as those of the Yaksha demidivinities.[34]

Above the image of Chakresvari on Bommalagutta are carved Adyanta Tirthankaras, Vrishabha and Vardhamana. The distinguishing features of these standing Jain figures are their long hanging arms and their mild form with youthful body and nudity. Each image has a trilinear umbrella over its head. There are three Jain divinities carved on either side of the Yakshini. The Jina Padas (feet) are also carved in a circle near these figures. The tribhuvanatilaka basadi and madanavilasa garden are now no more seen in the vicinity of the hill. perhaps they were not near the hill but in the village Gangadhara itself which can be judged from the Jain icons scattered in the fields around it.[35] The irrigation tank at the foot of the hill might be the tank called Kavitagunarnava built by Jinavallabha after the name of his famous brother Pampa, who had the title of Kavitagunarnava.

The Vaishnavite Temple

There is a Vaishnavite temple of the medieval period inside a walled compound. The main temple consisting of garbhagriha and antarala of the present order appears to be earlier than the mukhamandapa and porch. The garbhagriha and antarala stand on one and the same adhisthana, whereas the base of the mukhamandapa and porch differs from the earlier one. The base contains four petalled floral design. The walls of the temple are very plain which are separated from the Sikhara by a slightly projecting cornice decorated with semi-circular stones. The square mandapa has sixteen pillars including the four central pillars with a pial all along its length leaving a passage into the porch on the east through which the entry into the temple is obtained. The ceiling of the antarala and mandapa is flat-roofed whereas the ceiling of the central part of the mandapa and garbhagriha is laid in Kadalikakarana process.

The Sikhara of the temple is a stepped elongated pyramid. This appears to be the form, the temple Sikhara had taken when the stone-stepped sikhara of Jain temples of the Kadamba region was reproduced in brick in the Kakatiya Kingdom. The temples of Hanumakonda, Mattevada, Kasibugga, Kondiparti, Dharmasagaram were all built in the same pattern which can be noticed at Gangadhara.[36]

There are loose sculptures of garuda and Hanuman of 4' height placed on either side of the porch. Before the temple there is a garuda stambha of about 25' height, which reportingly contained at one time a miniature mandapa at its top enshrined with the image of garuda, which is now placed in a niche within the courtyard. This garuda stambha is similar to those found at Valgonda, Chilvakoduru, Nagunuru and Ramagundam. At present the garbhagriha contains the deities of Venkatesvara with his consorts Lakshmi and Padmavathi.

4. Repaka

The small village Repaka lies to the south-west of Karimnagar and can be reached via Bejjenki or Sircilla. The name of the village is referred to in the Parbhani plates[37] dated A.D. 966 issued by the

King Arikesari III of Vemulavada. It registers a gift of the village of Kuttumvritti-Venikatupalu in the midst of Repaka - twelve in the Sabbi-thousand to the famous Jain divine Somadevasuri for the white-washing, repairs, etc. to Subhadhama Jinalaya at Vemulavada. It appears that Repaka was a small administrative unit consisting of twelve villages. The pillar inscription[38] lying in the field near the middle school dated A.D. 968 reveals that Repaka was a Jain centre with a Jinalaya built by the King Arikesari III. The inscription is damaged and the first letter of the name of the Jinalaya is not identifiable. The name can be read now as Khalivuttu Jinalaya to which several gifts were made by a number of disciples of Jain faith. A certain list of Jain ascetics is also given. But unfortunately neither this Jinalaya is extant nor its ruins are found in the village.

5. **Dharmapuri**

Dharmapuri is situated on the bank of the river Godavari at a distance of 27 kms. from Jagtial. A direct road connects it from Karimnagar via Choppadandi. Here the Godavari flows from north to south forming a natural boundary between Karimnagar and Adilabad districts. The village contains fairly a good number of old temples which bear an eloquent testimony to the antiquity and the historical significance of this place.

Dharmapuri attained religious importance owing to the existence of the shrine dedicated to Narasima Swamy, an incarnation of Lord Vishnu. There is a Sthala purana known as *Dharmapuri Kshetra Mahatmyam* on palm leaves with 3500 Sanskrit slokas describing the puranic story and greatness of this Lord. It is dated in the saka year 850 which corresponds to A.D. 928.[39] The name of this village is mentioned in the inscriptions and literary works. The Kurkiyala inscription[40] of Jinavallabha datable to A.D. 945 mentions this village as Dharmavura or Dharmapuramu, gifted by King Arikesari II to his court-poet Pampa as an agrahara for his great work *Vikramarjuna Vijaya*. An inscritpion[41] of Kakati Ganapatideva dated A.D. 1246, now standing before the Ramalinigesvara temple, mentions the King's name and the gods Vaijanathadeva and Suryadeva and certain gifts. The details are not clear as it is a much abraded broken inscription. Madiki Singana in the introduction to his *Padmapurana-Uttarakhandam* states, that, when Muppa Mahipala was ruling from his capital Ramagiri-Pattana over Sabbi-nadu, Veligandala Kesana (14th-15th century A.D.) the Commander of his army is said to have celebrated festivals of god Narasimha in Dharmapuri.[42]

Old Narasimha Temple:

The old Narasimha temple contains a garbhagriha and a 48 pillared mandapa before it. The temple is inside a walled compound facing the east. The adhisthana members are very much obliterated. It contains a wide patta and Jagati decorated with Semi-circular stones. The wall is crudely plain. Above the wall there is a cornice, over which the stepped pyramidal sikhara rises. The garbhagriha contains the image of Lord Narasimha in the Yogic form and not in the ugrarupa. The mandapa before it appears to be a later addition with a parapet around it leaving passages on east, north and south.

There is a separate four pillared Kalyana mandapa before the temple. The pillars are richly carved with a typical Kakatiyan sculpture depicting several stories from the Epics. The figures of Matsya, Kurma, Varaha, dancing Siva, Narasimha, Rama and Lakshmana etc. appear on the rectangular and square panels of the pillars. This mandapa is definitely a later addition exhibiting the sculpture of the Kakatiya times.

Sculptures and Icons:

There are loose sculptures of Brahma and Balarama in the mukhamandapa of this temple. Balarama is rarely worshipped independently as a god. Usually his image is worshipped in association with that of Krishna.[43] But the sculpture of Krishna is not found here as it is shifted and now placed in the Museum at Karimnagar.

1. *Brahma:-* This is a standing figure of 6' height with four hands holding sruk in upper right hand, Vedas in upper left, while keeping the lower left in abhaya mudra with akshamala and the lower right crossed towards left resting on gada. Three faces are visible with a pointed beard for the middle face alone. He wears Jatamukutas, Kundalas, haras hanging on chest, armlets, wristlets, anklets and nupuras on feet. His Vahana Hamsa is carved on on right side at the base. This sculpture resembles the standing figure of Brahma at

Sopara in the Thana district of Maharashtra State with the similar pointed beard for the middle face alone.[44]

2. *Balarama:-* This figure is two handed, adorned with mukuta, graiveyakas, Keyuras, Kankanas, Katibandha, Vanamala, anklets and beaded nupuras. His left leg is stiff resting on the floor, while his right leg is crossed towards left so as to touch the ground with the toes. The flute is held in both the hands and one end of it is applied to the mouth. He wears rings to all the fingers of his hands. He is flanked by female chowry-bearers at the bottom. The image contains a makara torana behind it. Hala or the plough is carved on right side and the case of the flute is carved on the left side of the image.

3. *Krishna:-* This is a black granite image of 4' height with a makaratorana. Krishna stands in tribhanga with his left leg resting on the floor and right leg crossed towards left so as to touch the ground with the toes. He has eight arms. He is seen holding aloft the Goverdhana hill with the topmost right hand. He holds sankha and khadga in other two right hands. In three of the left hands, he holds padma, gada and chakra, with the remaining two hands the flute is held which is broken. He wears a mukuta, kundalas, katibandha, vanamala, keyuras, kankanas, rings to the little fingers, anklets and nupuras. He is flanked by lady attendants at the bottom holding fly-whisks. As this is an image of Goverdhana-dhari Krishna, cows and calves are carved on either side in front of the chowry-bearers. Now this figure stands in the Gandhi centenary Museum at Karimnagar.

4. *Garuda:-* This is a seated image with flying wings and hands folded in anjali.

The Sixty Pillared Temple:

The so called sixty pillared temple now contains only 48 pillars, perhaps the porch with the rest of the 12 pillars is now no more extant. This is a very old temple but now it houses Lord Venkatesvara. Its adhisthana consists of upana, patta, Jagati with semi-circular stones, Kumuda and vedi with inverted semi-circular stones. The mandapa is open without any pial around it. It has a plain projecting cornice with slight slant but it has now partly disappeared .

New Narasimha Temple:

This temple exists in the same courtyard facing the east with a garbhagriha, antarala and a mandapa before it. At one time there were eight dikpalas placed in separate niches around this temple. But now only two dikpalas Indra and Agni can be seen. Indra is seen standing with his vahana elephant. Agni is a two headed figure flanked by lady attendants. His vahana ram is carved behind him.

Venugopala Swamy Temple:

It stands at the back of the sixty pillared temple with an idol of Venugopala and several other small images of Alvars. It has a crudely carved garuda on right side and Hanuman on left side of the entrance.

Ramalingesvara Temple:

The temple is situated inside a square stone-walled compound of about 10'height. It faces the east and lies to the north-east of Narasimha temple. The main door leading to the courtyard contains a projecting cornice and a Gajalakshmi motif on lalata. The dvarapalas beneath the door jambs are flanked by lady attendants in dvibhanga bearing fly-whisks. The dvarapalas hold demaru and kapala in upper hands, gada in lower left while they keep lower right hand in abhaya. A mandapa of sixteen pillars is attached to this entrance inside the prakara. The mandapa consists of a passage corresponding to the doorway of this entrance with a raised platform on either side. The pillars rise over the platform. The lower part of the platform contains four petalled floral designs.

The temple consists of garbhagriha, antarala, mukhamandapa and small porch resting on two front pillars in the east. The temple stands on a highly elevated adhisthana which contains upana, Jagati, Kumuda and a vedi. The adhisthana has a cornice decorated with semi-circular stones over which the bhitti rises. The shrine is crowned by a curvilinear sikhara with an amalaka at the top, followed by a stone kalasa. A sukanasa projects to the east from the base of the sikhara, which is a Chalukyan feature.

A flight of steps leads to an enclosed rectangular mukhamandapa with eight pillars and corresponding pilasters which divide the ceiling into 12 compartments all filled by Kadalikakarana process. It has three entrances on east, north and south, the west being the shrine. The garbhagriha contains *Saikata linga* (sand pressed into the form of linga) supposed to have been set up by Lord Sri Rama during his sojourn in Dandakaranya. There is a seated female deity in the garbhagriha, perhaps the consort of Siva with damaru and trisula in upper hands, khadga and bowl in lower hands.

There is a small shrine exclusively dedicated to Ganapati to the north-east of the main temple in the same courtyard. The seated Ganapati is unusually big with four hands, wide ears and karanda mukuta over his head. Here Ganapati is given prominence with a separate shrine for him because Ganapati is worshipped as the popular guardian of households, remover of obstacles, patron of merchants, authors and school boys (for he is the scribe of gods) and god of common sense, who must be invoked before every enterprise and mentioned before any appeal to the divine spirit.[45]

Sculptures and Icons:

There are loose sculptures in the mukhamandapa of Ramalingesvara temple.

1. *Saptamatrikas:-* The seven goddesses are flanked by Vinayaka and Virabnadra with their respective vahanas carved below their seats. The saptamatrikas are four handed adorned with mukutas and usual ornaments.

2. *Mahishasuramardini:-* The image is well sculptured but all her hands are broken. Here Mahisha is found in the form of buffalo.

3. *Alinganamurti:-* Seated with the left leg folded and the right hanging, this god holds damaru encircled by a naga in the upper right hand, trisula in the upper left, keeps the lower right in abhaya holding askhamala and passes the lower left round the back of the devi. This sculpture can be compared with the images, found in the early Chalukyan temples of Alampur.[46]

4. *Skanda:-* The image is six faced with his vahana peacock.

5. There is a beautiful sculpture of Gautama and his consort Ahalya sitting with their hands folded in anjali.

The courtyard contains several other sculptures of Viragals, Nandis, Nagas and Naginis. There is a stambha of about 25' height standing before the temple, which reportingly contained at one time a miniature mandapa at its top housing a Nandi.

Satyavati Temple:

This temple stands at an elevated place facing the east with only one square garbhagriha. It contains a red sandstone Stambha of about 30' height bearing a miniature mandapa above it.

There is a detached mandapa of nine pillars before the temple. It contains a broken door jamb with a dvarapala of about 5' height standing in dvibhanga holding a khatvanga in upper right hand and damaru in upper left hand. He has his right hand crossed towards left resting on a club, while he keeps his lower left hand in abhaya. This figure is similar to the two dvarapala figures found in Kalesvaram.

The Mosque Temple:

The temple converted into mosque to the south of the courtyard of Narasimha temple is apparently a trikuta facing the east. A mandapa of 16 pillars, quite similar to that of the Ramalingesvara temple is attached to the entrance inside the prakara. The adhisthana of the converted temple contains upana, broad patta, Jagati and vedi. The Kakatiyan lattice work can be noticed beside the vertical door jambs on the southern part of the converted mosque. It contains ample traces of Hindu shrine even after its conversion into mosque.

According to a local Telugu book *Trisati,* this temple seems to have been damaged thrice, first by Malik Kafur, the military commander of Allauddin Khilji during his invasions on Warangal, next in A.D. 1425 by Azim Khan, the military officer of Bahamani Sultan Ahmed Shah (A.D. 1422-36) and the last by Rustumdil Khan, the

Subedar of Hyderabad, (A.D. 1687-1707) under the Mughal emperor Aurangzeb. It seems that Rustumdil Khan caused the conversion of this trikuta temple into a mosque in A.D. 1693 and appointed Abul Hasan Faras as its mouzan by allocating one hundred acres of land for its maintenance.[47]

Brahma Pushkarani: (The Holy Tank)

Brahma Pushkarani is a large and square temple tank with steps on all four sides. A passage of 6' width leads to the central Bhoga mandapa in the tank connected by a bridge with seven sluices under it. The holy tank has a parapet all around with four gates on four sides, the northern being the main which leads to the central mandapa.

An inscription[48] on a pillar of the mandapa in Brahma Pushkarani dated A.D. 1644 records the construction by certain Tirmalayya son of Chintala Narasa-boyi, of the compound wall around the Pushkarani and the mandapa on the platform, which was formerly constructed by Jupalli Dharmaraya. The latter is said to have built the steps around the Brahma Pushkarani.

6. **Choppadandi**

Choppadandi lies 16kms. north of Karimnagar on the P.W.D. road to Lakshettipet. There are two inscriptions in which the village is known as Cheppamdandi and Choppamdyandi. The first inscription[49] dated A.D. 992 lying at Melakunta near the village is of the reign of Taila II known as Ahavamalladeva. It records the construction of the tank Achabbe-samudra named after Achabbe, the daughter of Duggaraya, the follower of the prince Irvebedenga and the monetary gift of 70 drammas and the lands by the latter's dadi Divakabbe. Another inscription[50] carved on a pillar standing in the courtyard of the temple belongs to the reign of Irvebedenga Satyasrya. It is dated A.D. 1008 and records some gift of lands to the god Divakesvara, set up by Divakabbe, the dadi of the king Irvebedenga in the village choppamdyandi. This Divakesvara temple is now locally known as Sambhunigudi. It represents the architectural style of the 10th century A.D. prevalent in this region.

The Temple of Sambhunigudi

The temple stands in a stone walled compound. The walls of this enclosure are built of large blocks of stone fitted into each-other. This is a single shrine temple facing the east. It consists of a garbhagriha, an ardhamandapa and an enclosed hall with a porch before it. The adhisthana is simple and the walls rise with pilasters dividing their outer surfaces into well proportioned areas. The shrine is surmounted by a sikhara in stepped pyramidal form like the sikharas of the temples of those days at Vemulavada. The eight diminishing steps lead to a tapering circular member, crowned by an amalaka with a Kalasa above it. The eight steps of the sikhara are connected by a wide tapering band in the centre on all four sides.

The doorway leading to the closed mandapa measures 5' x 2 1/2' with Saivite dvarapalas carved at the base and turrets sculptured on the architrave. The mandapa with four pillars at the centre consists of a flat ceiling laid by means of large slabs of stone. The doorway of garbhagriha is plain while the ardhamandapa before it is open without a doorway.

Facing the above temple, there is another shrine, now housing the image of Vishnu. There are dvarapala figures on broken door jambs lying outside the prakara wall. There is a holy tank to the south of the temple constructed with steps on four sides which are in ruins.

Sculptures:

1. *Nandi:-* This is a Chalukyan Nandi of 3 1/2' length and 2' height lying in the porch at Sambhunigudi.

2. *Devi-* The figure has suffered having been exposed to sun and rain. This is a seated figure holding damaru in upper right hand, Khat-vanga in upper left hand, Khadga in lower right hand and a small bowl in lower left hand. She is adorned with a mukuta, kundalas, graiveyakas, girdles and anklets. She wears armlets and wrist-lets in pairs and an ardhoruka reaching below her knees. A hara of skulls hanging in between her large breasts reaches upto her navel. There is a naga hood carved on either side of the mukuta. The figure has

no symbol carved below her seat. This sculpture was shifted to Karimnagar in 1980 and now it is placed on pedestal in the museum.

7. **Jammikunta**

Jammikunta is situated at a distance of 53 kms. south-east of Karimnagar and can be reached via Huzurabad. It is a railway station on the Kazipet-Balharshah line of south Central Railway. There is an inscription[51] incised on two sides of the dhvaja stambha, which is about 25' high standing before the Siva temple in the old Jammikunta village. It is dated A.D. 995 and records the gifts of two *Khandus* comprising 20 *martars* of wet land and other dry lands and two ratanas to the god Aditya by Nagiya, the gavunda of Jammikunta village.The gift was made for the merit of his wife Vemakabbe. In the inscription the village is known as Dammikunte.[52] The Adityagriha mentioned in the inscription is now no more extant.

The Siva temple stands beside a tank facing the east. The present temple is reported to have been built over the ruins of the old temple. Some loose sculptures of the Kalyani Chalukyan period are found in and around the temple. The figures of Ganapati, Bhairava shaded by a hooded naga, a few naginis are half human and half serpentine in their form holding a shield and khadga in their hands. They are canopied by three, five or seven hoods. The nagini figures are similar to those found at Polas.

8. **Sanigaram**

Sanigaram is situated at a distance of about 40 kms. form Karimnagar on the way to Hyderabad. There are five Kannada inscriptions[53] of the Kalyani Chalukyan kings, which reveal, that it was a centre of Jain and Saiva worship. In the inscriptions the name of the village is mentioned as Sanagara. The first inscription dated A.D. 1051 registers a gift of ratana to the Duddhamalla Jinalaya. The second dated A.D. 1053 records the gifts of lands and a ratana to the god Madhupesvara of Khandi Sanagara. The third dated A.D. 1107 records similar gifts to the god Bhimesvara of Baliya Sanagara. The fourth dated A.D. 1128 registers the gifts of a ratana, ganuvu (oil-mill) and lands to the god Kommesvaradeva of Khandi Sanagara. The fifth and the last epigraph dated A.D. 1149 records similar gifts to the god Parthesvaradeva. Khandi Sanagara and Baliya Sanagara might be the names of the then localities which existed in the old Sanagara village. Now the temples of gods mentioned in the inscriptions are no more extant except the remains of their ruins noticed at various places all along the hillocks lying beside the present village. The traces of old fortifications and ruined walls can be noticed on the top of the hills.

Duddhamalla Jinalaya:

The renovation work and the gifts made to the Duddhamalla Jinalaya are mentioned in the earliest inscription of this place dated A.D. 1051. It might be a Jinalaya built by Yuddhamalla, probably one of the kings of that name belonging to the line of the Chalukyas of Vemulavada.[54] The Jinalaya is no more extant. But the present hillock, where the image of Parsvanatha is located, might have been the place, where this Jinalaya flourished in those days. The image of Parsvanatha is carved on a big boulder lying on the way to the tank. He stands nude in Kayotsarga posture. The coils of the serpent behind the Lord are close packed and its hoods canopy his head. As seen on the figure of Parsvanatha at Vemulavada, here too is a mother with her child standing to his left thanking the Lord in worship for his boon of the child. This sculpture is in all probability contemporaneous with the Parsvanatha of Subhadhama Jinalaya at Vemulavada as their faces are alike and legs are also similar.[55]

Bhimesvara Temple:

This temple is now at a deserted place beside the hillocks. It is perhaps the same old Bhimesvara temple mentioned in the epigraph A.D. 1107. The temple consists of 11' square garbhagriha, an antarala of 11' length and 8'-8" width and before it a mandapa of 18' length and 9'-2" width. The temple faces the east. The walls of garbhagriha and antarala are plain and the superstructure of the temple is lost. The mandapa, which leads to antarala, has a flat ceiling with a row of three pillars on either side. The pillars are typically Chalukyan in their treatment. The doorway of garbhagriha is very simple with Saivite dvarapalas carved at the base and a projecting stone shade over the lintel with a width of one foot. The pillar inscription of this temple is reported to be lying now before the

Mahalingesvara temple.

The Temple in the fields:

This is a ruined temple with a garbhagriha and antarala before it. The roof is lost. The doorway of antarala contains Gajalakshmi motif on lalata and Saivite dvarapalas at the base. This is a Siva temple facing the east.

Narasimha Temple:

This is a small temple situated on a hill near the Bhimesvara temple.

Mahalingesvara Temple:

This small temple is at the outskirts of the village and it does not merit any description. There is a linga placed on a pedestal in the garbhagriha. The height of the linga is 1'-8" with the circumference of 4'-6".

Loose Sculptures:

1. *Ganapati:-* This is a seated image before Mahalingesvara temple. He holds parasu in upper right hand, trisula in upper left, tusk in lower right and modakas in lower left hand towards which the trunk is twisted. He wears a short mukuta and his vahana mushika is seen below his seat.

2. *Nandi:-* This is of medium size lying at the same place carved in typical Chalukyan style.

3. *Mahishasuramardini:-* The broken piece containing the upper portion of the goddess is placed inside the garbhagriha of Bhimesvara temple. The devi has multiple hands and she is driving a sula downwards with one of her right hands. The lower portion of devi with asura is lost.

4. *The Saptamatrika piece:-* This is a broken piece lying at the same place containing only two out of seven matrikas.

5. *Bhairava:-* There is an image of Bhairava of 6' height outside the village on the way to Koheda. He holds damaru in upper right hand, trisula in upper left, Khadga in lower right and a human head in lower left hand.

9. Potlapalli

Potlapalli is situated about 30 kms. south of Karimnagar and can be reached via Husunabad. A pillar inscription[56] of the reign of Trailokyamalladeva dated A.D. 1066 records the gift of a ratana to a temple by Mahasamanta Chandayyarasar of Remgomda (Regonda) a nearby village. The first line on the second side of the inscription contains the word Nakaresvara (Nagaresvara) which denotes the name of a Siva temple to which the gifts were made. In the inscription the village is known as Pottapalliya. There is another inscription probably unrecorded, standing near a well before Mallannagudi. The Jain vestiges found here reveal that it was also a Jain centre. The old temples are no more extant but their ruins are found here and there in the village.

The present Ramalaya is reported to have been built over the ruins of the old temple, like the Siva temple at Jammikunta. On the base of this temple a few old sculptures of Matsya, Kurma, Primitive Mother goddess and motifs of gajas and simhas are found. A Chaitya window motif and a figure of dvarapala are noticed at a high level on a watch tower built in the middle of the village while a lion motif and a Chaitya window motif are found on the sluice of the tank. There is a well 3' x 3' before Mallannagudi probably built during the Chalukyan times with dressed stone blocks placed one over the other on all four sides right from bottom to the surface.

Sculptures:

1. *Ganapati:-* Ganapati in archaic form endowed with two arms and a natural elephant head without a mukuta is noticed in Mallannagudi.

2. *Saptamatrika Slab:-* A broken piece with three out of seven matrikas is now placed in Mallannagudi.

3. *Jain Image:-* A seated image of Jain Tirthankara with his hair in spiral ringlets and hands in dhyanamudra is noticed behind the tank bund. Both the arms are mutilated but the palms placed in dhyanamudra can be noticed now in the figure. It is carved smoothly in black granite. This figure is similar to those found at Vemulavada.

10. Koratla

Koratla town is 72 kms.form Karimnagar on Karimnagar-Nizamabad Road. The remnants of an old mud fort, its walls, moat and gateways drew the attention of the visitor. There is an undated Kannada inscription[57] of the reign of Trailokyamalla Somesvara I (A.D.1042-1068) in the *Koneru* or the holy tank inside the fort. It records a gift of some land for the worship, offerings and renovation etc., to the Rattamartanda Jinalaya by certain chief bearing the titles of Lattalurupuravaradhisvara and Suvarna-garudadhvaja, which indicate his Rashtrakuta affiliation like the rulers of Polavasa. A Jain sect of Koravattu-goshti belonging to Kranurgana and Tintrini-gachcha is mentioned. As this place was a centre of Koravattu Jains, the town might have derived its name as Koratla from the word Koravattu in the course of time.

Mahadeva Swamy Temple:

This is a small temple standing beside a rivulet known as Koratla-vagu. There is ample evidence to believe that this was originally a Jain temple known as Rattamartanda Jinalaya mentioned in the inscription. The presence of Parsvanatha figure and other Jain sculptures lying in the courtyard confirm that this temple was a Jinalaya in the place of the present Sivalaya. The practice of carving purnakumbha beneath the door jambs is believed to be a Jain tradition.[58] Here the doorway of the garbhagriha contains purnakumbhas and not the dvarapalas as seen in the Hindu temples. When there was bitter persecution of Jains during the 13th and 14th centuries, this Jinalaya appears to have been converted forcibly into Saiva temple. The temple originally contained only garbhagriha and a porch before it. The mandapa before the porch appears to be a later addition probably at the time of its conversion into Sivalaya. There are loose sculptures in the courtyard of the temple.

1. *Parsvanatha*: The figure of parsvanatha is of 5' height in red sand-stone with seven hoods of a serpent canopying his head. But three hoods on his left side are broken. The coiling of the snake several times behind the image is very appealing. He is nude in Kayotsarga posture exhibiting his youth. Now this figure stands inside the compound wall beside the entrance.

2. *Jain image*: This is another beautiful sculpture of 4' height in red sand-stone placed on another side of the entrance with a trilinear umbrella over the head. He is also in Kayotsarga posture extending his arms upto knees.

3. *Prabha Mandali*: At the back of the temple there is a beautiful ornamental device intended to be kept behind the head of a big Jain statue which is not traceable. The device contains a trilinear umbrella flanked by seated Tirthankaras in miniature shrines. It also contains flying gandharvas and semi-divine figures with fly-whisks. Beneath the umbrellas, the Prabhamandali is noticeable.

4. A broken piece of saptamatrika slab is fixed to a platform. The figures of Brahmi, Mahesvari and Kaumari are clearly visible.

5. *Surya*: This is a small image broken below the navel. He holds lotus buds in his two upraised hands. It is stated to have been recovered recently from the fort area.

11. Polas

Polas is about 56 kms. to the north of Karimnagar. It lies at a distance of 6 kms. from Jagtial on Jagtial-Dharma puri road. Once it was the capital of Polavasadesa ruled by some chiefs who had their affliation with the Rashtrakutas. There is an inscription[59] dated A. D. 1079 on a pillar near the local Panchayat office. It records only the date and the day, probably indicating that the pillar was set up as a part of the mandapa. Another important inscription[60] of Medaraja I standing before the Pulastyesvara temple dated A.D. 1108 records the name of the village as Polavasa and Pulastyasrama-Pattana and certain gifts made by the Virabalanja community consisting of Ayyavali-five hundred swamis, mummuridandas and Ubhaya-nandesis to the god Pulastyesvara. The ruins of temples and a large number of sculptures scattered in and around the village had a strong mud fort around it and the remains of which along with the moat can still be noticed in the village.

The famous Telugu literary work *Kreedabhiramamu* of 14th century mentions Polavasa as one of the famous six centres for the abode of a female deity known as Ekavira, the other places being Mandapaka, Penupaka, Mahuramu, Nagavaramu and Orugallu. It also mentions that deities of Ekavira and Kakatamma were set up side by side in Orugallu or Warangal.[61] The worship of Sakti in the form of Durga, Gauri, Gangamma, Kakati, Irukalamma, Ekavira and Yellamma etc., came into prominence in the medieval period.[62]

Pulastyesvara Temple:

This temple stands to the north of the tank and faces the east. This is a single shrine dedicated to Siva with a 10' square garbhagriha and an antarala with 7' length and 9' width. The exterior length of the shrine is 24' with a width of 16'. The doorway of garbhagriha contains Purnakumbhas beneath the jambs and a projecting cornice above the lintel. The ceiling of garbhagriha is laid in Kadalikakarana process with lotus medallion on the central square slab.

The adhisthana of the temple is plain and simple, above which the plain wall rises to the height of 6'. The spire is of curvilinear type, but the curve being very sharp at the top makes the spire disproportionate. It is crowned by a beaded amalaka, above which there is a large spherical stone Kalasa. The spire does not contain sukanasa before it.

The temple seems to have been renovated, when the mandapa before the temple was added to it. The connecting part of the mandapa with the porch of the shrine now stands collapsed, the traces of which can be noticed even today. As a mark of renovation one evidence can be cited. The doorway of the garbhagriha which presently contains Ganapati on Lalata, perhaps at one time contained Gajalakshmi motif which is displaced and improperly arranged at the same place.

Before the shrine is a mandapa with 32 pillars arranged in four rows. The mandapa looks to have been constructed in two phases. The first which is immediately before the temple, is enclosed by a parapet wall adorned with Kakshasanas or the stone seats with slop-ping backs to rest. The second phase of the mandapa contains porches on east, north and south with a passage on west leading into the mandapa of the first phase. The central part of the second man-dapa contains a circular ranga-sila. The whole mandapa is in a crum-bling condition. It contains all along a big projecting cornice with slight slant which is now seen damaged in certain parts.

There is a separate small shrine to the north of the mandapa with a stepped pyramidal spire of brick construction. The bricks used in the spire are strong and each brick measures 11" x 8" x 2". To the north of mandapa is a small holy tank in the shape of a big well with steps on south to reach the water.

Sculptures and Icons:

There are several loose sculptures in and around the temple.

1. *Saptamatrikas*: This is a rare early panel with seven figures of divine mothers seated in a row with their left legs folded and right legs hanging keeping the feet turned towards right. The figures are two armed and there are no vahanas or any other distinctive marks to separate them from each other. The head of each goddess is decked with a tapering kirita. They are adorned with graiveyakas, armlets, bracelets and anklets. The panel does not contain Vinayaka or Virabhadra carved on either side as noticed in later representa-tions. The panel no doubt represents earlier iconography of Sap-tamatrikas and resembles the panels of the Chalukyas of Badami. It can be dated to 8th or 9th century A.D. as the later panels are carved with the vahanas of their respective spouses. Moreover they are invariably shown flanked by Ganapati on one side, Siva or Virabhadra on the other.[63]

2. *Devi*:- This is a seated figure with four hands holding Khadga in lower right hand, damaru in upper right, trisula in upper left and a bowl in the lower left hand. She wears a Karanda mukuta. Her right leg is folded and left leg is hanging beside which Nandi is carved.

The presence of bull indicates that she is the consort of Siva. This image resembles the images of Patancheru[64] which was once the headquarters of the Chalukyas of Kalyani. Similar images of Devi are found in a large number throughout Karimnagar district.

3. *Viragal:-* This is a hero stone holding shield in left hand and Khadga held high in his right hand. His hair is combed and arranged into a side knot. An elephant is carved with a raised trunk to his left side.

4. *Viragal* He holds shield and Khadga in his hands. His hair is tied in the shape of a bun to his left side. He wears rings to his toes. He keeps a dagger tied to his waist. To his left is a standing female figure with her hands in anjali placed between the breasts.

5. *Viragal:-* This is similar to No. 4.

6. *Viragal:-* This is similar to No. 4 and 5. It is now placed in the sub-shrine lying to the north of the mandapa.

7. *Nandi:-* This is recently dug out and recovered from the ground. The chains of bells adorn its body. It is of medium size in Chalukyan style.

8. *Ganapati:-* He is two handed with a short mukuta over his head.

9. *Ganapati:-* He is four handed with wide ears wearing a mukuta.

10.*Nagini:-* This Nagini is shown in anthropomorphic form upto navel and below navel with the body of snake. She holds Khadga in right hand and shield in left hand as stated in the *silparatna.*[65] She has five out-stretched hoods canopying her head. She is adorned with necklaces and a hara hanging over her breasts. Her head is plain without a mukuta. The Naga stones are usually worshipped and installed with a belief to beget children.[66]

11. *Nagini:-* This is like No. 10 but small in size.

12. *Nagini:-* This is like No. 10 and 11 but wears a Karanda mukuta over her head. About a dozen beautiful sculptures of Nagas and

Naginis are noticed in the village. These figures are similar to those found in the temples of Alampur[67] in Mahaboobnagar district, Kolanupaka[68] in Nalgonda district and Biccavolu[69] in East Godavari district.

The Temple on the Tank-bund:

This temple has collapsed totally and its ruined pillars can be seen beside the tank-bund touching the water. However, a few beautiful sculptures still remain on the bund attracting the attention of the visitor.

1. *Annapurna:-* This is a four-handed seated image of about 3' height, carved in bas-relief on a black granite stone. She is a three eyed goddess with high breasts. In her lower left hand she carries a vessel and in her lower right hand, she holds a ladle touching the vessel as if ready to serve food. She holds damaru in her upper right hand and trisula in her upper left hand. She keeps her left leg folded and the right hanging. She is adorned with a Karanda mukuta, Patra kundalas, graiveyakas, armlets, wristlets, anklets and a hara hanging between the breasts. There is a makaratorana behind the image. A similar four-handed image of Annapurna comparatively smaller in size can be noticed in red sand-stone among the several loose sculptures now placed outside the Muktisvara temple at Kalesvaram.

2. *Ganapati:-* There is a big image of Ganapati with a single pair of arms holding modakas in his right hand on which the tip of the trunk rests. He holds a tusk vertically in his left hand. He keeps his left leg folded and right leg hanging. He is adorned with Yajnopavita, wristlets and a short mukuta over his head. As against the lack of crown in early images, the introduction of mukuta is after Kalinga tradition which developed in the later Eastern Chalukyan Ganapatis of the Golingesvara temple at Biccavolu.[70] The glaring contrast is that this image has a single pair of arms where as the Ganesas of Biccavolu are four handed.

3. There is a linga placed on a big round Panavatta of black granite.

4. Another linga is on a big round Panavatta of red sand-stone.

5. *Nandi:-* This is of medium size in typical Chalukyan style with a hara of bells.

Yellammagudi:

On the southern end of the tank-bund a few important sculptures are placed together on a little mound near Yerukalawada. The temple is now no more extant but its pillars and ceiling slabs are found scattered in its surroundings. Though the figures are greatly weathered, partly on account of the coarse-grained texture and brittle nature of the stone, they display considerable workmanship.

1. *Mahishasuramardini:-* Curiously enough this is a seated image with eight hands, three of which are broken. She holds chakra, khadga and trisula in her right hands and sankha and shield in her left hands. Her right leg is bent at the knee with the foot placed on buffalo. She wears Vanamala and all usual ornaments. Her Vahana lion is carved separately to her right side.

2. *Bhairava:-* This is a nude figure standing in tribhanga with a halo behind his head. He holds damaru and trisula in his upper hands and his lower hands are broken.

3. *Bhairava:-* This is like No. 2 but comparatively smaller in size.

4. *Naga:-* The body of the Naga from the waist upwards is in beautiful human form with the seven hoods on the head and below the navel, he is in serpentine form. He holds khadga and shield in his hands. He does not have mukuta but wears kundalas and armlets.

5. *Nagini:-* She is also with half human and half serpentine form with five hoods canopying her head. She does not wear mukuta. A beautiful hara hangs over her breasts. The figures of Nagas and Naginis of Polas are quite alike in comparison with the figures of serpent gods, which are also in half human and half serpentine form, carved on a big rock known as a panel of penance of Arjuna at Mahabalipuram datable to 7th century A.D.[71]

6. *A female Devotee:-* This is a seated female figure with legs folded and hands placed in anjali. The treatment of her coiffure is notewor-

thy. She is ornamented with kundalas, graiveyakas, bangles and wristlets.

7. *Bhairava:-* The figure is carved in low relief on an immovable boulder with damaru, trident, kapala in three hands while the fourth one is broken. The body below the navel is much damaged.

8. There is a panel containing two cavaliers attacking each other with swords.

9. *Ganapati:-* He is four-handed but his head is mutilated.

10. There is a central square slab of the ceiling carved with a full blown lotus.

Venugopala Swamy Temple:

The temple as seen now contains a garbhagriha, antarala and an open platform before it. It is in the middle of the village facing the east. The trisakha doorway of antarala is beautifully sculptured in Chalukyan style with a panel beneath the jambs on either side containing a four-handed dvarapala holding Vaishnavite symbols flanked by lady attendants. The treatment of the hair particularly the coiffure of the women is more appealing. The grace of their limbs and the charm of their jewellery are admirably represented. Their youthful bodies and high breasts attract the eye of the visitor. A hara from the neck hangs down between the breasts.

The adhisthana and the walls of the temple are plain. The sikhara is a stepped pyramidal one with a wide tapering band in the centre on its four faces. There is a column of about 20' height standing before the temple with a miniature mandapa above it.

Jain Vestiges:

The Polavasa chiefs patronised Jainism besides Saivism and Vaishnavism. An inscription of Banajipet dated A.D. 1082 in Narsampet taluk of Warangal district records that Virakamala Jinalaya was built by Medaraja I. It appears that Polas also contained at one time a Jain temple which can be evidenced by the Jain figures now found in the village. Curiously enough a nude Jain figure of 2' height in Kayotsarga posture is recovered recently from the foundations of a building belonging to Sri Kolichala Vishvanatham. This Jain image is not shaded by serpent hoods but his head contains the hair with spiral curls. Now this image is placed in the local Satyanarayana temple located beside the tank. Another seated image of Jain Tirthankara with his both legs folded and inter-crossed, keeping the soles of the feet upward and his hands placed in dhyanamudra is noticed on a hillock near the Pulastyesvara temple. The head of the image is mutilated. This worn our figure is similar to the figures found in Vemulavada.

Polas being the capital city during 11th and 12th centuries A.D. enjoyed royal patronage. It seems to have been a great centre of Saiva and Jaina worship.

12. **Nandi Mydaram**

The village Nandi Mydaram lies to the north-east of Karimnagar and can be reached via Dharmaram lying on the road to Lakshettipet. The village is situated behind a big tank formed by a bund connecting the two hillocks. There are beautiful temples standing on either end of the tank bund. The village Mydaram is now known as Nandi Mydaram because of the existence of a huge Nandi, perhaps the biggest in the district carved in typical Kakatiyan style. There is a fragmentary inscription[72] dated A.D. 1175 lying near Chinna Kondal Rao's house. The first side records a gift of land to the god Kesavadeva and mentions the name Bamdi Brammenayaka. The second side gives the above date and mentions the temple of trikuta installed by Medaraja. The third side mentions the name of Mahamandalesvara *Kaketa* Rudradeva. The word *Kaketa* probably stands for Kakati. The fourth side records some gift to Prolesvaradeva. The contents of all the four sides have no connection with each other.

Medaraja mentioned in the inscription was none other than Meda II who is stated to have installed the trikuta temple in A.D. 1175. The recorded date is illegible and doubtful because the authority of Meda II continued over Polavasadesa only upto A.D. 1159, when he was defeated by Kakati Rudradeva and his territory was annexed to the Kakatiya Kingdom.[73] As such there is no question of Meda II continuing upto A.D. 1175. The date is either wrongly recorded because of the illegible nature of the inscription or might be on account of an error committed in the carving itself. However, the fact, that the trikuta temple was installed by Medaraja, remains uncontested and indisputable. Therefore this trikuta temple represents the architectural style prevalent in the early half of the 12th century A.D. which was later imitated and improved in the Kakatiyan times.

Another inscription[74] of the reign of Kakati Ganapatideva, set up near Amaresvara temple on the tank bund is also illegible and undated. It introduces some subordinate chief of the Pallava lineage, who is said to be the right hand of Ganapatideva. Other particulars are not clear. There is an inscription perched at the entrance of the house of Gandla Gauraiah which is very near to the trikuta temple and remains probably unrecorded.

The Trikuta Temple:

This trikuta temple stands on the eastern end of the tank bund and faces the north. The shrines on the south and the east and the porch on the north are no more extant except their ruins. The mandapa and the western shrine are the only extant portions of the temple. The adhisthana is simple and the walls are plain. The mandapa has four central pillars with corresponding half pillars rising over the parapet wall. The ceiling in all the nine compartments of the mandapa is laid in Kadalikakarana process with full blown lotus medallions carved on the central square slabs. The special feature of the mandapa is that two miniature temples are erected on either side of western shrine over the parapet wall. Similar arrangement can be noticed at Raikal and the same was imitated later in the Kakatiyan temples at Kothapalli, Chandravelli and Palampet.

The extant western shrine consists of garbhagriha and ardhamandapa before it without a doorway as found in the trikuta temples at Raikal and Valgonda. This shrine is dedicated to Siva. The doorway of garbhagriha has a projecting cornice over the lintel decorated with pendants. The turrets are sculptured on the architrave, while the Saivite dvarapalas are carved beneath the jambs. The ruins of the door jambs with Vaishnavite dvarapalas, now lying on the south, reveal that the southern shrine was dedicated to Vishnu probably in the form of Kesava, to whom Bamdi Brammenayaka is stated to have made a gift of land. A typical Chalukyan Nandi is lying in the mandapa.

Amaresvara Temple:

This single shrine temple stands on the western end of the tank bund. The garbhagriha and antarala are extant but the mandapa is lost. The temple is surmounted by a stepped pyramidal sikhara crowned by a square member with a kalasa above it. The square member is decorated on all sides with lion motifs. The trisakha doorway of garbhagriha is fine with 2' x 2' panels beneath the jambs containing the Saivite dvarapalas. The flanking female chowry-bearers with a large knob of hair behind the head are quite pleasing though bulky in form. A Chalukyan Nandi and several naga stones are seen in the temple.

The temple before Nandi:

This temple is no more extant except its platform and a pillar still standing on it. A huge Nandi is lying before the platform. The Nandi, majestic in appearance is as big as the Nandi of the Thousand pillar temple at Hanumakonda. It is 8' long and 5' high, whereas the Nandi at Hanumakonda is 7 1/2' long and 5'-8" high. This Nandi is seated on a pedestal and ornamented with several bands running along and across its body. The Kakatiya mannerism and feel is best evidenced in its exquisite carvings. The festooned rump garland is clearly a feature of the Kakatiyas.[75]

Sculptures:

1. *Naga Kanya:-* This is the largest nagini slab 4' x 2 1/2' found in the district. She is in half human and half serpentine form with a multi-hooded canopy above her head. The figure is beautifully carved with a thin loin and large breasts with a hara hanging in between them. She holds shield in left hand and khadga in right hand. She wears mukuta, kundalas, necklace and a waist band. She is flanked by a hooded curled naga. This image is standing before Amaresvara

temple.

2. *Ganapati:-* He is holding tusk in left hand and modakas in right hand on which the tip of the trunk rests. He has no mukuta.

13. **Raikal**

Raikal is a big village situated about 70 kms. north-west of Karimnagar. It is only 20 kms. from Jagtial and can be reached by bus. There is a beautiful Triple Shrine temple, now known as Kesavanatha and Panchamukha Lingesvara temple. The temple stands at an elevated place inside the fort. The remnants of the fort and the crumbling mud walls can be noticed by the visitor. The temple is now under repairs and all the deities have been shifted to the courtyard to facilitate the renovation work.

An unpublished inscription of the reign of Kakati Prataparudradeva dated A.D. 1305, can be noticed in the courtyard on a broken stone pillar, carved on three sides with a Nandi at its top. The inscription is in Telugu script. It records that certain Rudradevani son of some Reddy has made a gift of 5 *marturs* of land near Donula Kaluva and another 5 *marturs* near Budumulagatu, total 10 marturs of land to Ramanathadeva and Lakumesvaradeva of Ravikanti for *Angaranga Vaibhogamu* of the deities on Sravana Bahuladvadasi, Vaddavaramu in Visvavasu year S. 1227 corresponding to A.D. 1305. The place is referred to in the inscription as Ravikanti which means an eye of the sun god. Ravi means sun and Kanti means eye. The worship of Sun was prevalent in this area and so the eastern shrine of the trikuta is dedicated to Sun god. The name Ravikanti became gradually corrupted into Rayikanti and today it is known as Raikal.

The Triple-Shrine Temple:

This temple has a cruciform plan. It has a square hall in the centre with three shrines projecting to the north, east and west and a portico projecting to the south. The temple faces the south. The adhisthana of the temple contains upana, broad patta, Jagati, Kumuda and Vedi, over which the plain wall rises. The wall and the spire are separated by a cornice in two tiers. The three shrines of the trikuta are crowned by curvilinear sickharas comparable to those of the temples at Alampur, Satyavolu and Mahanandi. The Sikharas are surmounted by amalakas over which there were stone kalasas which are found fallen in the temple surroundings. A sukanasa of Chalukyan tradition projects from the base of each sikhara.

A flight of steps leads to portico which further leads into mukhamandapa which is a 24' square hall. The parapet of the mandapa runs all along its circumference. The Kakshasanas are arranged over the parapet with slight slant at the top. The inner face of the parapet contains a band carved with four petalled floral designs usually found in the Western Chalukyan temples. The four central pillars of the mandapa are carved with various figures in low relief. The incarnations of Vishnu are carved in disorderly manner presenting the Matsya, Kurma, Varaha and Narasimha etc. The ceiling of the mandapa in all its nine compartments is covered by Kadalikakarana process. The bottom faces of the lintels are carved with multi-petalled lotuses.

All the three shrines are alike and consist of an ardhamandapa 8'-4" x 8' and a garbhagriha 8'-4" square. The ardhamandapa before the garbhagriha is open without any doorway. The doorways of the three garbhagrihas are similar in design with a Gajalakshmi motif on lalata and a projecting cornice above the lintel. The trisakha doorways contain a pilasteral motif in the middle flanked by floral and ornamental designs sculptured in vertical rows. The square panels beneath the sakhas are carved with dvarapalas. At the entrance of each doorway is a Chandrasila carved with conches and lotus buds on either side. Every ardhamandapa contains two miniature sitting elephants placed on either side of the doorway of each garbhagriha. The ceiling of ardhamandapas and garbhagrihas is laid in Kadalikakarana process.

The western shrine dedicated to Panchamukhalingesvara Swamy appears to be more important than the other two shrines because it contains two miniature shrines on the pial facing the mukhamandapa. These miniature shrines, perhaps intended to house Parivaradevatas, contain Purnakumbhas at their base. An interesting aspect of this village is that the Panchamukhalinga (idol of Siva with five faces) in this shrine is claimed to be one of the only two existing in India, the other being at Kasi (Benaras).[76] The doorway of the garbhagriha contains square panels beneath the door jambs, carved with Saivite dvarapalas flanked by male and female attendants with fly-whisks. In the left panel instead of a male attendant, Nandisvara is carved in human form with the face of a bull.

The northern shrine is dedicated to Kesavanatha. Beneath the door jambs are carved Vaishnavite dvarapalas flanked by male and female attendants holding fly-whisks.

The eastern shrine is dedicated to Suryadeva. Beneath the door jambs are carved dvarapalas each holding a lotus bud, gada, bow and a naga. The dvarapalas are flanked by beautiful figures of lady attendants with fly-whisks.

One of the Viragal sculptures in the courtyard contains a label inscription[77] in Nagari characters of 11th or 12th century A.D. with the emblem of sun and crescent at the top. Only the word Vikrama representing the name of the year is noticeable and the rest is illegible. Apparently this is a Chalukyan temple and can be dated to 11th century A.D.

Sculptures and Icons:

To facilitate the renovation work all the deities of the temple are placed in the courtyard.

1. *Panchamukha Linga:-* This linga has five faces, four on four corners and the other projecting from the centre. This belongs to the western garbhagriha.

2. *Kesava:-* This icon is of black granite and belongs to the northern garbhagriha. Here Vishnu is standing in Samabhanga and Samapada. He has four hands holding Sankha in upper right hand, Chakra in upper left hand, gada in lower left hand while he keeps the lower right hand in abhaya holding Padma. To his right side is a small figure of garuda knelt in anjali, while there is a figure of woman to his left side. The order of holding the four attributes in the four hands tallies with the order meant for Kesava as laid down in the *Rupamandapa.*[78]

3. *Devi:-* This is a seated female deity with her left leg folded and right leg bent at the knee and placed on the ground. She holds a bowl in her left hand and her right hand is broken, which probably held a Khadga. The image is carved of black granite.

4. *Surya:-* This is a small image of Surya holding two lotuses in his two upraised hands. The lotuses are crossing the shoulder level as laid down in the *agama-sastras.* He is adorned with Kiritamukuta, necklace, hara, Katibandha, Vanamala, anklets and nupuras. This Surya image belongs to the eastern shrine of the trikuta, but now this lone icon is placed near Bheemannagudi, which stands to the south of the village. Similar images of Surya with two upraised hands holding lotuses can be noticed in the Parasuramesvara temple at Gudimallam[79] near Renigunta and in the temples at Alampur[80] in Mahboobnagar district.

14. Valgonda

The village Valgonda is situated about 110 kms. to the north-west of Karimnagar. It is about 27 kms. from Metpalli connected by a concrete road. Both the temple and the village stand on the southern banks of the river Godavari. The village seems to have derived its name from a hillock sloping towards the village. Valu means slope and Konda means a hill or hillock. Valu plus Konda is known as Valgonda. There is a beautiful least ruined trikuta temple standing on the same hillock. In its architectural style this temple totally resembles the temple of Raikal containing three shrines crowned by lofty curvilinear Sikharas with a Sukanasa of Chalukyan tradition projecting from the base of each sikhara. The temple is set in a background of beautiful hillocks, luxurious vegetation and abundance of ever flowing water in the roaring gigantic river Godavari. The natural surroundings are beautiful and the place looks like a fine picnic spot leaving the picturesque memories on the mind of the visitor. There is a plain stone slab intended for an inscription with the emblems of sun, crescent, sword and other indistinct objects but curiously enough it is plain without any writing.

The temple of Valgonda is a triple-shrine with a hall entered through a porch on north and a shrine on each of the other three sides. It has a cruciform plan. It lies in a stone-walled compound but the walls are in ruins crumbling on all sides. The compound contains two entrances one on north and the other on south. The temple faces the north and about fifty steps from the sands of the river Godavari lead into a well elevated courtyard of the temple, where from one gets delighted by the beautiful sights and sounds of nature.

The base of the temple is very simple without any mouldings. The rows of large stone blocks one over the other form the base over which the plain wall rises to the height of about 6'. The walls and the spires are separated by a cornice in two tiers. All the three shrines are alike each consisting of a garbhagriha and an open ardhamandapa before it. The arrangement of an open ardhamandapa instead of an antarala before each garbhagriha found in this temple can be noticed similarly in the temple at Raikal. The shrine in the south is dedicated to Vishnu. At present it contains the deities of Rama, Sita and Lakshmana. The other two shrines in the east and west are dedicated to Siva in the form of Rajesvara and Ramalingesvara respectively. The hall is a 20' square and the central part of the mandapa contains a square form over which is a circular elevation known as ranga-sila. The mandapa has a parapet wall on all sides leaving an entrance on the north. On either side of the entrance there are loose dvarapala figures of about 5' height holding trident and damaru in upper hands, a gada in lower left hand keeping the lower right in abhaya. The whole mandapa has a big cornice all around with a slight slant. The three curvilinear spires are surmounted by amalakas which bear stone kalasas above them.

There are loose sculptures of Garuda, Bhairava and a few Vaishnavite saints. There is a Garuda stambha of about 25' height which reportingly once contained a miniature mandapa housing a small image of Garuda. The two other similar Nandi stambhas are now found fallen in the courtyard.

15. **Mallannapet** (Tirmalapuram)

Mallannapet is a small village situated about 62 kms. north of Karimnagar and 12 kms. east of Jagtial. It is a part of Tirmalapuram village. There is a single shrine temple dedicated to Siva known as Mallikarjuna locally called as Mallanna. The deity is worshipped mainly by the people of local Golla and Kurma castes. The village also derived its name as Mallannapet after the name of Mallanna, the deity of the temple. The temple represents the Kalyani Chalukyan style. Curiously enough this is a dvitala or two-storeyed temple, probably built by the Polavasa chiefs, in the last quarter of the 11th century A.D. This village is only 5 kms. east of Polavasa, which was the capital of a fief during 11th and 12th centuries A.D. The temple appears to have passed into the hands of the Kakatiyas and then to the Velama chiefs during the 15th and 16th centuries A.D. who in turn handed over the same to the Tammadis (drummers) of Polas in the middle of the 18th century A.D. Since then to this day the Tammadis are the pujaris of this temple. Though no earlier inscription is available, the later inscription[81] of a Velama chief dated A.D. 1753 records that Jupudu Dharmaravu Deshmukh made a gift of land in favour of Venna Jiyya, the Tammadi of Polas. The gift land is intended for growing a flower garden for the daily worship of the deity. Reportingly the south-east portion of the mandapa collapsed about 200 years ago and the debris of which has not yet been cleared from the spot.

The Mallanna Temple:

The temple consists of garbhagriha, antarala and sixteen pillared mandapa. It faces the east. The visitor finds plain walls rising from the ground as the adhisthana is buried in the ground. The walls are built of huge blocks of stone. The cornice is decorated with semi-circular tops at regular intervals. Above the shrine the upper storey consists of a small 6' square chamber having no idol at present. Outside the chamber there is a circumambulatory passage with a flat ceiling resting on pillars four on each side. The spire above the sanctum of the upper storey is in stepped pyramidal form with seven diminishing steps covered by a huge flat square slab, above which the sikhara ends in a vaulted hemispherical dome. The seven steps of the sikhara are connected by a wide tapering band in the centre on all four sides as seen at Choppadandi.

The mandapa is 31'square with four massive pillars in the centre. It is enclosed by a parapet wall leaving passages on the east, north and south. The Kakshasanas are arranged over the parapet wall on all sides. The central pillars are unusually large with 8' height and 2'-2" width. Instead of a four-armed bracket, the pillar contains a huge circular bracket, a novel member noticed nowhere in the temples of this region. The corresponding half pillars, which are in normal size rise over the parapet wall. The mandapa is flat roofed by means of large plain stone slabs placed one beside the other.

On either side of the antarala doorway, the dvarapalas stand cross-legged holding gada in left hand while keeping the right hand in abhaya holding a naga. At a little distance there stand two more dvarapalas cross-legged and carved in low relief with damaru and trisula in upper hands and club and naga in lower hands. The dvarapalas have a hooded canopy above their heads. The antarala is 9'-6" long and 11'-6" broad with two niches one on the north and the other on the south. The garbhagriha is a 14' square chamber. There are four pillars within the garbhagriha standing in the corners leaving a passage between the pillars and the walls. This is an early Chalukyan feature[82] found in the shrines at Vemulavada, Alampur and Mahanandi. This passage otherwise known as Pradakshinapatha around the deity seems to have existed within the garbhagriha, which is now closed by raising a pial. The trisakha doorway of garbhagriha is in typical Chalukyan style with Saivite dvarapalas flanked by chowry-bearers at the base.

The loose sculptures of two-handed and four-handed Vinayakas, naginis, Viragals, two broken pieces of saptamatrika slab, two Chalukyan nandis and the figures of Bhairava and devi etc. are noticed in and around the temple.

16. **Chilvakoduru**

Chilvakoduru or Silvakoduru is about 27 kms. to the east of Jagtial on Jagtial-Peddapalli road. There is a trikuta temple on the western bank of a rivulet. The temple stands in a stone-walled compound with entrances on the east and the north.

The Trikuta Temple:

The adhisthana of the temple is buried in the ground and the plain walls rise about 4 1/2' above the base. All the three shrines are surmounted by the curvilinear sikharas of different sizes, the main shrine containing the biggest. The temple is entered through a low level porch resting on two pillars which rise over the parapet wall. The porch is surmounted by a miniature shrine containing nandi inside it. A pair of dvarapalas stand on either side of the porch. The dvarapala rests the right hand on the hilt of the gada while he keeps the left hand in abhaya holding a naga. The crown, udarabandha, ardhoruka, armlets, wristlets and anklets, adorn the figures.

The doorway leading into the closed mandapa is very short 4 1/2' x 3' with purnakumbhas carved at the base. The mandapa is a 20' square with four central pillars of 6' height. The ceiling of the mandapa is flat and plain and it is only 7' high from the floor. The sculptures of Ganapati, devi and nandi are found in the mandapa.

On three sides of the mandapa there are three shrines of different sizes preceded by low-roofed antaralas. The main and the biggest shrine on west is dedicated to Siva. The doorway of antarala is 5' x 2 1/2' with Saivite dvarapalas carved at the base. On either side of the jambs there are three lattice holes one above the other. The garbhagriha is 9' square and its doorway contains purnakumbhas at the base. The southern shrine has a 7' square garbhagriha and its antarala is 5'long and 7' broad. The doorways are 4' x 2'. The loose sculptures of devi and Surya holding lotus buds in his two upraised hands are found at present in the shrine. The eastern shrine now houses the image of Vishnu. The garbhagriha is 6' square while the antarala is 5' long and 6' broad with a doorway of 4' x 2'.

The subsidiary shrines:

In the courtyard to the right of the entrance there are two separate shrines, the first one is bigger containing a garbhagriha of 7' square preceded by an ardhamandapa of 5' length and 7' width consisting of loose sculptures of Ganapati and a Chalukyan nandi. The second one comparatively smaller in size contains the trisakha doorway with Gajalakshmi motif on lalata and Vaishnavite dvarapalas at the base. The doorway is in typical Chalukyan style and its architrave is sculptured with turrets, some male figures and a kalasa. At present the shrine contains the loose sculptures of Bhairava, devi, naginis and a broken piece of Saptamatrika slab. These two subsidiary shrines in the courtyard are crowned by the brick built sikharas in stepped pyramidal form.

There is a nandi stambha of about 25' height with a miniature mandapa at the top containing a small nandi inside it. There are two more similar stambhas standing in the courtyard but their mandapas at the top are lost. On the right side of the main entrance in the north, there is a pillared mandapa attached to the compound wall. Both the compound wall as well as the walls of the main temple contain double shell, the core filled with mud and rubbles. No inscription is available in the temple, but the architectural style dates back the temple to the eleventh or twelfth century A.D.

17. **Thotapalli**

Thotapalli is about 30 kms. form Karimnagar lying on the way to Hyderabad. There is a trikuta temple in the village facing the south. It does not appear to have been ruined but left unfinished. There are three shrines projecting to the east, north and west with a square space in the centre. The space intended for the porch on the south and the mandapa in the centre is now plain without any structure.

The temple has no upapitha. Its adhisthana contains upana, patta, Jagati, Kumuda and Vedi above which the plain walls rise. There are no superstructures over the shrines. All the three shrines are dedicated to Siva. They are alike and consist of a garbhagriha 8' square and an ardhamandapa 8' square. The ardhamandapa before each garbhagriha is open without any doorway. The trisakha doorway of each garbhagriha is adorned with Saivite dvarapalas beneath the jambs, Gajalakshmi motif on lalata and turrets on the architrave.

There is a nandi of medium size lying in the open place. A large central slab intended for the mandapa is carved with a multi-petalled lotus in three concentric circles one beneath the other projecting downwards. It is curious that the flower has a slight convex shape unlike the flowers found in other temples. There are two hero-stones one before the temple and the other on the tank bund.

18. **Bejjenki**

Bejjenki is situated at a distance of 35 kms. south-west of Karimnagar. Although no inscription is traceable locally, the village is known as Bejavanke in the inscriptions of Sanigaram, a nearby village, which was an important centre of political and religious activity during the period of the Western Chalukyas of Kalyani. An inscription[83] of Trailokya-malladeva dated A.D. 1053 records that with the consent of Katereddy and others of Bejavanke village, one *mattar* (a land measure) of wet land was granted to the god Madhupesvara of Sanigaram. Another inscription[84] of the reign of Bhulokamalladeva dated A.D. 1128 records that a subordinate officer Repola Kuruvaraja made a gift of eight *mattars* of land in Bejavanke village to the god Kommesvaradeva of Sanigaram. From the above inscriptions it can be deduced that Bejavanke village, being very close to Sanigaram, was also an important centre of religious activity with a magnificent temple dedicated to Lord Narasimha. Traces of old fortifications, ruined walls and dilapidated bastions found here support the inference that a fort enclosing a big city must have existed.[85]

The Narasimha Temple:

The Narasimha temple at Bejjenki contains beautiful work of art. About 200 steps lead to the temple situated on the top of a hill. The temple faces the south. It consists of garbhagriha, antarala and mandapa with porches on south, east and west. Originally the sanctum is a cave, converted into the present form of garbhagriha. As the temple stands on a hill, the garbhagriha does not contain any adhisthana and the walls rise straight from the surface of the rock. But the adhisthana of mandapa contains upana, patta, Jagati and Vedi over which the bhitti rises. The gala part of adhisthana is cut into several compartments each filled with a four petalled conventional flower usually seen on all Western Chalukyan temples. The outer faces of the Kakshasanas, arranged over the parapet walls in the porches, are also cut into numerous compartments filled with gajas, simhas, asvas, Hamsas and four petalled flowers. Curiously enough there is a small panel depicting the image of primitive Mother goddess with legs wide apart showing prominently the genital organ. This figure is similar to the one found on the adhisthana of the platform before the Bhimesvara temple at Vemulavada. The walls of the garbhagriha are plain and the highly projected eave cornice is fine and slopy. The noteworthy feature of the temple is its superstructure. It consists of fifteen diminishing tiers arranged alternate with recesses to form the pyramidal shape. The tiers are decorated with semi-circular stones as seen on the steps of the sikharas of Kadamba temples.[86]

The hall, which is entered through the doorways of the porches, is enclosed by walls. A novel feature of the mandapa is its exquisitely carved central pillars. There is a considerable amount of excellent carving in the ceiling panels, but it was on the four central pillars that the sculptor was most prodigal with his art, as, from base to capital, these are intricately carved with both conventional designs and figure subjects. Each pillar on account of its wealth of imagery of gods in niches and figures in friezes, ceases to be structural element and becomes a complete tabernacle or altar in itself. The foot of the pillar or asvapadam is moulded and decorated with a miniature niche on each of its face with a deity inside it. The shaft consists of two square parts intervened by an octogonal section. This intervening portion is divided into moulding and recesses and is filled with rich ornamentation. The faces of the square portions are utilised for sculpturing several deities and beautiful female figures in bold relief. The transition from the shaft to the capital is marked by a circular part in the form of a vase with sloping top. A succession of mouldings leads to the projecting circular stone. The mouldings are connected by a triangular band sculptured with figures. A lotus shape is given to the bottom of the square abacus, above which the brackets are profusely carved. This is sculpturally one of the richest temples in Karimnagar region. The sculpturing is novel, minute and fine on the four central pillars. These pillars are similar to the most ornate pillars found in the temples of Warangal, Hanumakonda, Pillalamarri and Palampet. The figures carved on the square portions of the shaft are quite in high relief and stand out from the surface of the pillar. This sort of carving is rare and interesting, which is not found in the temples of Hanumakonda and Palampet, where the faces of the lower square portions of the shafts are entirely plain. The figures of several deities, dancers, drummers, cymbal-beaters, flute-players, lute bearers and huntresses are carved in bold reliefs. The joyous carefree attitude, the rhythm of movement and like effect of dancers are marvellous and exhibit a refined and highly developed art.

Several representations of Bhagavata, Bharata and other puranic episodes are found on the pillars. The sculpture of Amritamanthana contains three gods on one side and the three asuras on the other.

The panel with Siva seated on a pedestal and small figures of Vishnu and Brahma standing on either side indicates the darshan given by Lord Siva to them after they failed to find the bounds of the Jyotir-linga. This representation is not usually found in Kakatiya sculpture.[87] The figure of Narasimha flanked by garuda and Hanuman is amusing. Besides divine subjects, the general subjects are also sculptured beautifully on the pillars. There is a figure of huntress with a bow in her left hand and an arrow in her right pointing at a thorn in her left foot to some one attending to it. This is similar to the one found in a panel beneath the door jambs at Jakaram village lying on the way from Hanumakonda to Palampet.[88] The sculpture of a huntress is also noticed at Palampet and often at the doorsteps of Kakatiya temples. There is a naked figure of a woman holding a snake over her head. This figure is also similar to the figure carved to the right of the huntress at Jakaram in Warangal district.[89] But the glaring difference is that the figures at Bejjenki are short and stout and the figures at Jakaram are slim and tall. Another sculpture depicts a monkey trying to pull down the saree of a woman. This is also an oft-carved picture. It is seen on one of the bracket figures at Palampet and also at Tripurantakam[90] in Kurnool district. There is a *Kolattam* troupe of women playing with short sticks known as *Kolalu* in Telugu. The figures of dancers and drummers are amusing and elegant. Each figure has an attractive expression and a gay, carefree pose, the majority dancing form sheer joy in life. Apart from the dramatic effect, there is so much grace and beauty in the carvings that the art in its intellectual qualities and technical skill might have needed the practice and cultural development of many centuries before it could reach such perfection of craftsmanship. This sculpture has undoubtedly evoked great devotion through ages and our generations have derived great pleasure from its beauty and elegance.

The female figures have their hair arranged into a side knot in the shape of a bun. They wear ear rings, necklaces, haras, girdles, armlets, wristlets, anklets and nupuras. Though they are clad in scanty dress, they are charming and beautiful. But the only noticeable feature is that they are short and stout. This is due to the influence of Jain painting, wherein the dancers are short and stout. The deities wear crowns with rings arranged like the triple umbrellas above the Tirthankaras of Malkhed. Hence the influence of Jain art of Malkhed and Bodhan on its sculpture is no wonder.[91] The temple sikhara and the pial inside the mandapa are Jain influences. Moreover the famous Jain centres like Kollipaka (Kolanupaka) in the south and Pottalakere (Patancheru) in the south-west, which were once provincial capitals of the Kalyani Chalukyas, are not very far from Bejjenki. Therefore the influx of artists and architects from the Karnataka region is not impossible.

The ceiling of the mandapa is flat-roofed except the central compartment laid in Kadalikakarana process. The central square slab has a dome shaped lotus with upward circular rings as noticed in the temples of Nagunuru. The beams are decorated with floral designs. The triangular slabs carry the lion motifs comparable to those of the Thousand pillar temple at Hanumakonda.

To the north of the hall is the antarala with a doorway containing the Vaishnavite dvarapalas beneath the jambs. The doorways of the porches are simple without much ornamentation. The ceilings of the porches are laid in Kadalikakarana process with a shallow dome at the centre carved with upward circular rings and the triangular slabs contain the lion motifs.

Sculptures:

It is strange to notice a few sculptures of amorous couples on the outer side of the western walls of the temple. The mithuna figures are in the sex act which are not found in the Kakatiya sculpture. But the similar carvings can be noticed on the Eastern Chalukyan temples at Bikkavolu in East Godavari district.[92] The figures at Bejjenki, faintly carved on the walls in medium relief, deserve description.

1. There is a sculpture of the couple in sex act standing in opposite directions.

2. Beneath the above sculpture, there is an elephant rider looking back with a bow and an arrow aiming at a horse-rider, who is coming from the back holding a sword in his upraised right hand and the reins of the horse in the left hand.

3. There is a sculpture depicting a woman bent like the curve of a bow placing her hands in the front touching the floor, while a man standing at the back is in the sex act.

4. There is another sculpture depicting a man sleeping over a woman in opposite directions touching the sex organs of each other with their lips.

Bhairava:- This image is carved on a big boulder lying at a little distance to the west of the temple on the same hill. He is holding damaru in upper right hand, trident in upper left hand, a curled sword in lower right hand and a human head in lower left hand. The figure is shaded by a hooded serpent. A dog is jumping to his left to lap up the blood falling on the ground.

The architectural and sculptural features of the Narasimha Temple:

The details of style in architecture and the inference of certain elements in sculpture pertaining to this temple are indeed curious and confusing. The plain walls, the Kadamba type sikhara, unadorned doorways, absence of screen windows, an enclosed mandapa, the flat ceiling, the mithuna figures in the sex act and the presence of Mother goddess on adhisthana, are some of the features not found in the Kakatiya temples. They give an impression that it is a Kalyani Chalukyan temple. But the profusely carved central pillars with the sculptures depicting a huntress with a bow and an arrow, a woman holding a naga over her head, a monkey pulling down the saree of a woman, the lion face motifs on the triangular slabs of the ceiling, and a full blown lotus carved in a concave shape with upward circular rings, are some of the features quite akin to the Kakatiyan style. Hence it is difficult to assign a date to this temple in the absence of any epigraphic evidence. As the amalgamation of both the Chalukyan and Kakatiyan styles is apparent, this temple may be assigned to mid-twelfth century A.D. a terminal period when the Chalukyan style started waning and the typical Kakatiyan style started emerging with the erection of the Thousand pillar temple at Hanumakonda by Rudradeva in A.D. 1163.

19. Koheda

Koheda is situated about 35 kms. south of Karimnagar. It lies to the west of Husunabad. Outside the village on the way to Husunabad there is a single shrine temple known as Mallanna temple with a few subsidiary shrines in front of it.

Mallanna Temple:

This temple is dedicated to Mallikarjuna locally known as Mallanna. It faces the east. The plan of the temple is very simple consisting of a garbhagriha and an open pillared mandapa before it. The adhisthana of the temple is buried in the ground and the plain walls rise over the base. The sikhara of the temple is no more extant. The mandapa consists of a passage in the middle corresponding to the doorway of garbhagriha with a raised platform on either side. Twelve pillars, three in each row rise over the platform. The low level mandapa contains massive pillars of 4' height in crude form. The garbhagriha contains four pillars in its corners leaving 3' passage between the pillars and the walls, which is a feature generally found in the early Chalukyan temples.[93]

The subsidiary shrines:

There are two small shrines very close to the temple facing the south. The bigger shrine contains a closed mandapa with four pillars at the centre. The doorway of mandapa is 4' x 2' and contains Purnakumbhas at the base. This shrine is dedicated to Siva. Another smaller shrine contains at present the image of Bhairava holding damaru and trisula in upper hands and Khadga and bowl in lower hands. There are three viragals of 4' height holding sword and shield in their hands.

In the middle of the village there are two temples standing side by side facing the east. One is dedicated to Siva and the other to Vishnu in the form of Sri Rama. Each temple consists of garbhagriha, antarala and a sixteen-pillared mandapa. There is nandi stambha before Siva temple and garuda stambha before Vishnu temple. An image of nagini in half human and half serpentine form holding sword and shield in her hands with a canopy of seven hoods above her head is noticed in the courtyard. This nagini is similar to those found at Polas. The historical ruins reveal that Koheda was an important place during the Chalukyan and Kakatiyan times.

20. Kalesvaram

Kalesvaram lies in the interior of thick forest at the confluence of the river Godavari and its tributary Pranahita. This picturesque spot is situated at a distance of about 130 kms. north-east of Karimnagar and it is 16 kms. distant from Mahadevapuram. This place can be reached by bus from Karimnagar via Manthani or from Warangal via Parkal. This ancient place is near the meeting point of three states namely Maharashtra, Madhya Pradesh and Andhra Pradesh. On the other side of the Godavari there are the districts of Chanda in Maharashtra and Bastar in Madhya Pradesh.

The Siva temple of Kalesvaram is one of the most celebrated temples of Andhra Pradesh. God Kalesvara the presiding deity of this temple and Mallikarjuna of Srisailam in Kurnool district and Bhimesvara of Draksharama together gave Andhradesa its other name Trilingadesa. Kalesvara is celebrated in both tradition and literature. The puranic and literary evidences refer to the importance of this place from times immemorial. The existence of a small Jain image in dhyanamudra reveals that this place was also a Jain centre besides a great Saivite centre from the early times.

Ramaranya Sripada or Ramesvara Deekshita, a renowned scholar of Saivagamas got settled on the banks of the Godavari at Kalesvaram.[94] He was the religious guide to the king Prola II and he constructed several temples, and Saivite establishments. The Kalesvaram shrine was perhaps founded by him. The Nagunuru inscription[95] now lying in the Collector's Bungalow at Karimnagar dated A.D. 1171 records that Gangadhara, the minister of Kakati Rudradeva and the governor of Nagunuru, the capital of Sabbinadu, has constructed temples at several places including Kalesvaram. Another fragmentary inscription[96] recently unearthed on the tank bund near the new bus stand at Hanumakonda and now preserved in the local post-graduate centre also records that the minister Gangadhara installed the deities Murari (Vishnu) and Sankara (Siva) at the confluence of Pranahita and Godavari.

Visvesvara-Siva of Pasupata creed and religious preceptor of Kakati Ganapatideva is said to have founded a monastery called upala-matha at Kalesvaram and granted to it as a perpetual fief the

Brahmana village of Ponna-grama which he himself has founded.[97] An undated inscription[98] of the reign of Kakati Ganapatideva at Kalesvaram records that Visvesvara Sivacharya and his spiritual son Dharma Sivacharya are said to have constructed a Siva temple at Kalesvaram and endowed it with some lands. The Nidigonda epigraph[99] in Warangal district dated A.D. 1219 records that Kundaınamba, daughter of Kakati Mahadeva and sister of Ganapatideva is said to have constructed a temple to Ardhnarishvara at Kalesvaram.

Another inscription[100] at Kalesvaram dated A.D. 1397 records that the Vijayanagara Devaraya, son of Harihara II, while celebrating the festival of digvijaya at Kalesvaram on the banks of Gautami i.e. Godavari made the gift of *Tulapurusha* on Wednesday, the first day of the year Isvara. *Tulapurusha* is one of the sixteen *Mahadanas* (noble charities) prescribed by the canons of Hindu ethics (dharmasastras) and generally performed by royal dignitaries by giving in charity a lump of gold equal in weight to that of the donor. There is a votive label inscription[101] recording the name of Ramabhakta son of Yellabattu, who was a devotee of the god Muktisvara. Another label inscription[102] in characters of 16th-17th centuries A.D. records the gift of Nandi pillar by certain Baloju son of Valadu Tiduroju to the god Muktinatha.

Besides the above epigraphic evidences, the remnants of a mud fort with bastions built in stone reveal that this was an important place during the medieval period. When Ramagiri fort together with this area was controlled by the Mughals for some time, two mosques in Mahadevpur taluk one at Kalesvaram and the other at Sonipet are said to have been built by Aurangzeb.[103] Perhaps the mosque which now stands to the north-west of the main temple might be the same monument built by Aurangzeb.

There are good number of temples found in an utterly dilapidated condition at Kalesvaram. The Sangamesvara temple at the sangam, the Muktisvara temple lying at a distance in the forest area and the Chandrasekhara temple are important among the many other ruined temples. The Kalesvara and Muktisvara temple is the chief place of worship in the village.

The Kalesvara and Muktisvara Temple:

The unique significance attached to this shrine is that there are two Sivalingas namely Kalesvara and Muktisvara on a single *panavatta* (Pedestal). One of the lingas consists of two holes at its surface known as the nostrils of the deity. The legend tells that milk or water poured into these nostrils miraculously flows into the river Godavari. Even today it is a peculiar feature to be noticed that whatever amount of water is poured in these nostrils, they never get fully filled up.

The present magnificent temple is totally re-built during the recent times by the Government of Andhra Pradesh in the place of the old temple. Everything is new except the old deities Kalesvara and Muktisvara found in the form of lingas on a single *panavatta* in the present garbhagriha. A photograph taken before the demolition of the old temple, is now kept in the office of the present temple. It shows that the old temple facing the east contained a sikhara in stepped pyramidal form. Apparently there was a terrace erected over the pillared mandapa and the spire appears within the parapeted terrace. There was a pillar standing erect before the temple bearing a miniature mandapa at its top containing nandi inside it. Reportingly the small temple that existed to the north of the main temple contained the deity of Annapurna which is now found among the loose icons. A similar small temple that stood to the south of the main temple contained the deity of Praudha Saraswati. A flat roofed gateway with a ruined compound wall on either side for taking entry into the courtyard of the then temple can be noticed in the photograph.

Loose Sculptures:

There are a large number of loose sculptures placed in two rows outside the temple and beside the southern compound wall. The figures of dancers, archers, horse-riders, garuda, Mithuna, Arjuna's Matsya Yantra, Gopikavastrapaharana, Skanda riding on a peacock, lion in action at the back of the elephant holding its upraised trunk, male and female devotees with folded hands etc., depicted in different small panels can be noticed on the spot. The Nagas and Naginis found here are similar to those of Polas. Most of these loose sculptures are in red sand-stone and can be dated back to 11th and 12th centuries A.D. The following images deserve description.

1. *Annapurna:-* This sculpture of Annapurna, consort of Visvesvara, is the giver of food to mortals. The devi has only two hands. She holds a vessel of food in her left hand while she holds in her right hand a ladle touching the vessel for serving food. She keeps her left leg folded and the right hanging. She has a bejewelled crown, ear rings of precious stones and a jewelled graiveya round her neck. She has pointed breasts slightly looking down as they are heavy. She wears keyuras and kankanas. She has a Vanamala, a unique distinction. This figure rises in bold relief above a plain back-slab.

2. *Annapurna:-* This figure is smaller than the above. She has four hands like the image found at Polas. She holds damaru and trisula in her upper hands while she holds a vessel and ladle in her lower hands. The close tiaras of her crown exhibit the Hoyasala influence.[104]

3. *Ganapati:-* This worn out sculpture is an early form of Ganapati endowed with two hands and a natural elephant head without a mukuta.

4. *Ganapati:-* This sculpture is of 3' height in red sand-stone. He wears Karanda mukuta and has four hand. A naga is worn by him as udarabandha.

5. *Matsyavatara:-* This is a rare beautiful sculpture in black granite in the form of a very big fish. It is 8' long and 2 1/2 high with its mouth open. It is now placed in the corridor newly built all along the compound wall.

6. *Chaturmukha Linga:-* This linga is a fine sculpture in basalt with four faces carved on four sides. The linga is flat topped and it is now placed in the courtyard of the temple. Judging from its smooth polish and accuracy of carving, this sculpture resembles that of the Chaturmukhalinga of the ruined Swayambhu temple, which is now placed in the courtyard of the Sambhunigudi in the Warangal fort. A similar Chaturmukha linga is also found at Manikesvara temple in Kalahasti.[105]

7. *Surya:-* This is a beautiful Kakatiyan sculpture of 4'-6" height in basalt. It is well polished and exquisitely ornamented. There is a beautifully sculptured makara torana behind it and seven horses are carved on its pedestal. The figure is adorned with kirita mukuta, pendants on the ears, graiveyakas, a long hara hanging over the chest, Katibandha, Keyuras, wristlets, anklets and nupuras. He has two hands which are broken below the elbows. He wears an ardhoruka and a Vanamala. He is flanked by female chowry-bearers and women carrying bows and arrows.

8. *Vishnu:-* This sculpture is 3' in height adorned with all usual ornaments and a makara torana behind it. Garuda is seen with folded hands at the bottom to the right side of the deity.

9. *Lingas:-* There are several lingas of various sizes and some of them have the circumference of 8'.

10. *Nandis:-* There are nandis of several sizes in both the Chalukyan and Kakatiyan styles.

11. *Dvarapala:-* This beautiful sculpture of dvarapala is 6' tall in red sand-stone. He holds damaru in upper right hand and Khatvanga in upper left hand. He holds gada in lower right hand while his lower left hand is twisted to the right and rested on the hilt of gada. He wears mukuta, graiveyakas, Yajnopavita, armlets, wristlets, anklets and nupuras. He has a long hara of skulls beautifully stringed like large beads. This hara looks like Vanamala. This figure rises in bold relief above a plain back-slab.

12. *Dvarapala:-* This is similar to the above sculpture.

21. Nagunuru

Nagunuru lies about 8 kms. to the north of Karimnagar. The ruined temples, mutilated images and several inscriptions found here and the neighbourhood speak of the one time glory of the place. In the inscriptions the village is known as Nagaruru. It was a prominent centre of political and religious activities for about four centuries under the Chalukyas of Vemulavada, Western Chalukyas of Kalyani and Kakatiyas of Warangal. The village appears to have contained at one time a mud fort around it and the traces of which can be noticed even today.

The earliest inscription[106] of Nagaruru belongs to the reign of Arikesari II Vemulavada. It is dated A.D. 946 and records a gift of fifty *mattars* of land to a Brahmana named Dharapayya. Now this inscription lies in Karimnagar museum. Nagaruru was a flourishing town in Sabbinadu along with Vemulavada, Polavasa and Mantrakuta in the times of Chalukyas of Kalyani. An inscription[107] set up near Birannagudi dated A.D. 1112 records that Mahamandalesvara Pandarasa (Pandaraja) constructed the temple of Ravvisvara and endowed it with some lands irigated under tanks. The three label inscriptions[108] noticed on different hero-stones record the victories of the warriors named Kelan, Narappa and Sangama who struck their enemies in the presense of Dommaraja, the Lord of Nagaruru during the middle of the 12th century A.D. Another inscription[109] datable to A.D. 1159 refers to Dommaraja and his allies Medaraja and Jaggadeva with an army of eighty thousand and commemorates their victories over some enemy, believed to be Kakati Rudradeva. However, the Thousand pillar temple iniscription[110] of Hanumakonda records that Dommaraja and his allies were vanquished by Rudradeva in about A.D. 1159. Consequently the whole Sabbinadu together with Nagaruru was annexed to Kakatiya Kingdom.

The group of temples found here in the typical Kakatiyan pattern reveal that Nagaruru was a prominent centre in the Kakatiyan times alongwith Hanumakonda, Warangal and Palampet. The pillar inscription[111] of Nagaruru dated A.D. 1171, now lying at the Collector's Bungalow in Karimnagar, records that Kakati Rudradeva appointed his minister Gangadhara as the governor of the whole Sabbinadu with Nagaruru as his capital. There is also an unpublished epigraph of the reign of Rudradeva, locally known as Ramalin galagudi inscription.[112] This undated Telugu inscription records the gift of lands to the garland-makers of the temple.

An inscription[113] of Kakati Ganapatideva dated A.D. 1228 records that Nijarangala Malli Setti and his son Venni Setti established on behalf of all the Saliyas, Salesvaradeva, Ganapatisvara (in the name of Ganapatideva Maharaja) and Sakalesvara (in the name of all bhaktas). It is unfortunate that the pillar inscriptions are used for the basement of the local houses. One such inscription, believed to be of Ganapatideva can be noticed today near the house of Sri. K. Mallaiah. Besides stone inscriptions of Ganapatideva, his Karimnagar copper plates[114] dated A.D. 1246 record about a dispute over a canal of Chamanpalli village. It states that Maharaja Akshayachandradeva was the subordinate ruler of this region. As Chamanpalli is only 6 kms. from Nagaruru, the then capital of Sabbinadu, it can be presumed that the headquarters of Maharaja Akshayachandradeva was none other than Nagaruru itself.

All the splendour and glory of the village have vanished and it is today a small and unimpressive place. Several Kakatiyan temples important for their architectural and sculptural wealth are to be seen in the village as the vestiges of its past glory. These temples belong to 12th and 13th centuries A.D. However there are some early structures, old sculptures and a few remnants of the ruins which can be dated back to 10th and 11th centuries A.D. in view of their finishing, style and shape. Nagaruru was also a Jain centre which can be evidenced by a Jain figure carved on a big boulder in Kayotsarga posture overlooking the village from the top of a hill. Mostly the temples were constructed with red stone quarried locally. The stone available at the local hills is so fine that it is exported today to the countries like Korea and Japan.

1. *The Main Trikute Temple:*

The temple has a cruciform plan. It is triple-shrined with a square hall in the centre with three shrines projecting to the east, west and south and a porch projecting to the north. It stands on an upapitha and faces the north. The upapitha affords sufficient space all round the temple, which serves as Pradakshinapatha. The upapitha and adhisthana contain a number of similar mouldings horizontally. Mahapattika, Pattika, Padma and tripatta are the mouldings that are repeated with recesses intervening regularly. Some pattikas have semi-circular stones projecting over them. The walls which rise over the adhisthana are treated into a number of broad and narrow pilasters. The broad pilaster has folds on either side. Narrow pilasters surmounted by turrets are sculptured in the recesses. Sometimes they are crowned by an arched canopy on whose top is a Kirtimukha. The kapota of the temple takes a double curve. The spires are lost but the large blocks of stone placed over the garbhagrihas for the purpose of ceiling can be seen now.

A flight of 8 steps leads into the porch, the ceiling of which is lost. The doorway leading ito the hall consists of a moulded bhuvangama and door jambs consisting of five or six sakhas with a pilaster between them. Purnakumbhas are carved at the base. The lintel is broken. The mandapa is a 24'-4" square with four central pillars. The space between them is raised by 6". Inside this square is a circular elevation of 2" for the purpose of rangasila. Besides the central pillars the hall contains half pillars rising from the parapet wall. The ceiling of the mandapa in all its nine compartments is laid in *Kadalikakarana* process. The central square slabs contain three upward circular rings, each ascending ring being smaller than the lower, with a lotus bud hanging from the centre. A number of dripstones add beauty to the circular portion carved in concave shape.

The ceiling over the four central pillars is well-ornamented. The beams are decorated on their outerside with creeper designs forming several circles with swans inside them. Their inner sides are divided into several compartments by means of narrow pilasters. These compartments are adorned with the sculptures of dancers, drummers, trumpet-bearers and cymbal-beaters. The figures are not very large but their graceful features and spiritual expression can still be admired. The bottom faces of the beams contain three multi-petalled lotuses, each carved in three concentric circles with a lotus bud at the centre. The under faces of the triangular slabs are decorated with wide leaf pattern and small pendants, while their sides are cut into shallow compartments, each filled with a four petalled floral design. Swans, creepers, flowers and similar designs are seen in the various parts of the temple. This temple has the magnificence of its architectural style and its luxuriant decorative detail. The profusely carved ceiling of this temple can be compared with the ceilings found in the temples of Nagulapadu, Hanumakonda and Palampet.

All the three shrines of this temple are alike and consist of an antarala 9'-9" x 9-4" and a garbhagriha 9'-6" square. The doorways of the antaralas and garbhagrihas are almost similar in their architectural composition though they differ in their sculptural details. They consist of a moulded bhuvangama and three sakhas with a pilaster in the middle. The panels beneath the sakhas of the doorway of garbhagriha contain Saivite dvarapalas, flanked by chowry-bearers. The sakhas are decorated with gaja and simha motifs. All the doorways contain above the lintel a projecting cornice of 2'-3" width decorated with pendants and semi-circular stones. While turrets are sculptured on the architrave of the doorway of the garbhagriha, Siva is represented on the architrave of the doorway of antarala. Siva is seated with his right leg folded and left leg stretched downwards. He holds damaru and trisula in his upper hands. He places his lower left hand on his folded right leg, while he keeps his lower left hand on his folded right leg, while he keeps his lower right hand in abhaya. He is flanked by female drummers in pairs and another female figure holding Kalasa in her hands.

Each garbhagriha contains a linga placed on a high pedestal carved with several mouldigs. Both the linga and *panavatta* are in black basalt. The circumference of the linga is 4'-4" with a height of 1 1/2' over the *panavatta*. The linga is flat topped and its edge bevelled. In the case of antarala, lattice windows are arranged on either side of the doorway. They are apparently meant for decoration as their rears are closed. The panels beneath the lattice windows and the sakhas of the antarala doorway are carved with beautiful female figures in dvibhanga posture holding fly-whisks in their upraised right hands. The grace of the pose and the plastic beauty of the limbs in each figure attract the eye of the visitor. The varied treatment of the coiffure is specially noteworthy. Some of them have their hair arranged in the shape of a bun. Majestic dignity and happy serenity are expressed in the figures holdig the purnakalasa and the mother holding a child in her lap. All the figures are well-ornamented with necklets, haras, armlets, wristlets, anklets in pairs and nupuras. The rich imagination and perfect skill of the sculptor have caused the doorway to be considered one of the most magnificent examples of Kakatiyan art.

2. *The single shrine temple to the north of the Trikuta:*

This temple stands at a distance of few yards from the main trikuta. It faces the east and consists of a pillared mandapa, an antarala and a garbhagriha. The mukhamandapa, which is now extant, measures 25' either way. A small parapet wall runs round the hall leaving entrances on east, north and south, the west being the shrine. The outer surface of the parapet contains a band divided into several compartments filled with gaja motifs and four petalled floral designs. The ceiling of the mandapa is laid in *Kadalikakarana* process. But the carving over the central slab differs from that of main trikuta. Here each compartment is adorned with a flat multi-petalled lotus carved in three concentric circles with a lotus bud hanging from the centre. These lotus medallions are similar to those found in the temples of Palampet and Hanumakonda.

There is an interesting sculpture on a pilaster beside the doorway of antarala. It depicts the story of the tortoise from *Panchatantra*. A similar sculture is noticed at Alampur on a pilaster on the northern wall of Visa Brahma temple.[115] The ceiling of antarala is lost and the walls of the garbhagriha are now reduced to a heap of stones. It can be deduced by the Saivite dvarapala figures carved on the doorway of garbhagriha that this temple was dedicated to Siva.

3. *Temple next to the single shrine temple:*

This ruined temple stands to the north of the single shrine temple. It faces the east. A doorway and a porch before it resting on two granite pillars are the only remains of this temple. The pillars, doorway and the ceiling of the porch in their design and decoration are similar to those found in the main trikuta temple. A big nandi carved in Kakatiyan style is thrown out alongwith its pedestal.

4. *The temple situated to the north-east of the main trikuta temple:*

This temple is situated on the other side of the road. All that remains of this temple is a sixteen pillared mandapa with four pillars in the centre. There is a garuda stambha standing before this temple. The stambha is about 40' high containing a small mandapa at the top with garuda figure in it. Garuda is depicted in human form with the wings of a bird and a beak-like nose keeping his hands folded in *namaskaramudra*. This figure has two faces one looking at the north and the other at the south. There is another similar garuda stambha standing in the fields at a little distance. But this double-sided garuda faces the west and east. The garuda figures of this place are double-sided facing opposite directions in consonance with the *Agama Sastras.*[116]

The existence of garuda stambha before the extant mandapa reveals that this was a Vishnu temple. The Karimnagar inscription dated A.D. 1171 records that twenty four forms of Vishnu were carved in the Vishnu temple of Nagaruru.[117] But the 'Chaturvimsati-Vishnu' figures are now no more seen at this place. This feature in Vaishnavite art is interesting and rare. These forms of Vishnu are now found on the Jagamohana before the Simhachalam temple in Vishakhapatnam district.[118]

5. *The temple beside the hill:*

This temple faces the east and stands on a little mound beside the hill. The temple consists of garbhagriha, antarala and an open mandapa which is in ruins. This temple is dedicated to Siva. The walls of the temple are built of large blocks of stone. Fillets of various sizes run round the walls of garbhagriha. The only note-worthy feature of the temple is its superstructure. It consists of diminishing tiers arranged alternate with recesses to form the pyramidal shape. The tiers are decorated with semi-circular stones. The crowning member is a four sided stone with a flattened top. The ante-fix is in the front. A minor shrine is attached to the south of the main shrine. The north-east portion of the mandapa is lost. The pillars of the extant portion of the mandapa and the doorways of garbhagriha and antarala are similar to those of the main tirkuta temple. The spire of this temple resembles the spires of the Lakshmi Narasimha temple at Bejjenki and a small ruined temple about $1\frac{1}{2}$ furlongs west of the main temple at Palampet.

6. *Ramalingala gudi:*

There is a temple known as Ramalingalagudi dedicated to Siva. This temple is distant and lies beside a rivulet flowing to the south of the village. The temple is in total ruins. An unpublished inscription of Kakati Rudradeva records the gift of lands to the garland-makers of the temple. A big image of Ganapati is reported to have been shifted form here to Karimnagar museum.

7. *The temple in the midst of the village:*

This Siva temple is in a ruined condition. It faces the east and consists of garbhagriha, antarala and a pillared mandapa. A low level doorway made of balck granite, perhaps belonging to another temple, leads into the low level mandapa. The lalata contains Gajalakshmi motif while there are niches beneath the sakhas with an arched canopy crowned by Kirtimukha. Within the niche stands a Saivite dvarapala flanked by chowry-bearers. The sculpture of Mahishasuramardini is reported to have been shifted to some other place. The low level doorways and the low level mandapa with crude pillars give an impression that it is a pre-Kakatiyan temple probably belonging to 11th century A.D.

8. *The trikuta temple beside the P.W.D. road:*

This trikuta temple is about a kilometre from the village. It lies to the right side of the P.W.D. road leading from Karimnagar to Lakshettipet. The whole temple is in a ruined condition. It faces the south and stands on an upapitha. The mouldings of upapitha are lost. As visible now, a band running along the upapitha is divided into several compartments each filled with a four petalled flower. Swans, bulls, elephants and flowers are carved on the adhisthana. The treatment of the walls slightly differs from that of the trikuta temple situated in the village. The garbhagrihas appear to have remained either unfinished or ruined.

9. *Small temple near the bus stop:*

This temple faces the east and stands to the north of the above temple. It consists of a garbhagriha and a porch before it. The adhisthana contains several mouldings and the walls are treated into broad and narrow pilasters. This is also in ruined condition and does not merit any description.

Several temples scattered over distant places in and around the village reveal that Nagunuru was a very big city weilding political power during the early medieval period.

Sculptures and Icons:

Some loose sculptures are collected and placed in a small room containing a door of iron rods with a wooden frame. This has now become a place of worship in the midst of the village.

1. *Vishnu:-* He is standing in samabhanga with four hands. He holds sankha in upper right hand and chakra in upper left, while his lower hands are broken. He is flanked by chowry-bearers at the bottom. He is adorned with all the usual ornaments with a makara torana behind him. Garuda is seen sittig with his palms folded in anjali mudra to his right side.

2. *Siva as Uma Mahesvara;-* Siva is seated with Parvati. His left leg is folded while the right is stretched downwards. Parvati is seated on his left leg. Nandi is squatting at the bottom. Siva holds trisula in upper right hand, damaru in upper left hand. He keeps his lower right hand in abhaya while he passes his lower left round the back of the devi. Parvati also passes her right hand round the back of Siva while she holds a kalasa or fruit in her left hand. The god wears jatamukuta, haras, yajnopavita and other ornaments. Ganapati is found to the right of Siva. Similar alinganamurti sculpture is found in the Siva temple at Dharmapuri.

3. *Nagini:-* She is in half serpentine and half human form shaded by three hooded naga. She holds khadga in right hand and shield in left hand.

4. *Devi:-* This is a seated figure holding trisula and damaru in upper hands, khadga and bowl in lower hands.

5. *Vinayaka:-* This is a very small figure holding tusk in right hand and modakas in left hand towards which the trunk is twisted.

6. *Bhairava:-* This is carved on a big boulder standing before the Siva temple located beside the hill. He is standing with four hands. Trisula in upper left hand and skull cup in the lower left are found. A dog is jumping to his left. Similar image is carved on the other side of the same boulder.

7. *Mahishasuramardini:-* Devi is standing with right leg steady on the floor and the left kept on the neck of Mahisha. The asura form is emerging from the neck of Mahisha. She has eight hands. Her lower right hand is driving sula into the body of the asura. Two of the left hands hold khetaka and bow. Her lower hand is twisting the head of the asura. Devi is wearing a mukuta, hara, keyuras, valayas and ardhoruka. The asura is holding a sword and shield in his hands.

8. *Mahishasuramardini:-* This sculpture is on a boulder lying between the bus-stand and village. Devi is standig with the left leg steady on the ground and the right leg placed on Mahisha, who is in animal form. She has four hands.

9. *Surya:-* This image is on the same boulder. He is standig in samabhanga holding lotuses in his two upraised hands.

10. *Ganapati:-* He is seated and two handed. He has no head-gear and the trunk is twisted to the right. This is also sculptured on the same boulder.

11. *Nandi:-* This is a well polished nandi carved in typical Kakatiyam style. It is thrown out alongwith its pedestal. Now it lies in an open area near the main trikuta temple. The meticulous carving of the details of the ornaments speak volumes about the Kakatiyan chisel. The *Muvvalapatta* and the hara of bells adorn the rear and fore parts of the nandi. The Kirtimukha tassels that span the girth of nandi are knotted in Brahmamudi alongwith the *Muvvalapatta* and hara of bells on its back. Kantha haras adorn the sacred bull but its face is defaced and snout is damaged.

12. *Ganapati:-* Now this big image, brought from Nagunuru, lies before the gate of Karimnagar museum. This is an image of 4' height endowed with two hands and a natural elephant head without a crown. He holds tusk in his left hand while his right hand holds a cup of modakas on which the tip of the trunk rests. His forehead is adorned with haras. He wears Yajnopavita, armlets, wristlets and anklets. This is an early form of Vinayaka carved in Chalukyan style. Vinayaka figures of similar size and shape are found at Kolanupaka museum in Nalgonda district.[119]

13. *Nagini:-* This is a much worn out figure with half human and half serpentine form with seven hoods canopying her head. Now it is placed in Karimnagar museum. Similar images are found at Alampur, Kolanupaka, Bodhan and several other places.

14. *Mahishasuramardini:-* This is also brought to Karimnagar museum from Nagunuru. She places her right leg on the head of Mahisha, who is in animal form, while she holds the tail with one of her left hands. She has four hands but all are mutilated. The head of the devi is lost.

22. **Kothapalli**

Kothapalli is 5 kms. from Karimnagar and lies on the road to Jagtial. A dilapidated trikuta temple, in typical Kakatiyan style is found in the village. This temple is similar in style to the main trikuta temple at Nagunuru, which is very near to this place. The temple faces the south. It consists of a square mandapa with three shrines towards the east, west and north and a porch on the south.

The temple stands on an upapitha. It is divided into horizontal mouldings. Pattikas of various sizes and Padma are arranged alternate with recesses. The upapitha stands ruined at several places. There is a band running all along the upapitha decorated with four petalled floral design as seen on the upapitha of the ruined trikuta temple lying outside the village and beside the P.W.D. road at Nagunuru. This upapitha is 6'-6" high and affords a space of 10'-6" on its surface all around the temple, which serves the purpose of Pradakshinapatha. Adhisthana is also similarly moulded. The walls are treated into broad and narrow pilasters alternate with recesses. The shallow recesses are filled with narrow pilasters surmounted by turrets. The sikharas have fallen and the heaps of bricks grown with grass are now found over the shrines.

A flight of steps on the south leads tot he proch. The mandapa has four pillars in the centre with floor between them slightly raised. A parapet runs round the hall on which the miniature shrines are arranged as at Palampet. It was the practice of the Hoyasalas to put such miniature shrines on either side of the stair case at the entrance outside the temple.* The ceiling of the mandapa in all the nine compartments is laid in *Kadalikakarana* process. Each shrine contains a garbhagriha and an antarala with beautifully carved doorways. The figures of dancers and the motifs of turrets are sculptured on the architraves. The perforated screen windows are arranged on either side of the antarala doorways.

23. **Sundella**

Sundella is a small village situated on the banks of the Godavari and can be reached via Godavari-khani. There is a pillar inscription[121] of the reign of Kakati Mahadeva lying in the field near the Narasimha temple. It is dated A.D. 1197 and mentions King's subordinate who made a gift of land.

The Narasimha Temple:

This is an old temple dedicated to Narasimha. The doorways of the temple are short decorated with a projecting cornice above the lintel. An open mandapa, which appears to be a later extension made probably during the Kakatiyan times, is attached to the Narasimha temple on its western side. Two shrines on the north and two shrines on the south each consisting of a garbhagriha and antarala are attached to the mandapa. The doorways of the shrines and the pillars of the mandapa are in typical Kakatiyan style. The ceiling of the central part of the mandapa has a dome-shaped lotus with upward cirular rings similar to those found in the temples at Chandravelli and Manthani.

The Siva Temple:

There is another small temple dedicated to Siva lying at a little distance to the above temple. It is in ruined condition. The garbhagriha and antarala are the extant portions of the temple. The trisakha doorways are decorated with projecting cornices above the lintel, while the purnakumbhas are carved at the base.

24. **Jangoan**

Jangoan is situated on the banks of the Godavari and can be reached via Godavarikhani. The village is a pre-historic site. Early and middle stone age artefacts, like hand-axes and flake-scrapers were reported by Munn from Allur and Jangoan villages.[122] There is a beautiful trikuta temple facing the north. All the three shrines are dedicated to Siva. The special feature of the manda is that it contains a cluster of four pillars in each corner. Thus there are sixteen pillars in the centre of the mandapa. The pillars are beautifully carved and decorated with lion brackets. To the west of this temple, there is another ruined temple with a garbhagriha and a mukhamandapa.

To the north of this main temple on the other side of the road, there is another trikuta temple in a ruined condition. The existence of two trikuta temples reveals the prominence of this place during the Chalukyan and Kakatiyan times.

There are several loose sculptures around the temple. Among them the loose sculpture of a Saivite dvarapala 5' in height and the image of a devi are important. The seated devi holds damaru and trisula in upper hands, bowl and khadga in lower hands. This is a much worn out sculpture and is similar to the image of Choppadandi, now placed in the Karimnagar museum.

25. **Manthani**

Manthani town once known as Mantrakuta in the Puranas has a rich cultural heritage and historical background from the times immemorial. It is situated about 72 kms. north-east of Karimnagar on the banks of the river Godavari. Every part of the town is interspersed with the ruins of ancient shrines and temples and grandiose sculpture impressing the visitor with its hoary past. A rivulet by name Bokkalavagu, which kept the town isolated till recent times, joins the Godavari near Manthani.

The *Skanda-purana* states that Mantrakuta was a hermitage of sage Gautama.[123] Sages from different places used to come to Gautomashram to receive the blessings of the sage and learn Vedamantras. This place was thus called Mantrakuta which means the centre for learning vedic mantras.

Gundaraja, the younger brother of Medaraja II of Polavasadesa ruled over Mantrakuta as a feudatory of the Western Chalukyan kings. The Gangapuram inscription[124] near Manthani mentions Gundaraja as a subordinate of the Western Chalukyan King Bhulokamalladeva. The Govindapuram epigraph[125] dated A.D. 1122 and an undated inscription at Venkatapur[126] reveal that Gundaraja had his control over the Narsampet and Mulug areas in Warangal district. The Palampet inscription[127] giving the genealogy of Recherla Rudra incidentally records that his grand father Kama, the general of Prola II defeated Manthenya Gunda in a battle. This inscription mentions the village name as Manthenya. The Thousand pillar temple inscription[128] at Hanumakonda records that Prola II beheaded Gunda with his head shaved and his chest marked with the symbol of Varaha as a mark of humiliation. This inscription mentions the name of the village as Mantrakuta. The pillar inscription of Nagunuru dated A.D. 1171, now lying in the Collector's Bungalow at Karimnagar records that the minister Gangadhara established in the excellent city of Mantrakuta a temple for the three-eyed God.[129]

The manthani inscription[130] in the Hanuman temple near the tank called Tammicheruvu is dated A.D. 1199, the first regnal year of Kakati Ganapatideva. It records that a subordinate chief named Alluprolaraja the ruler of Chennuridesa made a grant of land to Manchibhattopadhyaya, the priest of Ganapatideva. The donee in turn founded a village, excavated a tank and gave house sites to Brahmanas of Mantrakuta. He also installed temples for Kesavadeva and Mahadeva and gave a garden to the god Gopijanavallabha of Mantrakuta. The record which is in Nagari script mentions the name of the village both as Mantrakuta and Manthena. D.C. Sircar thinks that Manchibhattopadhyaya and Manchanarya are identical and refer to the one and the same person.[131] The priest is said to have flourished under the patronage of the Kakatiyas some time towards the close of the 12th and the beginning of the 13th centuries A.D.

A reference of Manthani is found in the inscription at Gaya which was examined by D.C. Sircar, who later on visited Manthani and found similar inscription in the Hanuman temple. Both the inscriptions read as "Sri Mantrakuta Gopijana Vallabhayanamaha". According to the inscription at Gaya, Mallikarjuna Suri, the preceptor of the Kakatiya King visited holy places like Kasi and Gaya alongwith his wife Gauri and offered worship on behalf of the King. The inscription was installed by his consort at that time.[132]

Visvesvara Siva or Visvesvara Sambhu, the religous preceptor of Kakati Ganapatideva is said to have established temples and Mathas at mantrakuta, Kalesvaram, Chandravelli, Khambampalli and other places.[133] The Nidigonda epigraph[134] in Warangal district dated A.D. 1219 records that Kundamamba daughter of Kakati Mahadeva and sister of Ganapatideva is said to have constructed temples to Uma Mahesvara at Mantrakuta and Ardhanarisvara at Sri Kalesvara. This inscription also mentions the village name as Mantrakuta.

Manthani is famous for many temples built during the Kakatiya period or even earlier. Seelesvara, Siddesvara and Gautamesvara are the most important among the many more temples scattered in all directions of the town.

Seelesvara and Siddesvara Temples:

These two single shrine temples stand in a single complexon an elevated place. Each temple consists of garbhagriha, antarala and mukhamandapa. It is said that the Kakatiya army of Prola II, which defeated Gundaraja of Mantrakuta, was headed by two army chiefs named Seelappa Naidu and Siddhappa Naidu, who in memory of their victory over Gundaraja, constructed these two Siva temples after their names known as Seelesvara and Siddhesvara at Mantrakuta.[135] Reportingly these two temples were in ruinied condition till recent times. Consequent to the renovation work undertaken by Sri Loke Ramanna the resident of manthaṇi in 1942, these temples now stand in a good state of preservation. On architectural and stylistic grounds these two temples appear to have been built earlier to Gautamesvara temple probably in 12th century A.D.

Gautamesvara Temple:

This is a trikuta temple standing on the banks of the Godavari. It faces the south. This temple evolved elaborate ornamental sculpture indicating a final stage as it is believed to have been raised during Prataparudra's reign probably in the closing years of the 13the century A.D. This trikuta is in red sand-stone and resembles the plan of the Thousand pillar temple at Hanumakonda. The upapitha of the temple is completely lost all around while the adhisthana part is visible partly at a few places. In the wall patterns, this temple recalls

Ghanapur example. On the outer walls of this temple Narasimha is seen not with Lakshmi sitting on his thigh, but tearing out the intestines of the demon and wearing them as a garland in the Hoyasala fashion. Naked Naginis, chowry-bearers, Vasudeva, Varuna and Brahma are carved in relief. On the eastern face Andhakasura Samahara is seen. Same figures are greeted with a changed arrangement on the south facing temple too. The spires on the eastern and northern shrines are lost and the spire on the western shrine as it exists now is a stepped pyramidal one.

The common mandapa connecting the western and northern shrines is lost. The extant portion of the mandapa with four central pillars now serving as the ardhamandapa before the present Gautamesvara shrine contains a typical Kakatiyan Nandi beautifully carved and highly polished in basalt stone. The four central pillars are exquisitely carved and in the capital portion of the pillar, there is a full blown lotus looking upward lying in between the projecting ciruclar member and the square abacus. These pillars are similar to those of the temple at Chandravelli hamlet of Khammampalli near Manthani. The ceiling above these central pillars is domeshaped and constructed of ring upon ring of stones, each ascending smaller than the lower and closing in towards the top, which is covered by a single circular slab with a graceful pendant hanging from the apex. This dome-shaped ceiling is comparable to the ceilings found in the Mahadeva temple at Ittagi[136] in Raichur district and Venugopala Swamy temple at Magala[137] near Hirahadgalli in Bellary district.

All the three shrines are alike each consisting of a garbhagriha and an antarala. Noteworthy are the niches found on either side of the antarala doorways. The small temples on the pial raised at the corners of the square mukhamandapa at Palampet are fixed up here on either side of the antarala of the eastern shrines. This is a significant change, which incorporates the minor temple introduced by the Hoyasalas as an ornament to the main temple at its entrance instead of the mandapa.[138] On the vertical door jamb of the antarala of the eastern shrine, the Jain figures in Padmasana posture are noticed on the perforated plate rising to a man's height. Elaborately carved coffered ceiling showing concentric rings with a lotus bud at the apex is noticed in the antrala of the eastern shrine. But the ceiling in the antrala of the northern shrine is not in concentric circles but it consists of five squares each ascending square being smaller than the lower and finally covered by a square slab. The figures of dancing Brahma, Ganapati, Nataraja, Kali and Vishnu are seen on the architraves.

26. **Chandravelli** (Khammampalli)

The small village Chandravelli now known as Chandrarelli, the hamlet of Khammampalli is situated at a distance of about 16 kms. south-east of Manthani. There is a beautiful Kakatiyan temple standing on the banks of the river Maner. The place around the temple as visible now is totally deserted. The temple can be reached from Khammampalli after covering about 4 kms. on foot through a hilly track. An undated and much abraded Telugu inscription[139] of the reign of Kakati Ganapatideva mentions the village name as Chandravelli and records certain gifts to the god Visvanathadeva installed by Rajaguru Visvesvara Sivacharya. The epigraph contains the names of the villages such as Chandravelli, Khammampalli and Peddapalli.

The Siva Temple

This is a majestic single shrine temple dedicated to Siva. The temple faces the river Maner on the east. It is cruciform in its plan with a central hall having four projections constituting three porches in the east, north and south and the garbhagriha on the west. The plan of the temple is similar to the plans of the Erakesvara temple at Pillalamarri and the single shrine temple standing to the north of the mosque at Nagulapadu in Nalgonda district. Placed on an upapitha the temple at Chandravelli commands a panoramic view of the entire neighbourhood with green pastures, glittering waves of Maner and beautiful sights and sounds of nature. The upapitha and adhisthana of this temple have several mouldings horizontally similar to those of the trikuta at Hanumankonda and the main temple at Palampet. The walls are treated into broad and narrow pilasters alternate with recesses. The offsets of the bhitti project forth till they reach a projecting niche at the centre on the three sides of the walls of garbhagriha. The superstructure of the temple is lost.

A flight of steps leads to the northern porch, while the eastern and southern porches are in a ruined condition. The mandapa is very large and measures 38'-6" x 44'-3". It consists of four rows of pillars and some of the pillars contain a full blown lotus looking upward bearing the square abacus. The brackets above the abacus are massive and short ending in scroll design and decorated with hooded nagas at the centre. The hall at its western end consists of two miniature shrines placed on the parapet wall facing each other. This sort of arrangement of placing the miniature shrines in the mandapa is found in the temples at Kothapalli and Palampet. The ceiling of the mandapa stands damaged.

The antarala doorway measuring 7'-3" x 5' is richly carved and decorated with perforated screen window on either side. The projecting cornice above the lintel is decorated with pendants. The architrave is sculptured with Nataraja dancing over *Apasmarapurusa*. Siva is eight-handed. His left leg is bent at knee with the portion below angularly kept and the foot resting on *Apasmarapurusa*. The right leg is lifted up in dance movement. To the left of Siva the figures of Vishnu and Vinayaka are carved while to his right are the figures of Brahma and another probably Kumara. The ceiling of the antarala consists of four octagons each ascending octagon being smaller than the lower and finally covered by a full blown lotus. A number of dripstones add beauty to the central part of the octagonal dome. The doorway of garbhagriha is also similarly carved but less elaborately. This temple stands as one of the most magnificent examples of Kakatiyan art.

27. Katkuru

Katkuru is situated about 40 kms. south of Karimnagar. It can be reached from Husunabad and Huzurabad. A pillar inscription[140] of the reign of Kakati Ganapatideva dated A.D. 1202, now standing before the temple gives a lengthy genealogy of both the Viriyala and Malyala chiefs. It also records that Mailama, who hails from Viriyala family married Chaunda of Malayala family. The latter was the commander-in-chief of Kakati Ganapatideva.[141] Mailama is stated to have constructed the temples to the god Siva at Katkuru and endowed them with tanks and lands.

The Trikuta temple:

The temple is situated inside a walled compound with an entrance on the north. The walls on the south and the west are no more but the traces of their basement can be seen now. The Prakara wall is built of massive stone blocks with a double shell, the core being hollow in the middle. The temple is a trikuta with a hall entered through a porch on the north side and a shrine on each of the other three sides. It has no upapitha. The adhisthana of the temple is 2' high with plain pattas over which the plain bhitti rises with a cornice in two tiers. The superstructures are in ruins and now only a few bricks remain.

The mandapa measures 19'-4" either way. The height of the mandapa is only 8' and the height of the pillars from base to the bracket is 6'-4". The ceiling of the mandapa is flat except the central compartment laid in *Kadalikakarana* process with a lotus medallion at the centre. The mandapa contains around it a parapet wall over which the Kakshasanas are arranged. A finely carved and well polished nandi is seen in the mandapa. There is a slab of Saptamatrikas flanked by Virabhadra and Vinayaka with their respective Vahanas carved below their seats.

All the three shrines are alike and consist of an antarala 6'-6" x 5' and a garbhagriha 6'-6" square with the doorways measuring 4'-4" x 2'-2". Each antarala doorway is decorated on either side with a screen window. The female figures of dancers, drummers and cymbal-beaters are carved at the base as well as on the architrave of the antarala doorway. The trisakha doorway of each garbhagriha contains Saivite dvarapalas at the base and turrets on the architrave.

The special feature of this temple is that it consists of miniature shrines six on the east, four on the north and two on the west inside the courtyard. All of them are attached to the Prakara wall at regular intervals. Each shrine has a sikhara of two steps crowned by a flat four-sided square member.

28. **Godisala** (Upparapalli)

Godisala is situated at a distance of about 50 kms. south-east of

Karimnagar. It is connected by a rough road of 10 kms. from Huzurabad. This village is otherwise known as Upparapalli.[142] Godisala is perhaps the corrupt name of Gudisala which means a palce where there is a temple. An inscription[143] dated A.D. 1236 records the installation of Siva temples, tanks, gardens and the gift of the village Pincharapalli to the deities Panchalingas by Kataya, son of Rajayanayaka, a minister of Recherla Rudra, who was a great general of Kakati Ganapatideva. Of the panchalingas mentioned in the epigraph, three are enshrined in the trikuta temple and the other two are set up in two separate temples constructed to the south of the main temple. Upparapalli is an important historical site, where the earliest expedition of the armies of Alauddin Khilji against Telingana was repulsed for the first time in A.D. 1303.[144] The temples of this place are set in the background of beautiful hills and hillocks. The local granite stone appears to have been used for therir construction. Now the temples stand at a deserted place, which can be approached by a cart track of 3 kms. from the village.

The Main trikuta temple:

The temple has a cruciform plan. It has a square hall in the centre with three shrines projecting to the north, west and south and a portico projecting to the east. All the three shrines are dedicated to Siva in the form of linga, the emblemof cosmic energy. The general architectural effect of the temple is grand and shows the high ideals and consummate skill of the builders. The temple faces the east.

The temple has no upapitha. The adhisthana contains upana, Jagati, Kumuda, and Vedi, over which the bhitti rises. The highly projected eave cornice is arranged in two tiers all round the temple. The superstructures of all the shrines are lost. The walls are built of large blocks of stone and they have a double shell, the core being hollow in the middle. This method of building is exposed to view, as the outer shell of the walls of the northern and western shrines have been destroyed by climatic or other causes. A sad defect of the Kakatiya temples in general is that they are not provided with adequate foundations and as they were built of large blocks of masonry, sinkage has occured in the majority of cases, so that cracked walls, broken lintels and out-of-plumb columns are features, which frequently obtrude themselves on one's notice.[145]

A flight of four steps lands into the porch, which measures 12' east-west and 9' north-south. The main hall measures 27'-6" each way and has a square apartment enclosed by four pillars in the middle. Inside the square is a circular elevation known as rangasila. This rangasila has smooth polish like a mirror, where the temple dancers gave their performances and the musicians and singers recited the sacred hymns. The pillars are exquisitely carved and exhibit the consummate skill of the Kakatiyan craftsmen both in carving and polishing the stone. Black stone is used for pillars as carving could be sure and accurate. The sculpture on four central pillars is so sharp and crisp that it might have been finished only yesterday. The asvapadas of the pillars are decorated on their faces with the figures of dancers and drummers on four sides. The facets, the floral designs and the religious motifs are all deeply cut and the human figures stand out from the main surface of the stone. These pillars are as elegant and charming in their carving and polishing as the pillars of the temples at Palampet and Hanumakonda in Warangal district, Pillalamarri and Nagulapadu in Nalgonda district.

The ceiling of the mandapa is laid in Kadalikakarana process in all its nine compartments. The ceiling in the central compartment is the principal and highly ornate of the many ceilings of the Kakatiya temples in Karimnagar region. The inner faces of the beams are decorated with hamsamala, while their outer faces are plain. Three flat multi-petalled lotuses are carved on the bottom surface of each beam. The carvings from the underside of the square central slab upward are circular, each ascending ring being smaller than the lower one. The large and finely carved drop or central piece is in a single block let down from the top. A number of drip-stones add beauty to the circular portion carved in concave shape. The carving presents a great variety of design and its effect can be but faintly presented by any drawing.

The highly ornate doorways of antaralas and garbhagrihas of this temple are the best examples of superb workmanship. Each doorway is of 6'-2" height and 3'-2" width. The doorway of antarala has side screen windows of exquisite fret work admitting plenty of light in. The sakhas of the doorway are adorned with floral designs and beneath them the figures of dvarapalas, dancers and chowry-bearers are beautifully sculptured. The lintel contains Gajalakshmi motif at the centre. A projecting roof decorated with semi-circular stones and a sculptured architrave are the other sections of the doorway. On the architraves, Siva is seen dancing on the prostrate body of *Apasmarapurusa*. This is a ten handed variety of Siva. To his left are the figures of Vinayaka and Vishnu while there are Brahma and Kumara to his right. The antarala behind this doorway is 8'-6" long and 9'-3" broad. The doorway of garbhagriha is carved like that of antarala except the purnaghatas carved at the base and turrets carved on the architrave. The garbhagriha is 11'-2" square. Though the architecture of the temple is conventional to a degree, none can deny its magnificence, nor can any one ignore the righ imagination, patient industry and skilful workmanship of the builders of this temple.

The single shrine temple:

This temploe stands to the south of the trikuta temple at a distance of a few yards. The temple consists of garbhagriha, antarala, mandapa and a porch before it. The porch rests on two front pillars. The sixteen pillared mandapa with four central pillars is open without any parapet wall around it. The pillars are plain without any ornamentation. The mandapa is in ruined condition. The temple faces the east and it is dedicated to Siva.

Another single shrine temple:

This temple is quite adjacent to the above temple and the slanting eave cornices of both the temples in the mandapa portion touch each other. Apparently there is no demarcation between the mandapas of both the temples and one can pass freely from one mandapa to the other. The plan, size and shape are quite similar to those of the above temple. This temple is also dedicated to Siva. The garbhagriha and the porch are lost. There is a typical Kakatiyan nandi in the ruined mandapa of this temple. The architectural style and the poor workmanship reveal that these two Siva temples were constructed earlier to the trikuta temple.

Loose Sculptures:-

1. *Bhairava:-* This is an image of 7' height carved on a big stone slab.

He holds damaru in upper right hand, trisula in upper left hand, a curled khadga in lower right hand and kapala in lower left hand. A dog is jumping to his left. Now this image stands before the trikuta temple.

2. *Nandi:-* This is a typical Kakatiyan nandi now lying before the trikuta temple. It is 5'-9" long with several ornamental bands running along and across its body. It has a collar ornamented with haras of bells around the neck. The festooned rump garland is clearly a feature of the sculpture of the Kakatiyas.[146]

3. *Nandi:-* This is similar to the above and lies in the ruined mandapa of the single shrine temple.

29. **Pothgal**

Pothgal or Potuganti is situated about 60 kms. south-west of Karimnagar. It can be reached via Sircilla. There is an inscription[147] in Nagari script on the main door of the Vishnu temple now known as Ramalaya. It is dated A.D. 1235 and records the installation of some deity by Mahapradhana named Narayana son of Vamideva of Vasishtha gotra. There are two temples on a hillock facing the east. They stand side by side in a stone walled compound.

The Siva temple:

The temple consists of garbhagriha, antarala and a sixteen pillared mandapa. The mandapa is enclosed by a parapet wall leaving a passage on the east. There is a tall column of about 25' height standing before the temple with a miniature mandapa at the top containing a nandi inside it.

The Vishnu Temple:

The temple consists of garbhagriha, antarala, a closed mandapa and an open mandapa with a porch before it. As the temple is built on the plain surface of the rock, the walls rise straight from the ground without any adhisthana. Kakshasanas are arranged over the parapet wall of the open mandapa. The doorway of the closed mandapa is beautifully decorated with female figures at the base. There is a loose sculpture of Surya standing in samabhanga with seven horses carved at the base. The hands of the figure are broken. The garbhagriha at present contains the deity of Sri Rama. Loose sculptures of garuda and Hanuman of 6' height are placed in the courtyard. There is a garuda stambha of about 25' height standing before the temple. Outside the village and beside the P.W.D. road there are two viragals of 4' height holding sword and shield in their hands. Pothgal was an important place during the Chalukyan and Kakatiyan times because it lies on the way from Kolanupaka to Vemulavada.

30. **Mutharam**

Mutharam is a small village lying to the south-east of Karimnagar at a distance of about 60 kms. by road. It can be reached from Huzurabad or Husunabad via Mulkanur. There is a beautiful trikuta temple in typical Kakatiyan style lying in the fields near the village. This temple is similar to those found at Nagunuru and Kothapalli. The temple faces the east. The porch on the east and the mandapa in the centre remain either unfinished or ruined. Three shrines are appended on three sides of the square platform intended for the mandapa.

The upapitha of the temple is high and runs all-round the temple. This is divided into a number of mouldings horizontally. Pattika, Padma and tripatta of various sizes are repeated with alternate recesses. The third band from the ground has a row of stones with semi-circular tops and the last band has the same decoration inverted. The adhisthana is also similarly moulded. The walls are treated into broad pilasters and recesses. Narrow pilasters surmounted by turrets are sculptured in the recesses. The *Kapota* of the temple is in three tiers. The superstructures are lost but the huge blocks of stone laid for the purpose of ceiling remain over the shrines.

A flight of ten steps leads to the open square platform containing a heap of large blocks of stone, either ruined or intended for the erection of the mandapa. Each garbhagriha of this triple shrine temple is preceded by an antarala and every one of them has a door way. The door frames are alike in their architectural composition. All the doorways are decorated with a wide projecting roof over the lintel sculptured with pendants. The architraves are sculptured with turrets. Dvarapalas are carved beneath the jambs of the antarala doorways while the doorways of the garbhagrihas remain plain at the base. The western and the southern shrines are dedicated to Siva while the northern shrine is dedicated to Vishnu. On stylistic grounds grounds the temple may be dated to the first half of the 13th century A.D.

Sculptures:

1. *Vishnu:-* This is a typical Kakatiyan sculpture of 4' height placed in the northern garbhagriha. He stands in samabhanga holding sankha in upper right hand and chakra in upper left hand, while his lower hands are broken. He is adorned with kirita-mukuta, kundalas, haras, graiveyakas, udarabandha, triple girdle, ardhoruka and vanamala. He wears armlets, wristlets, anklets and nupuras. He is flanked by chowry-bearers and garuda is seen to his right at the bottom.

2. *Ganapati:-* This is a big image with four hands lying under the trees at a little distance to the north of the temple. He wears Karanda mukuta and naga as udarabandha. This image is similar to the one found in the mandapa of the Thousand pillar temple at Hanumakonda.

31. **Gudimettapalle** (Sultanabad)

Gudimettapalle is a very small village lying on the road to Peddapalli at a distance of only a kilometre from Sultanabad. It is almost like one of the localities of Sultanabad town. The place seems to be an early historical site with a mound where several pieces of black and red ware pottery are noticed. This region is studded with a large number of early historical sites almost in every alternate village.[148] There is a single shrine temple dedicated to Siva. It lies in the fields, nearer to the P.W.D. Road. It consists of garbhagriha, antarala and a sixteen pillared mandapa. The temple faces the north. The walls of the garbhagriha are in dilapidated condition. The outer shell of the wall is lost and the stone blocks of the inner shell are exposed. The superstructure is also lost.

The mandapa has a parapet wall around it leaving passages on north, east and west. The western portion of the mandapa is totally lost. The ceiling of the remaining compartments in the mandapa is laid in Kadalikakarana process each decorated with a full blown lotus at the centre. The doorway of antarala is typically Kakatiyan with a perforated screen window on either side. Purnakumbhas are carved beneath the door jambs. The doorway of garbhagriha contains Saivite dvarapalas at the base and Gajalakshmi motif of lalata. The projecting cornice above the lintel is decorated with pendants. The architrave is sculptured with turrets. There is a typical Kakatiyan Nandi in the mandapa with its face mutilated.

32. **Vilasagar**

Vilasagar is situated at a distance of about 25 kms to the west of Karimnagar and can be reached via Kudurupaka cross-roads. There is a beautiful trikuta temple facing the east in the middle of the village. An illegible inscription,[149] on a slab lying in the compound of the temple records the date S. 1224 and the name of the year Subhakrit which corresponds to A.D. 1302. The other details are not clear but the single word *Malyala* is noticed, probably indicating the name of the family of the Malyala chiefs, who served under the Kakatiya rulers.

The Trikuta Temple:

The temple consists of a square mandapa with three shrines towards the north, west and south and a porch on the east. It does not contain upapitha. Some of the mouldings of the adhisthana are buried in the ground. One of the bands has a row of stones with semi-circular tops at regular intervals and the top band immediately above it has the same decoration inverted, with a recess between both the bands. The plain walls rise over the adhisthana. A fillet prominently decorated with four petalled flowers runs round from the centre of the walls of each garbhagriha. The Kapota is in two tiers. The shrines are surmounted by the sikharas in stepped pyramidal form. Each sikhara consisting of ten diminishing steps in brick is crowned by a round member with a Kalasa above it. This elongaged pyramid appears to be the form, the temple sikhara had taken, when the stone-stepped sikhara of the Jain temples of the

Kadamba region was reproduced in brick in the Kakatiya temples.[150*] The sikhara of Padmakshi temple at Hanumakonda is also built in the same form by Mailama, the wife of Betana, the minister of Kakati Prola II.[151]

The porch on the east leads to the 24' square mandapa with four central pillars which are plain without any ornamentation. The ceiling of the mandapa, porch, antaralas and garbhagrihas is laid in Kadalikakarana process. All the three shrines are alike and each shrine consists of a garbhagriha and an antarala which measure 8'-8" x 8'. The linga in the garbhagriha is 1'-3" high with the circumference of 3'-10" and the height of its pedestal is 2'-4". The doorway of the antarala has a vertical perforated stone plate on either side decorated with four petalled floral designs. The doorway of the garbhagriha contains sakhas decorated with floral designs and lion motifs with a pilaster in the middle. The Saivite dvarapalas flanked by female chowry-bearers are carved beneath the jambs. The lalata contains Gajalakshmi motif. The projecting cornice over the lintel is plain and the architrave is sculptured with turrets.

There are two hero stones of 5' height standing outside the village on the way to cross-roads.

33. **Chittapur**

Chittapur once an important centre of Saivism with a trikuta temple, is today a small village lying at a distance of about 80 kms. north-west of Karimnagar. It can be reached both from Koratla and Metpalli by a rough concrete road of about 10 kms. It lies to the west of a big rivulet. There is a pillar inscription[152] of the reign of Kakati Prataparudradeva (A.D. 1295-1323) of Warangal. The exact year is not identified but it contains Phalguna Suddha Somavaramu i.e. Monday and the Saka year Sobhakrit.

The inscription introduces a local subordinate named Chinni Rudradeva, the nayamkara or military chief of the village Peddapariyala included in Chinnapariyala-Sthala, which is perhaps the old name of Chittapur. The names of its surrounding villages Sripuram (Siripuram) and Dharmavuramu (Dharmaram) also appear in the inscription. It records that certain Bairisetti of the

Virabalinja community had installed the gods Bairesvara, Sakalesvara and Nagesvara in a trikuta temple and endowed them with one third of the produce in the land irrigated under the tank Sakalasamudra newly constructed by him. The remaining two thirds is said to be the share of the king. Perhaps the big tank now existing beside the village was the old Sakalasamudra. The king Prataparudra is said to have visited the temple and made gifts of lands. But unfortunately not even the ruins of the temple exist today in the village except a few traces of its foundation at a little distance from the rivulet. Local information reveals that the ruins of the temple were used by a local Velama chief for the construction of his building about a century ago. This reminds us the case of Amaravati in Guntur district where the ruins of Buddhist Stupa were used by the local chief in the same manner. The pillar inscription seems to have been shifted to local Hanuman Tota or garden, when no more ruins remained on the temple spot.

34. Thimmapur

Thimmapur is about 81 kms. from Karimnagar and 31 kms. from Jagtial on Jagtial-Lakshettipet road. There is a ruined Trikuta temple just beside the P.W.D. road at the 4th kilometre stone form Dharmapuri. The temple faces the east and stands to the south of the river Godavari at a distance of about a furlong. Now the temple is surrounded by barren lands.

The whole trikuta complex stands on a big rock of red sand-stone and the same type of stone is employed for the construction of the temple also. As the temple stands on a rock at the height of about 6' it does not contain any adhisthana. The walls rise straight for about 6' from the base of the rock.

A flight of steps leads directly to the 17' square mandapa. Three shrines are appended on three sides of the mandapa with an entrance on the east. The ceiling of the mandapa is flat roofed except the central portion, which is laid in *Kadalikakarana* process.

The western shrine seems to be the main with Siva in the form of linga. The door frame is very simple with Saivite dvarapalas carved on either side beneath the door jambs. The lintel contains

Gajalakshmi motif at the centre. The shrine on the north is totally ruined except a door frame still standing. The southern shrine is also ruined but the door frames with a narrow antarala are still extant. The north and south doorways contain purnakumbhas beneath the door jambs. All the three shrines contain narrow antaralas of 2'-4" length and 6'-4" breadth. The only spire that is extant on the western garbhagriha is in stepped pyramidal form. This spire is also in ruins. Neither any inscription nor any loose sculpture is noticed in and around the temple except a panavatta and linga in the mandapa. A beautiful nandi of this temple is reported to have been shifted to Dharmapuri. The architectural style of the temple is very simple, perhaps built by a local chieftain during the twelfth century A.D.

35. **Peddampet**

The small village Peddampet is situated at a distance of about 60 kms. north-east of Karimnagar. It can be reached via Peddapalli and it is only 5 kms. from Ramagundam. To the south of Peddampet there is a hillock known as Peddadevulla gutta. The hillock appears to have contained at one time a beautiful temple, the ruins of which can be noticed now on the spot. The broken door jambs, a beautifully carved central pillar, a big nandi, a huge linga of basalt and broken pieces of dhvaja stambha are important finds among the ruins. The remains reveal that the temple was built of red stone. Besides a Saivite temple, it appears that a Vaishnavite temple also existed at Peddampet.[153] A beautiful figure of Yakshini from the Vaishnavite temple is reported to have been shifted to Hyderabad museum. Another beautiful sculpture of a woman and broken door jambs of this place now stand in the Karimnagar museum.

Sculptures:

1. *Yakshini:-* The idea of the exuberance of youth combined with unfettered emotion is well illustrated in this figure. The sculpture possesses some very striking characteristics, notably the extraordinary plumpness of the hips, which feature is further projected by the sharp curve of the body line near the waist.[154] The waist is thin, as is usual in Indian sculpture, but in this figure this characteristic has been accentuated by the over development of bosom and abdomen. The arms have been thrown up and the hands gracefully joined

above the head. But in carving the arms, the artist has again exaggerated their girth in contrast to the elbows, which look comparatively thin but more shapely. This exaggeration of certain parts of the body suggests an exuberance of life or swirl of emotion combined with bold sweep of the line of the body.[155]

2. *Sculpture of woman*:- This beautiful sculpture of a young woman in red stone, now stands in Karimnagar museum. Her face is totally defaced. Her left hand is broken below the elbow and above the wrist, while her right hand is completely lost. Yet this stands as a sculpture of exceptional beauty and elegance. This standing figure is perhaps a huntress holding a bow which is also broken. But still the upper curve of the bow is seen to her left above her shoulder. A monkey sitting to her right is trying to pull down her saree to make her nude, while she is trying to hold it up with her left hand placed on left thigh. Yet her efforts prove in vain and her genital part is exposed. Her loin is slim and her breasts are high and heavy. She is adorned with a necklace, a long hara hanging in between breasts, armlets, anklets and nupuras. A monkey pulling down the saree of a woman is an oft-carved feature found in the Kakatiyan sculpture.[156]

3. *Door jamb*:- This is a trisakha door jamb in red stone decorated with gaja motifs and four petalled floral designs with a pilaster in the middle. A Saivite dvarapala is carved in a niche at the base. Now it stands in the Karimnagar museum.

4. *Door jamb*:- This is another door jamb in red stone with a female figure carved at the base holding a bunch of fruits. It stands beside the above mentioned one in the same museum.

36. **Yelgedu**

Yelgedu is situated about 20 kms. north-east of Karimnagar and 10 kms. west of Sultanabad. There is an old temple dedicated to Siva. It is known as Ramalingesvara temple and stands beside a big tank. There is an inscription[157] dated A.D. 1301, which records the gift of some local taxes to the god Ramanathadeva by the queen of Prataparudradeva Maharaja named Lakmadevi for increasing the merit of her father Paldevanayiningaru.

Ramalingesvara Temple:

This appears to be a pre-Kakatiyan temple by its simplicity in architecture and execution. The temple faces the east. It consists of a garbhagriha 10' square, an antarala 6' x 8' and a sixteen pillared mandapa with four pillars at the centre. The mandapa is enclosed by a parapet wall leaving a passage on the east. A sub-shrine is attached to the mandapa on the north. It contains garbhagriha and antarala. At present it houses a female deity with Saivite attributes. A seated image of Jain Tirthankara carved on a pilaster to the left side of the sub-shrine can be noticed in the mandapa. The spires of both the main shrine and sub-shrine are in the stepped pyramidal form.

There are loose sculptures in the antarala. Among them there is an image of Ganapati in archaic form endowed with two hands and a natural elephant head turning the trunk towards right. A Chalukyan nandi is noticed in the mandapa. To the north of this temple is another temple known as Ramalaya.

37. **Kasipet**

Kasipet is situated at a distance of about 15 kms. north-west of Manthani and can be reached via Gunjapadge village. Now the village totally stands deserted for the unknown reasons except the group of temples standing on the bank of the river Godavari which can be reached after covering 3 kms. on foot from Gunjapadga. Kasipet is an early historical site with several mounds where pieces of black and red ware pottery and large number of brickbats are noticed.

The Double shrine temple:

This temple stands in a stone walled compound facing the east. The prakara wall on the east with an entrance facing the Vishnu shrine is extant while the walls on the other sides stand collapsed. The prakara wall appears to have contained another entrance facing the Siva shrine but it is in total ruins. The temple consists of two separate garbhagrihas standing side by side dedicated to Siva and Vishnu with a common antarala and a multi-pilared mandapa twith porches on the east, north and south. There is a sub-shrine situated on either side in the north-west and the south-west corners of the hall. The brick sikharas over the shrines are in ruins.

The mandapa has six rows of pillars five in each row. Thus there are 30 pillars excluding the corresponding half pillars rising over the parapet wall which runs all around the mandapa. The shaft consists of two square parts and curiously enough their faces are sculptured with several figures in low relief which are simple in design and exhibit less workmanship. The figures of dancers, huntresses, a woman holding a Kalasa, the palanquin of a woman being carried by two women on either side, the nude figure of a young woman standing cross-legged laying her right hand on breasts and hiding her yoni with her left hand, a man standing with folded palms, the scene of *Gopika Vastrapaharana,* the entwined nagas and the friezes of elephants, lions and deer are the most important among the sculptures found on the pillars.

The Single Shrine Temple:

This temple stands facing the east at a little distance to the south of the main temple housing at present the seated image of Sri Rama along with his consort Sita sitting on his folded left leg. He keeps his right hand in abhaya, while he passes his left hand round the back of the devi. The makara torana behind the image is carved with dasavataras.

38. **Mulkanuru**

The village Mulkanuru is on the way form Huzurabad to Husunabad. There is an old temple in Kummarivada dedicated to Siva. It consists of garbhagriha, antarala and a sixteen-pillared mandapa. The temple faces the east. There are a few old sculptures of Ganapati and female deities. The Devis hold trisula and damaru in upper hands while they hold Khadga and bowl in lower hands. This place was also a centre of Jain worship. An unfinished Jain image seated in dhyanamudra is shifted from this place to the Karimnagar museum. This image is now placed on a pedestal in the courtyard of the museum. The image is in black granite and the face is left unfinished.

39. Nancherla

Nancherla is about 24 kms. to the east of Jagtial connected by a concrete road. There is a temple now known as Ramalaya in the middle of the village. It faces the east. As seen now the temple consists of garbhagriha, antarala and mukhamandapa. Originally the temple consisted of only garbhagriha and a porch resting on two pillars, which are quite similar to the pillars found inside the garbhagriha. The mukhamandapa and the two small shrines behind it projecting to the north and south in the antarala portion of the present order appear to be later additions, as the walls of the garbhagriha and porch consist of large blocks of stone whereas the shrines appended later contain comparatively smaller stones. Outwardly the temple looks like a trikuta but it does not contain the common mandapa as found in the other trikuta temples, which have a cruciform plan.

The adhistana of the temple is very simple without any mouldings, over which the bhitti rises. The wall and the spire are separated by a cornice in two tiers. The spire over the main shrine is in stepped pyramidal form, whereas the spires over the small shrines are no more extant. The mukhamandapa measures 26' east-west and 28' north-south. The eastern portion of the mandapa to the extent of 10' length appears to have collapsed. The central part of the mandapa is slightly elevated with a rangasila in circular form.

The trisakha doorway of antarala contains Gajalakshmi motif on lalata and a projecting cornice above the lintel. The architrave is decorated with turrets. The panels beneath the door jambs contain four handed Vaishnavite dvarapalas flanked by two female chowry-bearers. The doorway of garbhagriha is plain without any decoration. The garbhagriha measures 14' either way. Curiously enough there are four pillars inside the garbhagriha leaving a passage of 1 1/2' width between the pillars and walls. This is an early Chalukyan feature generally found in the temples constructed in this area during the 10th and 11th centuries A.D.

The main shrine at present contains the seated image of Rama along with his consort Sita sitting on his folded left leg. He keeps his right hand in abhaya, while he passes his left hand round the back of the devi. The makara torana behind the image is carved with dasavataras within the circles formed by creepers. There are loose sculptures of Lakshmana, Bharata, Satrughna and Hanuman in the same garbhagriha. The northern and southern shrines contain the loose sculptures of Balarama and Krishna respectively.

40. **Gambhirraopet**

Gambhirraopet is a fairly big village situated about 80 kms. south-west of Karimnagar and can be reached via Sircilla by bus. The village stands about a kilometre away from the river Maner. There are two single shrine temples standing side by side overlooking the Maner. Both the temples face the east. They are enclosed by a prakara wall with a separate gateway for each temple. The gateway of each temple consists of a double storeyed mandapa with twelve pillars in each floor. The similar arrangement of double storeyed mandapa can be found at the gateway of the old Siva temple, which is Chalukyan in style, at Duddeda village lying on the P.W.D. road from Siddipet to Hyderabad in Medak district.

There are neither loose sculptures nor inscriptions in and around the above temples. Both the temples are in a dilapidated condition. They look Chalukyan in their style and can be assigned to 12th century A.D.

The Northern temple:

This temple consists of garbhagriha, a narrow antarala and an open mandapa. The garbhagriha is vacant and it is 6'-9" square, while antarala measures 6'-4" north-south and 3'-10" east-west. The doorway of antarala is 4'-7" x 2'-3" and the doorway of garbhagriha is 4' x 2'-9". Purnakumbhas are carved at the base of the antarala doorway while the doorway of garbhagriha is plain. The mandapa measures 16' each way. A small broken nandi in Chalukyan style is found in the mandpa. This temple is probably dedicated to Siva. A monolithic pillar broken at the top stands before the temple.

The Southern Temple:

This temple consists of garbhagriha, antarala, a closed mandapa and an open mandapa before it. The northern portion of the open mandapa is no more extant. The closed mandapa measures 16' each way. The four central pillars are richly carved and the square base of each pillar is decorated with a miniature niche on each of its face with a deity inside it. The garbhagriha is vacant and it is 9'-4" square while the antarala measures 9'-4" north-south and 5'-3" east-west. This temple is probably dedicated to Vishnu in view of the Vishnu mark found on the lintel of one of the doorways.

Sitarama temple and Yellammagudi are other important places of worship in the village.

41. **Ramagundam**

Ramagundam is situated at a distance of about 64 kms. north-east of Karimnagar on the banks of the Godavari. It is a railway station on the Kazipet-Balharshah section of the South Central Railway. The village appears to have been a place of historical significance during the early medieval period. A fragmentary and damaged stone inscription[158] set up on the steps of Ramalaya mentions certain Mahamandalesvara Edaraja bearing the titles Lattaluru-Puravaresvara and Suvarnagaruda-dhvaja which are similar to those borne by Medaraja in his Polavasa epigraph[159] in the same Godavari region. Both the chiefs, in view of their titles, must have belonged to the same stock of Rashtrakuta family of generals. Kakati Rudra's Thousand pillar temple inscription[160] dated A.D. 1163 refers to Edaraja as one of the enemies of Prola II, who made the former flee form the battle-field like a child in the presence of the Chalukyan King Jagadekamalla II. Edaraja appears to have ruled over Ramagundam area contemporaneous with Medaraja of Polavasa and Gundaraja of Mantrakuta.

Ramalaya:

This is a single shrine temple consisting of garbhagriha, antarala and a mandapa with a porch before it. The gala part of adhisthana is divided by means of short pilasters into several compartments filled with Hamsas, simhas, gajas and four petalled floral designs. The walls are plain and the sikhara is in stepped pyramidal form. The garbhagriha at present contains the deity of Sri Rama. There is a tall column standing before the temple with a miniature mandapa at the top.

The Torana-gateway:

The special distinction of this temple is the possession of a Torana-gateway. The tall Torana-gateway, a typical feature of the architectural style of Telingana, among the known instances, may be considered as the earliest in date.[162] It stands before the temple consisting of two upright posts with a profusely sculptured cross-beam above them. This is a makara Torana, the predominant ornamentation being makara. The lintel contains a niche at the centre and on its either side four lotus buds hang down from the lintel like those of Hamsa-Torana at Warangal. This Torana is very archaic and similar to the Torana at Kulpak (Kolanupaka) in Nalgonda district and Nandikandi in Medak district.

The erection of Torana-gateway in Wanrangal region, started at Hanumakonda near Padmakshi temple,improved at Kolanupaka and beautified at Ainavolu. The Hamsa Toranas at Warangal famous for their size, grandeur and beauty appear to be the final culmination of the effort to build up an imposing doorway to a fort or temple.[162] The Toranas at Warangal and Ainavolu in Warangal district consist of double pillars, whereas the Torana at Ramagundam has a single pillar on either side. The Torana at Ramagundam contains graceful lions serving as brackets. At present only the left side lion bracket is seen, the other being lost. The pillars consist of several sakhas decorated with floral designs and motifs of birds and animals. The four-handed Saivite dvarapalas flanked by the female chowry-bearers are carved beneath the jambs, which is a special feature not found on the Toranas at Warangal and Ainavolu. The rear side of Torana is also similarly fashioned as in the front. The presence of Saivite dvarapalas on the Torana gives rise to a doubt that there should have been another Siva temple in the same compound which can be evidenced by the several ruined pillars found on the spot. On the way to Ramagundam, there is a dilapidated temple on a hillock known as Boda gutta.

42. Vellulla

Vellulla is about 90 kms. from Karimnagar and 5 kms. from Metpalli. There is an old Narasimha temple on a hillock to the south of the village. Though no older inscription is available, the later inscription[163] dated A.D. 1613 records the construction of a sluice at the Nagula tank for the pleasure of the deity lord Narasimha by certain Minnayya of Munnuri caste at the instance of a Velama chief named Juvvadi Dalapatiraya.

The old Narasimha temple on the hillock is very simple with three small rooms connected to a mandapa at an unequal distance. The temple faces the east with an entrance leading into the mandapa rectangular in form. The main shrine is like a small cave type cell formed by a big boulder resting on another big boulder. The natural cell with the depth of about 5' contains a loose Narasimha sculpture. The shrine is covered by boulders on three sides with a wall and a door on the east. The pillars of the mandapa are very crude with square members intervened by a round member. To the north end of the mandpa is a small shrine with a female deity locally known as Lokamata. Another small shrine on the south contains a few loose sculptures.

At another spot there is a big image of Hanuman around which walls are constructed recently, so as to give it a temple form. Near the image there is an inscription[164] on a boulder dated A.D. 1665 recording the installation of Hanuman image by three sons of Anisetti Prataparavu of Munnuri caste named Prataparavu Konaya, Venkataya and Potaya Jaggaya. The work was executed by Bhupaludu Tomdaya.

Vellulla is famous for a female deity locally known as Yellamma. There is a beautifully carved female deity lying flat under a banian tree to the north of the village. An unidentifiable triangular stone slab beside the female deity is also worshipped perhaps as the severed head of Renuka, the wife of the famous sage Jamadagni.

The traditional story[165] relates that Renuka the wife of Jamadagni once became the victim of a momentary excitement on seeing the royal couple sporting in the waters of a river. Consequently she could not make a pot as usual with the clay and failed to bring water. Jamadagni got frowned and commanded his sons to behead their sinning mother. Parasurama came forward and carried out the behest of his father. Pleased with this, Jamadagni asked his son to ask for a boon and the latter desired for the restoration of his mother to life. Jamadagni regretted his inability to grant the request but conceded that the two parts of Renuka's body will become objects of popular worship. As such the severed head of Renuka is generally worshipped as Yellamma and headless body as Bhudevi.

The sakti cult started flourshing in the form of Gangamma, Ekavira, Kakati, Irukalamma, Gauri, Mahalakshmi, Yellamma, Maisamma and Pochamma during the Kakatiya times. These deities are generally associated with the communities like Gollas, Yadavas, Kuruvas etc.[166]

43. **Konapur**

The village known as Pembetla-Konapur lies to the north of Jagtial at a distance of about 8 kms. connected by a concrete road. There is a small temple dedicated to Siva in the form of Linga known as Sri Dubba Rajesvara Swamy. at present the temple is totally a rebuilt one. According to local information, there existed an old temple simple in size and structure standing at the same place, which can be further confirmed by an inscription standing near the temple datable to 15th century A.D. in view of the characters of letters carved in Telugu.[167] It contains Krodhi, Vaisakha Su 14 Guruvara on which certain Sarvabhumuni Narusaya was gifted some land for this holy centre by Dhannapaneni Ghamtaya Dhamsagi Singarayya. But it does not contain the numerical figure of Saka year to judge its accurate antiquity. As this inscription can be dated back to 15th century A.D. it can be presumed that the temple existed still earlier probably in the 13th century A.D., when this region was under the sway of the Kakatiyas.

In the vicinity of the temple there are two old Vaishnavite dvarapala images carved beautifully in high relief. Both the images are four handed flanked by female chowry-bearers at the bottom. They hold Chakra in upper right hand and Sankha in upper left hand while their lower hands perhaps holding gada are found broken. They wear mukutas, kundalas, graiveyakas, haras, keyuras, armlets, wristlets, katibandha, vanamala, anklets, and nupuras. A broken piece of door jamb containing elephant and lion motifs is perched near these images.

44. Neerakulla

The village Neerakulla is only 5 kms. from Sultanabad. There is an old temple standing on a very big boulder in the middle of the river Maner. The natural surroundings are beautiful with hillocks and luxurious vegetation. The spot is picturesque as the boulder containing the temple is surrounded by water. The temple is dedicated to Vishnu in the form of Sri Ranganayaka. The walls of the temple are plain and the spire is in stepped pyramidal form. The pillars in the open mandapa are massive and short and appear to be of an early origin.

In the vicinity of the above temple there is a hillock on the northern bank of Maner containing a small temple with garbhagriha and an ardhamandapa before it. At present there is no deity in this temple. The doorway of garbhagriha contains Gajalakshmi motif on Lalata and Purnakumbhas at the base. There are two miniature shrines at the same place provided with the vimanas of south Indian style.

45. Kotilingala

Kotilingala otherwise pronounced as Kotalingala is situated about 65 kms. north of Karimnagar at the confluence of Peddavagu and Godavari. The village is about 3 kms. from Karimnagar-Lakshettipet road on eastern side and can be reached from Valakaturu. A few label inscriptions in the Brahmi characters of 2nd century B.C. were noticed on the way to Munulagutta form Kotilingala. On a sand stone pillar now lying in a paddy field about a kilometre away, there is a label inscription which reads *NAGAGOPINIKAYA* in bold double lined ornamental characters of first century A.D.[168] The Buddhist stupa on a hillock at Pashigaon and the hill locally known as Munulagutta, probably inhabited by the Jain monks near Kapparraopet are in the close vicinity of this village. It is from this place that the coins of Chimuka or Simuka, the founder of the Satavahana dynasty were collected.[169] A few early uninscribed punch-marked copper coins were also found at this place.[170] In view of the description of the river in *Gatha Saptasati* and surface finds including large sized bricks and pottery, it can be inferred that the site was one of the strongholds of early Satavahanas.[171]

The early historical site of Kotilingala is now under excavations conducted by the Archaeological Department of Andhra Pradesh. Several brick wells big and small with well laid out sewage system have come to light in the recent excavations. As at Dhulikatta the mound at Kotilingala is also encompassed by a mud fort with several gates opening towards the cardinal points. The fortification on the Godavari side was much ruined due to flooding and erosion. However a gate in the middle of the rampart was traced, which served as an inlet and outlet for merchandise. Towards the north of the fort and adjacent to the water course of the river, the brick structures in a long row indicate the presence of a wharf. These brick structures near the water course are reminiscent of once a commercially and politically important town. The large sized bricks used for the structures, were ransacked by the villagers to be utilized for the construction of their houses. In fact the entire village of Kotilingala is now built with the early historical bricks.[172]

At all the corners of the fortification there are bastions, presently appearing like high mounds. On one of the mounds there exists a temple dedicated to Siva. The temple is of late Chalukyan type with stout pillars.[173]

Siva Temple:

The temple consists of two shrines with a common mandapa containing four pillars at the centre. Each shrine consists of a garbhagriha and an antarala. The western shrine facing the east is considered to be the main shrine dedicated to Kotisvara and the other southern shrine facing the north is dedicated to Siddesvara. The mandapa is enclosed by a parapet wall with passages on the east and the north. In the courtyard of the temple there is an image of Bhairava 4' in height containing a hooded canopy over his head. A dog is seen jumping to his left at the bottom.

The sculptures of Venugopala and Ganapati are noticed in the mandapa. Scattered images can be spotted on the river banks and at one place is a beautiful specimen representing Kaliya-mardana.[174] A beautiful sculpture of Vishnu reclining on the serpent known as Shayana-murti is shifted and now placed in the Karimnagar museum.

46. Aravelli

Aravelli is situated about 50 kms. north of Karimnagar and can be reached via Mallial. There is a ruined Venugopalaswamy temple of late medieval period outside the village. The temple faces the east and it is now surrounded by fields. The walls of the temple are plain and the sikhara built in brick is in stepped pyramidal form. The doorway of antarala contains above the lintel a projecting cornice decorated with pendants. The Vaishnavite dvarapalas are carved beneath the sakhas. Lattice windows are aranged on either side of the doorway. They are apparently meant for decoration as their rears are closed with a back plate. The loose sculptures of Vaishnavite dvarapalas 3' in height stand on either side of the doorway.

Aravelli is famous for a female deity locally known as Nayakuralu. The devi is housed in a separate temple in the village. This temple is built of brick walls covered by country tiles. The sculpture of devi is small in size. She holds sword in right hand and a bowl in left hand.

There are some important sculptures outside the temple. The image of Vishnu with a makara torana behind him is flanked by chowry-bearers. Garuda is seen sitting to his right at the bottom with folded hands. The hands of the god are mutilated. There is another sculpture of Shanmukha riding on his vahana peacock with his consort. The sculpture of Nagini is in half serpentine and half human form shaded by seven hoods. She holds sword and shield in her hands. There is a viragal found outside the village on the way to Bathikapalli.

47. Anantagiri

The village Anantagiri lies to the south-west of Karimnagar and can be reached via Sircilla. The village appears to have derived its name as Anantagiri because of the existance of a temple on the hill dedicated to Vishnu in the form of Anantashayana. There is an inscription[175] dated A.D. 1517 which introduces certain Lakhayamantrin of Srivatsa-gotra and his descendants Sri Krishna, Rama, Lakhaya and again Rama and Krishna. The last named Krishna is said to have built a tample to the god Ananta on the hill.

48. Peddapalli

Peddapalli town, the headquarters of the revenue division, is situated at a distance of 32 kms. from Karimnagar. It is a railway station on Kazipet-Balharshah line. An undated inscription[176] of the reign of Kakati Ganapatideva at Khammampalli village near Manthani records the names of certain villages and the name of Peddapalli village figures among them. In view of the above mentioned epigraph one can be sure of the existence of Peddapalli village during the Kakatiyan times.

There is a Siva temple known as Ramalingesvara temple in the old town of Peddapalli. It consists of garbhagriha, antarala, an open pillared mandapa and a porch before it. The walls are plain and the spire is in stepped pyramidal form. The trisakha doorway of antarala is beautifually sculptured and it contains a well projected cornice above the lintel while purnakumbhas are carved at the base. This temple stands as an example for the traditional pattern of architecture which was upheld in raising temples in the later times.

There is a loose sculpture of Bhairava near the entrance. He holds trisula in upper left hand, damaru in upper right, khadga in lower right and kapala in lower left hand. The image is 5' tall in black granite.

49. Sircilla

Sircilla town is situated at a distance of 40 kms. west of Karimnagar on the banks of the river Maner. There is a single shrine temple dedicated to Vishnu in the middle of the town. Reportingly it contained at one time the deity of Chenna Kesava. But at present it houses Lord Venkateshvara. The temple consists of garbhagriha, antarala, and an open-pillared mandapa. The spire is in stepped pyramidal form. Though no older inscription is available, there is a much abraded Telugu inscription[177] in late characters on a stone near the temple. It mentions the name of certain devotee, name nor clear, who was the son of Angabokhala Konayya. It also records the name of another devotee Ramabhadraiah who was the son of Vittala. There is another label inscription[178] which simply records the date in saka year 1812 which corresponds to A.D. 1890.

There is another single shrine temple in the town dedicated to Siva. In the courtyard of this temple, there is a beautiful sculpture of Ganapati 4' in height with single pair of arms holding modakas in his left hand on which the tip of the trunk rests. He holds a tusk in his right hand. He keeps his left leg folded and right leg bent at the knee. He wears a mukuta and a hara on his fore-head. A Naga is adorned as udharabandha, while his vahana mushika is carved below his seat. A medium size nandi in typical Chalukyan style is also found in the same courtyard.

50. **Karimnagar**

Karimnagar is situated on the northern banks of river Maner, the tributary of Godavari. A small village by name Aripirala is known to have existed beside Maner.[179] Probably the purana bazar of Karimnagar might be the then Aripirala village, where a Siva temple of late medieval period still exists. It is said that during the reign of the Asafjahis, Syed Karimuddin, the well-known Qiladar of Elgandal fort, founded a village near the fort at a distance of 8 kms. and named it after him as Karimnagar.[180] The old Aripirala village is believed to have formed a part of the present Karimnagar town. As a result of reorganization of the districts in the erstwhile Hyderabad state, the headquarters of the district was shifted form Elgandal to Karimnagar in A.D. 1905.[181] Since then the town has grown enormously by leaps and bounds.

Siva Temple:

There is a single shrine temple dedicated to Siva in the purana bazar of Karimnagar town. It faces the east. It consists of garbhagriha, antarala and an open mukhamandapa. The adhiṡthana of the temple is partly buried in the ground. Some of the visible bands of adhisthana are decorated with semi-circular stones. The bhitti is plain and the spire is in stepped pyramidal form. The mukhamandapa consists of three passages on the east, north and south. The ceiling above the four central pillars is in *Kadalikakarana* process and the central square slab contains upward circular rings, each ascending ring being smaller than the lower with a lotus bud looking down from the centre. This carving is similar to the carvings found on the central square slabs of the ceiling in the main temple at Nagunuru.

The antarala doorway is richly carved. The architrave is sculptured with turrets, while the purnakumbhas are carved at the base. The doorway of garbhagriha is similarly decorated but it contains Saivite dvarapalas at the base.

Loose Sculptures:

There are some important old sculptures placed around the temple within the courtyard.

Saptamatrikas:- This slab contains seven figures of divine Mothers with Vinayaka at one end. Their Vahanas are carved below their seats. The figures are four handed and adorned with mukutas.

Mahishasuramardini:- She is standing with left leg steady on the ground and the right leg kept on the neck of Mahishasura who is in animal form. The goddess has eight hands. She thrusts trisula into the body of the animal with her lower right hand while she holds the tail of the animal with her lower left hand. She holds bana, khadga and Agni in upper right hands and shield, bow and spear-like object in upper left hands. She is adorned with mukuta, Kundalas on the ears, Keyuras, Kankanas and Katibandha.

Brahma:- This is a standing figure with three heads, the fourth being the stone slab at the back cannot be carved. He has four hands. He holds pustak with lower right hand and gada with lower left hand while the objects in upper hands awre indistinct. His vahana Hamsa is carved to his right at the bottom. He is adorned with mukuta, graiveyakas, Yajnopavita, Katibandha and Vanamala.

Saraswati:- She is seen riding on her vahana Hamsa which is carved in big size. The deity has four hands. She holds Vedas in her upper right hand and keeps her lower right hand in Abhaya holding an akshamala. The objects in her left hands are indistinct.

Parsvanatha:- This is a nude Jain figure of about 4'height standing in *Kayotsarga* posture. The coils of the serpent behind the lord a re close-packed and its seven hoods canopy his head. He holds akshamala in his right hand.

Naga:- He is in half human and half serpentine form holding sword and shield in his hands.

Nagini:- She is also in half human and half serpentine form holding sword with her right hand and shield with her left hand.

Door Jambs:- There are two ruined door jambs placed on either side of the entrance. They contain four-handed Saivite dvarapalas at the base.

A detailed study of the above mentioned 50 sites reveals that the majority of the temples are dedicated to Siva, while a few of them belong to the Vaishnavite deities. Besides the temples of the Hindu pantheon, a considerable number of Jain vestiges are also noticed in the district.

REFERENCES

1. B. Rajendra Prasad, *Art of South India*, p.64.
2. *iAPKD*, Nos. 40, & 41.
3. N.S.Ramachandra Murthy, *Op.Cit.*, Section II, pp.1-.
4. *IAPKD*, Nos. 2,4,6,13,18,20,21.
5. *APGKD*, 1974, p.252.
6. B.B. Havell, *Indian Architecture Through Ages*, p.73.
7. N. Venkataramanayya, *Chalukyas of Vemulavada*, pp.44, 82, 84.
8. B. Rajendra Prasad, *Op.Cit.*, pp.141 & 142.
9. M.L. Nigam, *Sculptural Art of Andhra*, p.20.
10. B. Rajendra *Temple Sculpture of Andhra Pradesh*, p.42.
11. M. Rama Rao, *Early Chalukyan Temples of Andhradesa*, pp. 13 & 17, Pl.II & V.
12. *Ibid.*, p.33.
13. *Ibid.*, p.38.
14. *Telangana Sasanamulu* (Telugu), No.21, pp.173-177.
15. N. Venkataramanayya, *Op.Cit.*, p.45.

16. *Telangana Sasanamulu* (Telugu), No.19, pp.120-122.
17. Percy Brown, *Op.Cit.*, p.144.
18. *Ibid.*, p.145.
19. Stella Kramrisch, *Op.Cit.*, p.203, Pl.57.
20. *IAPKD*, No.2, p.5.
21. *EHI*. Vol.I, Part II, p. 306.
22. *RE*, 1966, No.169, p.42.
23. S. Gopalakrishna Murthy, *Jain Vestiges in Andhra*, p.44.
24. *Ibid.*, p.45.
25. *Ibid.*
26. B. Rajendra Prasad, *Op.Cit.*, p.34.
27. N. Venkataramanayya, *Pallavulu-Chalukyulu* (Telugu), pp.270, 271.
28. N. Venkataramanayya, *Chalukyas of Vemulavada*, p.41.
29. *EHD*. p.511.
30. *EA*. Vol.II, pp.21-28.
31. B.C. Bhattacharya, *The Jaina Iconography*, p.87.
32. C. Sivaramamurti, *An Album of Indian Sculpture*, p.82.
33. R.P. Hingorani (ed), *Digambara Jaina Iconography*, p.37.
34. B.C. Bhattacharya, *Op.Cit.*, p.87.
35. *EA*., Vol.II, p.26.
36. S. Gopalakrishna Murthy, *The Sculpture of the Kakatiyas*, pp.8, 9.
37. N. Venkataramanayya, *Op.Cit.*, pp.42 & 93.
38. *IAPKD*. No.5, p.12.
39. Rotte Visvanatha Sastry, "Dharmapuri Kshetra Mahatmyamu", *Andhra Prabha*, Telugu weekly, dt.19.6.1963.
40. *EA*., Vol.II, p.22.
41. *IAPKD* No.31, PP.93-96.
42. *ea*. Vol.II, p.25.
43. *EHI*. Vol.I, Part I, p.201.
44. *Ibid.*, Vol.II, Part II, p.508, Pl.CXLV.
45. E.B. Havell, *Indian Sculpture and Painting*, p.66.
46. M. Rama Rao, *Op.Cit.*, p.23.
47. M. Shyamasundara Sastry (ed), *Trisati* (TeluguPI, pp.17-23.
48. *IAPKD*. No.49, pp.120-122.
49. *Ibid.* No.8, p.21.
50. *Ibid.* No.11, p.29.
51. *EA*., Vol.II, pp.36-38.
52. *IAPKD*. No.9, p.25.
53. *EA*. Vol.IV, pp.67-89.
54. *Ibid.*, p.68.
55. S. Gopalakrishna Murthy, *Jain Vestiges in Andhra*, p.44. Pl.XI.
56. *IAPKD*. No.16, p.42.
57. *Ibid.* No.17, pp.44-47.
58. S. Gopalakrishna Murthy, *Op.Cit.*, p.51.
59. *IAPKD*. No.42, p.113.
60. *Ibid.* No.75, pp.139-141.
61. Kreedabhiramamu (Telugu), Verse 128, (Kakatammaku Saidodu Ekavira)
62. B. Rajendra Prasad, *Art of South India*, p.171.
63. M.L. Nigam, *Op. Cit.*, p.55.
64. M. Radhakrishna Sarma, *Temples of Telingana*, pp.62, 63.
65. *EHI*., Vol.II, Part II, p.556.
66. *Ibid.*, pp.555, 556.
67. M. Radhakrishna Sarma, *Op.Cit.*, pp.52 & 54.

68. S Ramakantham, *Guide Book to Kolanupaka Site Museum,* pp.13 & 15.
69. M. Rama Rao, *Eastern Chalukyan Templess of Andhradesa* p.8.
70. C. Sivaramamurti, *Early Andhra Art and Iconography*, p.12. Pl.60.
71. G. Jouveau Dubreuil, *Iconography of Southern India*, Pl.LXXXII.
72. *IAPKD*. No.26, p.71.
73. *EHD*. p.586.
74. *IAPKD*. No.33, p.99
75. B. Rajendra Prasad, *Temple Sculpture of Andhra Pradesh*, p.44.
76. *APGKD*. 1974, p.246.
77. *IAPKD*. No.68, p.134.
78. *EHI*., Vol.I, Part I, pp.228, 229.
79. Late Jitendranath Banerjea, *The Development of Hindu Iconography* p. 440.
80. M.L. Nigam, *Op. Cit.*, p.58.
81. *IAPKD*. No.53, p.125.
82. M. Rama Rao, *Early Chalukyan Temples of Andhradesa*, pp.17 & 38.
83. *EA*. Vol, pp.70-74.
84. *Ibid*., pp.81-84.
85. *APGKD*. 1974, p.246.
86. S. Gopalakrishna Murthy, *The Sculpture of the Kakatiyas*, p.21.
87. *Ibid*., p.42.
88. *Ibid*., p.23, Pl.22(a).
89. *Ibid*.
90. *Ibid*., p.23.
91. *Ibid*., p.42.
92. M. Rama Rao, *Eastern Chalukyan Temples of Andhradesa*, pp.5-7.
93. M. Rama Rao, *Early Chalukyan Temples of Andhradesa*, pp.17 & 38.
94. S. Gopalakrishna Murthy, *Op.Cit*., p.7.
95. *IAPKD*., No.25, pp.64-71.
96. *JAHRS*., Vol.XXXVI, Part I, pp.58-62.
97. *EHD*., p.710.
98. *IAPKD*., No.32, pp.96-99.
99. P.V. Parabrahma Sastry, *Select Epigraphs of Andhra Pradesh*., No.20, pp.50-55.
100. *IAPKD*., No.45, p.117.
101. *Ibid*., No.70, p.135.
102. *Ibid*., No.71, p.136.
103. *Census Hand Book, Karimnagar District*, 1961, P.VI.
104. S. Gopalakrishna Murthy, *Op.Cit*., p.7.
105. M. Rama Rao, *Select Andhra Temples*, Pl.XIV-1
106. *IAPKD*. No.1, pp.1-5.
107. *Ibid*. No. 77, pp.143-145.
108. *Ibid*., No.74. pp.137-139.
109. *Telangana Sasanamulu* (Telugu), Vol.I, No.17.
110. *IAPWD*. No.36.
111. *IAPKD*. No.25, pp.64-71.
112. An unpublished inscription at Nagunuru is collected from Sri K. Mallaiah, the local head-master.
113. *Corpus*, Part III, p.2.
114. *JAHRS*. Vol.XXXV, pp.183-188.
115. M. Radhakrishna Sarma, *Op.Cit*., p.129, Pl. 131.
116. Late Jitendranath Banerjea, *Op.Cit*., p.533.
117. *IAPKD*. No.25, p.70.
118. S. Gopalakrishna Murthy, *Op.Cit*., p.28.

119. S. Ramakantham, *Op.Cit.*, p.9, Pl.2.
120. S. Gopalakrishna Murthy, *Op.Cit.*, p.25.
121. *IAPKD*. No.27, p.73.
122. V.V. Krishna Sastry, *Op.Cit.*, p.11.
123. T. Vedantam (ed), *Town Study of Manthani*, p.19.
124. *IAPKD*. No.23, p.58.
125. *JAHRS*. Vol.XXXVI, Part I, pp.33-47.
126. *IAPWD*. No.31, p.87.
127. *Ibid.*, No.50, pp.141-149.
128. *Ibid.* No.36, pp.94, 95.
129. *IAPKD*. No.25, pp.65-70.
130. *Ibid.* No.28, pp.75-80.
131. *JAHRS*. Vol.XXXV, p.169.
132. T. Vedantam (ed), *Op.Cit.*, pp.22, 23.
133. *Corpus*, Part I, p.20.
134. P.V. Parabrahma Sastry, *Op.Cit.*, No.20, pp.50-55.
135. T. Vedantam (ed), *Op.Cit.*, p.159.
136. P. Sreenivasachar (ed), *The Archaeological Bulletin No.II*, Pl.XXXVII B.
137. Alexr Rea, *Chalukyan Architecture*, pp.11, 12. Pl.XVII.
138. S. Gopalakrishna Murthy, *Op.Cit.*, p.41.
139. *IAPKD*. No.34, pp.101-103.
140. *Ibid.* No.29, p.80.
141. *IAPWD*. No.48, p.131.
142. *ARE*. 1967, p.7.
143. *Ibid.* No.385, pp.124-127.
144. *EHD*. pp.644, 645.
145. *Ibid.* p.742.
146. B. Rajendra Prasad, *Op. Cit.*, p.44.
147. *IAPKD*. No.35, p.103.
148. V.V. Krishna Sastry, *Op.Cit.*, pp.120-127.
149. *IAPKD*. No.43, p. 114.
150. S. Gopalakrishna Murthy, *Op.Cit.*, pp.8, 9.
151. *Ibid.*, p.9.
152. *IAPKD* No.38, pp.106-111.
153. *EHD*. p.759.
154. *Ibid.*, Pl.XL B.
155. *Ibid.*, p.760.
156. S. Gopalakrishna Murthy, *Op.Cit.*, p.23.
157. M. Somasekhara Sarma (ed), *Corpus of Telangana Inscriptions*, Part IV, No.38, p.84.
158. *JAHRS*. Vol.XXXVI, Part I, pp.63, 64.
159. *IAPKD*. No.75, p.139.
160. *IAPWD*. No.36, p.94.
161. *JAHRS*. Vol.XXXIV, Parts (1-4), p.11.
162. S Gopalakrishna Murthy, *Op. Cit.*, p.30.
163. *IAPKD*. No.48, pp.119, 120.
164. *Ibid.* No.51, pp. 1123, 124.
165. M. Rama Rao, *Early Chalukyan Temples of Andhradesa*, p.7.
166. B. Rajendra Prasad, *Art of South India*, p.171.
167. *IAPKD*. No. 62, p.131.
168. V.V.Krishna Sastry, *Op. Cit.*, p.126.
169. *Ibid.*

170. D. Raj Reddy and P. Suryanarayana Reddy, *Uninscribed Coins of Andhra*, Nos. 65, 67-70, pp.59-62.
171. V.V. Krishna Sastry, *Op. Cit.*, p.126.
172. *Ibid.*
173. *ARDAM*. 1977-1978, p.2.
174. *Ibid.*
175. *IAPKD*. No.46, pp.117, 118.
176. *Ibid.* No.34, pp.101, 102.
177. *Ibid.* No.67, p.134.
178. *Ibid.* No.55, p.127.
179. *Karimnagara Mandala Charitra* (Telugu), p.34.
180. *Census of India, Karimnagar District* 1961, P.IX.
181. *APGKD*. 1974, p.2.

FOUR

Architecture

The origin of the structural Hindu temple is shrouded in mistery. The erection of sanctuaries for the images of gods dates back perhaps to the 2nd century B.C. Several deva-grihas (houses of gods) of pre-Christian centuries have been excavated in extremely fragmentary state. The earliest available examples are mostly of brick. The foundations of Vishnu temple have been unearthed at Besnagar in Bhopal and this shrine is assigned to the 2nd century B.C.[1] These sanctuaries, presumably built of perishable materials, afforded little scope for the application of the principles of architecture as an art.

The Gupta period ushered in the practice of building with lasting materials especially in dressed stone and brick. It marks the beginning of the temple architecture. The well-known group of temples in north India such as the brick temple at Bhitargaon in Uttar Pradesh, the Siva shrine at Bhumara, Parvati temple at Nachana Kuthara, Vishnu and Varaha temples at Eran and the temples at Tigawa all in Madhya Pradesh are assigned to fifth century A.D., while the Dasavatara temple at Deogarh in Jhansi district is assigned to the early sixth century A.D.[2]. The earliest known free standing stone structure to have survived in tact is temple No. 17 at Sanchi dated to about 415 A.D.[3] The two dilapidated temples at Ter in Sholapur district and Kapotesvara temple at Chejerla in Guntur district also belong to the fifth century A.D.[4]

After the decline of the Buddhist art in the Deccan, a cultural renaissance was started by the Chalukyas of Badami, who built several beautiful shrines for Hindu pantheon at Aihole, Pattadakal and Badami par-excellence in artistic merit and aesthetic qualities. The influence of this early Chalukyan art and architectural tradition travelled from its epi-centre to the far distant areas in Andhra Pradesh. The Nava Brahma temples at Alampur and the temples at Mahanandi and Satyavolu stand as a living testimony to the genius of great builders who followed the course of this great art tradition which also excercised great influence on the temple architecture during the later times in Karimnagar district.

To trace the history of architecture in Karimnagar district, there are no concrete evidences of the existence of temples of Brahmanical origin pertaining to the early historical period, although there is an evidence of the existence of a Buddhist stupa at Dhulikatta datable to 2nd century B.C.[5] There is a single evidence noticed in the recent excavations at Peddabankur, which yielded a single brick cell that appeared like a temple without giving any knowledge as to what deity it was dedicated to. The so-called brick temple measured 5.30 x 4.90 metres.[6] Structural monuments of the early centuries of Christian era built of perishable materials have not survived. There is a gap of several centuries to study the temple architecture of Karimnagar district except the surviving cave temples at Adavi Somanapalli datable to 7th or 8th century A.D.

The temple building activity in Karimnagar district gained momentum with the advent of the Chalukyas of Vemulavada, who built their shrines with lasting materials especially in dressed stone. A rich variety of temples came to be constructed in Karimnagar region through the patronage of the Chalukyas of Vemulavada, Chalukyas of Kalyani, Polavasa Chiefs and Kakatiyas from the beginning of the tenth century A.D. to the beginning of the fourteenth century A.D. The majority of these temples are dedicated to Siva, but some belong to Vaishnavite group, while the number of fanes built by Jains is not inconsiderable.

The Kakatiya temples bespeak of high degree of excellence in the technique and art of building. Their temples are characterized by breadth of vision and loftiness of spirit on the one hand and by superior craftsmanship on the other.

1. Site

The site is the most important factor to be considered in temple-building. Selection of the site and examination of the soil are elaborately treated in the vastu sastras, since they were regarded as important preliminaries to actual construction of the temples. Hindu temples are constructed on sites which satisfy the canons of beauty, religious sanctity, convenience and architectural stability. *Brihat Samhita* says that the gods always play where the groves are near rivers, mountains and springs and in towns with pleasure gardens.[7] *Tantra-samuchchaya* reveals that the site, for the purpose of installing the deity, should be chosen in a sacred place, on the bank of a river, the shore of the sea, the place where the rivers meet, the top and slope of mountains, in a forest, grove or garden, in a village, capital or city or in any other lovely place.[8]

The temples in Karimnagar district seem to have been constructed on such sites which are preferred for temple building by vastu sastras. The temples of Valgonda, Dharmapuri, Thimmapur, Kotilingala, Kasipeta and Manthani are situated on the banks of the river Godavari and the temple of Kalesvaram is situated at the confluence of the rivers Pranahita and Godavari. The cave temples of Adavi Somanapalli and the temples of Gambhirraopet and Chandravelli face the river Maner, while the temple of Neerakulla stands on a big rock in the midst of the same river. Vemulavada with its temples stands on the banks of Mulavagu, a rivulet which joins the Maner. The other temples which stand beside the rivulets are found at Koratla, Chilvakoduru, Chittapur, Kodmial and Thangallapalli.

One of the important considerations in the selection of the site was the availability of water. It appears that the construction work of the tank and the temple went on simultaneously in some villages. The two epigraphs[9] at Choppadandi dated A.D. 992 and A.D. 1008 reveal that the tank and the temple were constructed almost in one and the same period. In certain cases the tank-bund itself was chosen as the site for the construction of the temple. The temple of Raja Rajesvara at Vemulavada built on the tank-bund in A.D. 1083[10] is still in tact exhibiting its architectural stability. But the foundations of the trikuta temple and Amaresvara temple built on the tank-bund at Nandi Mydaram are shaken and failed to withstand the pressure of tank water for centuries together. Now they are in a dilapidated condition. The temple of Polas built on the tank-bund is in utter ruins. The existence of a temple near the tank was felt convenient as the water could be useful for both the deity and the devotees. The temples, located in the close vicinity of the tanks, are found at Choppadandi, Jammikunta, Vemulavada, Sanigaram, Potlapalli, Polas, Raikal, Yelgedu and Vilasagar.

The temples located on the hills are found at Ramagiri, Anantagiri, Sundaragiri, Kothagattu and Kindagattu. The site for the Narasimha temple was chosen generally on the top of a mountain. The conception underlying the name Girija-Narasimha is that the lion comes out of a mountain cave.[11] As the abode of Lion is a mountain cave, it appears that the Narasimha temples were constructed often on the top of a mountain or hill as noticed at Ahobilam, Simhachalam, Yadagiri and other places. The Narasimha temples located on the hills in Karimnagar district are found at Bejjenki, Elgandal, nampalli, Nandagiri, Beerpur, Dumpeta and Vellulla.

The temples were also built in the centre of the capital cities like Vemulavada, Polas, Mantrakuta and Nagunuru. The inscription[12] of Gangadhara, a minister, dated A.D. 1171 records that he built a Vishnu temple in his capital Nagunuru. It is difficult to ascertain today the exact direction in the village or town, where the temples under study are constructed, since the set-up of these places have undergone many changes during the centuries of progress and decay. There are certain temples located at present far from the villages and surrounded by fields. Such temples are found at Godisala, Mutharam, Katkuru, Koheda, Chelpur, Gudimettapalle, Thakkalapalli and Aravelli.

2. **Ground Plan**

The direction which a temple is to face was not left to the fancy of the architect, and the rules governing this point were elaborately dealt with in all treatises on architecture, as this aspect was considered to be of supreme importance. Generally temples face the east and this direction seems to have been preferred most as the rays of the rising sun illuminate the image of worship. The eastern facet of structures both in plan and elevation, gets a full and direct exposure to the solar radiation. Most temples in Karimnagar district face the east. But there are also shrines facing north, south and west.

Temples facing the East:

1. The temples of Vamulavada
2. The temples of Dharmapuri
3. The temple of Choppadandi
4. Siva temple at old Jammikunta
5. Bhimesvara temple at Sanigaram
6. Pulastyesvara temple at Polas
7. The main temple at Kalesvaram
8. The temple at Chandravelli
9. The temples of Godisala
10. The temples of Pothgal
11. The Trikuta at Mutharam
12. The Trikuta at Vilasagar

Temples facing the North:

1. The Triple-shrine at Nandi Mydaram
2. The Trikuta at Valgonda
3. The Trikuta at Chilvakoduru
4. The Main Trikuta at Nagunuru
5. The Trikuta at Jangoan
6. The Trikuta at Katkuru

Temples facing the South:

1. The Triple-shrine at Raikal
2. Narasimha Temple at Bejjenki
3. The Trikuta at Kothapalli
4. Gautamesvara temple at Manthani

Temples facing the West:

1. The cave temples of Adavi Somanapalli
2. Mahadeva temple at Koratla

The principal units of the ground-plan of the Chalukya and the Kakatiya temples in Karimnagar district are (1) Garbhagriha (2) Antarala (3) Mukhamandapa or hall (4) Ardhamandapa or porch. The growth and variety in ground-plan of these temples depend upon the alignment of these units and the number of deities for whom shrines are provided in the temple. The alignment and arrangement of these units slso decide the shape of the temple from the exterior.

1. *Garbhagriha:*

Garbhagriha literally means the womb of the house. This is the inner-most chamber or cell or sanctuary of the temple containing the image or symbol of the main divinity. It is the presence of the sanctum sanctorum that makes permissible the use of the designation 'Temple'.

2. *Antarala:*

Antarala literally means the intermediate space and is used to refer to the chamber before the garbhagriha which usually connects it with Mukhamandapa.

3. *Mukhamandapa:*

Mukhamandapa is used to refer to the hall before the antarala. The middle hall of a temple is also used to refer to the Navaranga.

4. *Ardhamandapa or Porch:*

Porch is a covered entrance way.

The earliest temples found at Vemulavada are single shrines built by the Chalukyas of Vemulavada, who were the subordinates of the Rashtrakutas. Their ground-plan consists of garbhagriha, antarala and mukhamandapa. But the antarala in these early temples has not yet acquired the definite shape of a closed chamber with a doorway. The space intended for it connecting the garbhagriha and the pillared hall is open in the shape of an ardhamandapa without a doorway. In the garbhagrihas of the Bhimesvara and Kedaresvara temples, four pillars are arranged around the pedestal with linga, making a sort of passage and gallery around it. The is an early Chalukyan feature found in some of the temples at Alampur and Mahanandi.[13]

In the temples of the Chalukyas of Kalyani and the Kakatiyas in Karimnagar district, the ground plan consists of garbhagriha, antarala, mukhamandapa or pillared hall and porch. The temples can be classified on the basis of the number of shrines they possess into two forms. (1) Single shrine temples (2) Trikutas or triple shrine temples.

The single shrine temple with porches on the three sides of the hall and the trikutas with a porch at the entrance are resolved into cruciform plan.

Important single shrine temples of Kalyani Chalukyas and Kakatiyas:

1. Siva temple at Choppadandi
2. Bhimesvara temple at Sanigaram
3. Raja Rajesvara temple at Vemulavada
4. Temple at Chandravelli with three porches
5. Temple at Gudimettapalle

Trikuta temples of Kalyani Chalukyas and Kakatiyas:

1. The Trikuta at Raikal
2. The Trikuta at Valgonda
3. The Main temple at Nagunuru
4. The Trikuta at Kothapalli
5. The Trikuta at Jangoan
6. Gautamesvara temple at Manthani
7. Siva temple at Katkuru
8. Siva temple at Godisala
9. The Trikuta at Mutharam
10. The Trikuta at Vilasagar

Measurements of Some Temples:

1. *Siva temple at Choppadandi:-* Hall 20' each way; Garbhagriha 7'-6" square and the porch 10'-6" x 8'-3".

2. *The Trikuta at Raikal:-* Hall 24' square; square garbhagrihas 8'-4" each way; Ardha mandapas 8'-4" x 8'; the porch 14' x 7'.

3. *Siva temple at Mallannapet:-* Hall 31' each way; Garbhagriha 14' square; Antarala 9'-6" x 11'-6".

4. *The Trikuta at Thotapalli:-* Garbhagrihas each 8' square and Ardhamandapas 8' each way.

5. *The Main Trikuta at Nagunuru:-* Hall 24'-4" each way; Garbhagrihas each 9'-6" square and antaralas 9'-9" x 9'-4".

6. *The Trikuta at Godisala:-* Hall 27'-6" each way; Garbhagrihas each 11'-2" square; antaralas 8'-6" x 9'-3"; porch 12' x 9'.

7. *The Trikuta at katkuru:-* Hall 19'-4" each way; Garbhagrihas each 6'-6" square; antaralas 6'-6" x 5'.

8. *The Trikuta at Vilasagar:-* Hall 24' square; Garbhagrihas 8'-8" x 8'; antaralas 8'-8" x 8'.

3. **Adhisthana and Upapitha**

When one stares at the temples under study, he notices either one or two sections occuring beneath the pabhaga or the lower most part of the wall. Both the sections have mouldings and while one member is optional, the other is essential. The optional member, when it appears, is below the essential member. The essential member is the Adhisthana (socle) and the optional member is the upapitha (Pedestal).[14]

The term 'Adhisthana' is derived from 'Adhi' (upon) and 'Stha' (to stand).[15] Etymologically 'Adhisthana' denotes an object on which something stands. Base, basement and socle are the English terms used by the modern writers to denote this part. Dubreuil[16] and Percy Brown[17] translate it as 'base'. Srinivasan[18] and Mallaya[19] have used the word 'basement', Kramrisch[20] translates 'Adhisthana' as 'socle'.

The term 'upapitha' is derived from 'Upa' (under) and 'pitha' (seat). The Vastu texts and the moder writers use 'upapitha' to denote the member constructed beneath the Adhisthana. Dubreuil and Kramrisch use the term in the same sense. A temple may be built with or without an upapitha below the Adhisthana. Ancient texts and the extant temple monuments under study point to its optional character.

The upapitha is a distinguishing characteristic of the Kakatiya temples, while it is lacking in the temples of the Chalukyas of Badami and Kalyani. The Kakatiya temples usually stand on a high and broad platform or upapitha. In most of the temples of Rajputana, Gujarat or South india, where upapitha occurs in a temple plan, it does not take the form of a broad platform.[21] It is only again in the case of Hoyasala temples, the upapitha is a broad platform on which the temple stands in the middle. The uniqueness of the Kakatiya temples lies in the presence of the upapitha with its varied mouldings.

The following are the important Kakatiya temples in karimnagar district, which have an upapitha.

1. The Main Trikuta at Nagunuru
2. The ruined Trikuta beside the P.W.D. road at Nagunuru
3. The Trikuta at Kothapalli
4. Gautamesvara temple at Manthani
5. The temple at Chandravelli
6. The Trikuta at Mutharam

According to the vastu sastras, the upapitha serves a three-fold function.[22] (1) It contributes to the stability or security of the temple (2) It gives unnati or height to the building (3) It enhances sobha or beauty to the monument. In the Kakatiyan temples the upapitha, which runs round the temple, is considerably wide and serves the purpose of Pradakshinapatha. Generally both the upapitha and Adhisthana are beautified with the similar mouldings like patta or pattika, Gala or griva, tripatta, Padma and Kumuda.

The Adhisthana and upapitha enhance the beauty of the temple through their mouldings. They are the most important type of non-representational decoration and the chief distinction and the crowning beauty of many important Kakatiya temples consist in their mouldings and their perfection of form and placing. Their myriad delicacies of form and the subtle play of light on their changing surfaces is the secret of the striking beauty of the exterior of the

Nagunuru, Kothapalli and Mutharam temples.

4. Stambha

Stambha or Pillar is one of the most important architectural members in the Hindu temple. It was put to several uses and different names were given to it depending upon the purpose it served. Several types of Hindu free-standing pillars are seen in Karimnagar district as in other parts of the country. Among these are the Garuda Stambhas, the earliest example of which found in India, is the Besnagar column.[23] Garuda Stambhas are erected near Vishnu temple at Nagunuru in Karimnagar district. A similar Garuda stambha is also found before the Viranarayana temple at Kolanupaka in Nalgonda district. A stone inscription of the reign of Trailokyamalla (Somesvara-I) at Bodhan in Nizamabad district makes a reference to Garuda Stambha.[24]

The two pillars of Garuda at Nagunuru are similar. They are situated in the fields before the ruined temple north-east of the main trikuta temple. From base to the top they consist of a four-sided part, an octagonal part, a circular section with an octagonal part, circular section with an octagonal belt in the middle, again an octagonal part, a sixteen sided part, a circular part, the capital, a miniature mandapa with Garuda figure in it. The Stambhas are about 40 feet in height. The Garuda Stambhas found at other places are short ranging from 20' to 25' in height containing the miniature mandapas at the top. Such pillars are found before the Vaishnava temples at Polas, Gangadhara, Valgonda, Pothgal and Ramagundam.

Similar to the Garuda Stambhas there are also Nandi Stambhas containing a miniature mandapa with Nandi figure in it. These pillars are normally 25' high and they are found before the Saiva temples at Chilvakoduru, Pothgal and Valgonda.

Next come the Torana-pillars. The makara torana at Ramagundam consists of two upright posts with a profusely sculptured lintel above. These torana-pillars contain several sakhas decorated with floral and creeper designs. The Saivite dvarapalas flanked by female chowry-bearers are found at the base of each pillar. This torana is similar to those found at Kollipaka and Nandikandi. It is different from the Warangal gate-way which has double pillars on either side.

The pillars which are part of the temple structures in Karimnagar district may be analysed into the following sections.

1. The Asvapadam or base or foot of the pillar.
2. The shaft is the portion of a pillar, between the Asvapadam and the capital.
3. The capital or upper portion of a pillar including phalaka or abacus which is generally a square table forming the crowning member of a capital and corbel or brackets.

The pillars of the cave temples at Adavi Somanapalli are very simple and crude in form consisting of a square section at the foot with a square shaft of 3' height, followed by an octagonal part. The capital is again a square part containing a bracket with two arms stretching along the lintel.

The four central pillars of the Bhimesvara temple at Vemulavada are unusually tall because the slopy pent roof is adopted. These pillars are fashioned in chitrakhanda form of decoration. The base of the pillars contains niches on four sides.

The pillars in the old dilapidated temple at Thotapalli near Husunabad and the pillars at Yelgedu are very crude in form. The pillars in the temple at Mallannapet are unusually massive and instead of a square abacus and four-armed bracket, they contain a huge circular bracket which is a novel member noticed nowhere in the temples of this region. The pillars at Thotapalli near Karimnagar are square throughout in form with several square divisions from base to the abacus. The four central pillars of the halls at Bejjenki and Godisala are most elegant and superb with smooth finishing and exquisite carvings. The faces of the square portions of the shafts at Bejjenki are utilised for carving several deities and beautiful female figures in bold relief.

The following are the general characteristics of the pillars found in the temples of the Kalyani Chalukyas and Kakatiyas in Karimnagar district.

Chalukyan and Kakatiyan periods contain porches. In this scheme only the shrine is enclosed by walls, whereas the hall and porches are open and have a short parapet wall.

The wall treatment of some of the Chalukyan temples differs from that of the other temples in the area under study. The walls of the Nagaresvara, Kedaresvara and Raja Rajesvara temples at Vemulavada and the Siva temple at Choppadandi rise with pilasters consisting of slender shafts dividing the outer surface of the walls into well proportioned areas and giving to the whole a functional framework of great architectural value. On the outer surface of the walls of Kedaresvara temple, the figures of Ganapati, Brahma, Siva, Vishnu and Saraswati are carved beautifully in between the pilasters. In the Bhimesvara temple at Vemulavada the walls of the antarala portion contain Vatayanas admitting plenty of air and light into the temple. The northern Vatayana houses the beautiful figure of Mahishasuramardini. The architectural grandeur and artistic qualities imbibing the peculiarities of the typical architecture of the Chalukyas, the old temples at Vemulavada are inspiring and instructive examples of ninth and tenth centuries A.D.

The central section of the shrine walls is left unornamented being composed of large blocks of stone in some of the Kalyani Chalukyan and Kakatiya temples of this area, as evidenced by the temples at Raikal, Valgonda, Polas, Mallannapet, Godisala and Katkuru. In some cases the fillets of various sizes run round the walls of garbhagriha as seen at Nagunuru temple, which stands just beside the hill and to the south of the main trikuta temple. This type of treatment is slightly different at Vilasagar, where a fillet prominently decorated with four petalled flowers runs round from the centre of the walls of each garbhagriha of the trikuta temple. The shrine walls of the Narasimha temple at Bejjenki built with large blocks of stone are plain but they contain on their outer surface a few sculptures of amorous couples, cavaliers and elephant riders.

The walls of the temples at Nagunuru, Kothapalli, Chandravelli and Mutharam are broken up by ratha off-sets, the central one in each wall generally being larger than the rest. The treatment of walls into broad and narrow pilasters alternate with recesses is a common feature found in the Kakatiya temples. The broad pilasters have folds on either side. The shallow recesses are filled with a narrow pilaster surmounted by a turret and sometimes as at Nagunuru it is arched over by a cusped scroll of the most beautiful character rising from two slender pilasters at the flanks. In some cases as noticed in the Gautamesvara temple at Manthani, the figures of various deities are carved at the bottom of the broad pilasters. In the case of Chandravelli temple, the offsets of the walls project forth till they reach a projecting niche at the centre on the three sides of the walls of garbhagriha. These niches are similar to those found on the walls of the garbhagrihas of the Thousand pillar temple at Hanumakonda.

This type of treatment of the walls is one of the chief characteristics of the Kalyani Chalukyan art of the neighbouring regions and clearly the Chalukyan art must have been the source from which the Kakatiya architects drew.[25] The Mahadeva temple at Ittagi,[26] the temples at Lakkundi and several other temples in the Karnataka region, when studied from this angle, make the point clear.

The walls carry the weight of the beams, roof and superstructure, wherever present and transmit it to the adhisthana and upapitha. The walls of the temples are generally built of large slabs of masonry and they have a double shell, the core being hollow in the middle or sometimes filled by mud mixed with gravel or rubbles. This method of building is exposed to view, where the outer shell of the wall has been destroyed by climatic or other causes, such examples being found in Nagunuru, Godisala and Gudimettapalle. As the foundations of the walls have not been laid deeply enough, sinkage has occured freely, causing the ruin of many temples. Even those which have survived have broken lintels, cracked walls and out-of-plumb columns, this unfortunate state of affairs being entirely due to the insecure nature of the foundations.[27]

The top part of the wall is called Kapota or cornice. The Kapota of the temples at Mutharam, Kothapalli and Chandravelli consists of several mouldings as in the case of upapitha and adhisthana. But in the Kalyani Chalukyan as well as some of the Kakatiya temples a well-formed Kapota decorated with semi-circular stones is common.

The prakara walls were also built of massive stone blocks with a double shell as is evident from the survivals at Choppadandi, Chilvakoduru and Katkuru. The parapet wall is short and the most common decoration is dividing it into numerous compartments by means of pilasters and inserting a four petalled flower in each of them.

6. Doorways

The door-frames, architraves and friezes on them are so richly carved that they all illustrate the immense devotion and masterly skill of the architects in building and adorning the abodes of their gods. Invariably the garbhagriha is entered through a doorway. Antarala, when present, also generally possesses one, though instances of antarala without a doorway are to be seen in the temples at Vemulavada, Nandi Mydaram, Raikal, Valgonda and Thotapalli. The Vemulavada Chalukyan hall-temple of Bhimesvara is entered through a doorway, while the halls in the Kalyani Chalukyan and Kakatiya temples do not have one as they are entered through the porches. However, the Kalyani Chalukyan hall-temple at Choppadandi, the Raja Rajesvara temple at Vemulavada and the Narasimha temple at Bejjenki with doorways on three sides of their halls are exceptions. The following are the chief characteristics of the various parts of the door-frame.

Bhuvangama:- Bhuvangama is the foot-rest or threshold i.e. the lower horizontal part of the door-frame. This is plain in the Vemulavada Chalukyan temples at Vemulavada. But in the Kalyani Chalukyan and the Kakatiya temples, it is mostly moulded being divided horizontally into projecting bands and recesses and vertically into projecting and receding sections as noticed in the temples at Raikal, Nagunuru, Godisala and other places. The moulded and sculptured character of the Bhuvangama of the doorways is a feature which is common to the Chalukyan doorways of neighbouring regions.

Sakhas (Door-jambs):- The section of the door-frame on either side of the opening is horizontally divided into the lower and upper sections of which the former is of less height than the latter. Dvaradevatas, dvarapalakas, chowry-bearers or purnaghatas and other allied figures are sculptured on the lower section. In many of the Kalyani Chalukyan and Kakatiya temples these figures are carved with ornamented canopies above. Generally the carvings on the lower section correspond to the sakhas or door-jambs occuring in the upper section. Beautiful figures of dvarapalas flanked by female chowry-bearers carved at the bottom of the door-jambs are found in the Raja Rajesvara temple at Vemulavada, Venugopalaswamy temple at Polas, Amaresvara temple at Nandi Mydaram and in the trikuta temples at Nagunuru, Kothapalli, Katkuru and Godisala.

The upper section of the sides of the door-frame always consists of a succession of mouldings of jambs or sakhas. The doorways of the Kalyani Chalukyan and Kakatiya temples usually contain trisakhas with a pilaster in the middle. Generally speaking the sakhas are more in number in the Kalyani Chalukyan temples than those in the Vemulavada Chalukyan temples. Sometimes their number is still more in the Kakatiya temples than those of the Kalyani Chalukyan Period. For example the doorway that leads into the mandapa of the main trikuta temple at Nagunuru contains five or six sakhas with a pilaster between them. In most of the Kakatiya temples the common feature of the antarala doorways is to adorn them with a beautifully perforated screen window on either side. The perforated stone windows, besides providing ornamentation to the doorways, serve the function of letting into the dark interior of the shrine sufficient light and air. It is interesting to notice Jain figures in Padmasana posture carved on the perforated plate adorned on either side of the antarala doorway of eastern shrine in the Gautamesvara temple at Manthani. Another noteworthy feature in this temple is to find niches fixed up on either side of the antarala doorways.

Generally the sakhas of the doorways are adorned with creeper and floral designs, gaja and simha motifs or scroll designs with figures in them.

Patanga or Urdhvapattika (Lintel):- Patanga is the lintel which contains a tablet carved at the centre with a little projection known as Lalatabimba or mangalaphalaka. The usual lalatabimba devatas are Gajalakshmi and Vinayaka in the Kalyani Chalukyan and Kakatiya temples of Karimnagar district. Very few doorways are without them. Above the mangalaphalaka some of the sakha patterns are carried over.

Another feature present in most of the Kalyani Chalukyan and Kakatiya doorways is the stone shade or the roof projecting over the lintel moulded and decorated with hanging lotus buds and projecting semi-circular stones. The purpose of this member, seems to be, to give definition to the doorway as a whole separating it from the part coming above and to add to the beauty of the structure. Besides, it also lends greater support to a deeply sculptured beam above.

Much variety in the doorways is achieved by the pattern of carvings over the patanga of the doorway. Generally turrets or representations of miniature pavilions are carved on the architraves of the doorways. The number of turrets is three and sometimes five. The figures of deities, dancers and drummers are also carved on the architraves of the doorways at Nagunuru and Kothapalli. The figures of Nataraja dancing over the prostrate body of Apasmarapurusa flanked by the deities Vishnu and Vinayaka on one side and Brahma and Kumara on the other are beautifully carved on the architraves of the doorways at Godisala and Chandravelli.

The doorway leading into the hall of the Bhimesvara temple at Vemulavada is crowned with a makara torana. The Vemulavada Chalukyan doorways in the temples of Bhimesvara and Nagaresvara are simple and less elaborately ornamented when compared to the doorways found in the temples at Raikal, Polas, Nandi Mydaram and Mallannapet of the Kalyani Chalukyan period. The highly ornate doorways with exquisite fret work and beautiful side screen windows are found in the Kakatiya temples at Nagunuru, Kothapalli, Katkuru, Godisala, Manthani and Chandravelli. They exhibit superb workmanship and great craftsmanship of the Kakatiya period. The simplest and unadorned doorways are those used for the prakara entrances at Katkuru, Kasipeta, and Gambhirraopet.

The doorways are the chief ornamental members in the temples. The Kalyani Chalukyan doorways bear resemblance and exhibit the features found in the adjacent areas of Telingana and northern Karnataka in the contemporary period. The Kakatiya door-frames differ from the earlier ones only in ornamentation and not in architectural composition.

7. Ceiling and Roofing

The method of ceiling and roofing in the Vemulavada Chalukyan temples differs from that of the Kalyani Chalukyan and Kakatiya temples. The hall of the Bhimesvara temple at Vemulavada consists of four central pillars which are unusually tall and the other pillars are short because slopy pent roof is adopted, which is a peculiar feature not found in any other temple of the Karimnagar district. The halls of some of the temples are flat-roofed. The early tradition of laying flat-roof, as found in the temple No. 17 of the Gupta period at Sanchi[28] is continued in the medieval times also. Such roofing is found in the halls of the Nagaresvara and Kedaresvara temples at Vemulavada, Bhimesvara temple at Sanigaram and in the temples at Mallannapet and Chilvakoduru. The halls of the temples at Bejjenki, Katkuru, Thimmapur and Gangadhara are also flat-roofed but the ceiling of their central compartments between the four central pillars is laid in Kadalikakarana process.

In most of the Kalyani Chálukyan and Kakatiya temples, the ceiling of the mandapa is divided into nine compartments by beams resting on the capitals of pillars supporting the roof. These compartments are square in plan. The closing of these compartments follows the principle which the vastu texts call as 'Kadalikakarana' process[29]. This process involves the insertion of triangular slabs at the angles of the square compartments. Five stones are used instead of one. Usually instead of two tiers and five stones, three tiers and nine stones are used. In case of five tiers, seventeen stones are used. This device has a pleasing effect because it removes the flatness of the ceiling which otherwise would have been apparent. In the Kalyani Chalukyan and Kakatiya temples of Raikal, Valgonda, Nandi Mydaram, Nagunuru, Kothapalli and Godisala, the ceiling of the hall in all its nine compartments is laid in Kadalikakarana process. The method of laying the ceiling in Kadalikakarana process was also prevalent in the north Indian temples of the contemporary period. This process is found in the Siva temple of tenth century A.D. at Panderthan which is 5 kms. to the south-east of Srinagar in Jammu and Kashmir State.[30]

In the second variety the ceiling of the central apartment of the hall is dome-shaped. It is constructed of ring upon ring of stones, each ascending ring being smaller than the lower and closing in towards the top, which is covered by a single circular slab with a graceful pendant hanging from the apex. This sort of ceiling is found in the central apartment of the Gautamesvara temple at Manthani and it is similar to those found in the temples at Ittagi,[31] and Magala[32] both in Karnataka state. But the ceiling of the antarala in the northern shrine of the same temple at Manthani is different. Instead of circular rings it contains five squares, each ascending square being smaller than the lower and finally covered by a square slab.

In the third variety, at first triangular stones and then circular rings are used. Examples of these are found in the trikuta temples at Nagunuru Godisala and single shrine temples at Bejjenki and Karimnagar. The ceiling of the antarala in Chandravelli temple is different as it is an octagonal dome consisting of four octagons, each ascending octagon being smaller than the lower and finally covered by a full blown lotus. A number of dripstones add beauty to the octagonal dome.

Generally the ceiling of the central compartment supported by four central pillars is beautifully sculptured. The beams and their undersides, the triangular stones and the concentric circles are made use of for the most pleasing and skilful ornamentation. When the circular rings are used, the inside of the vault is carved into ascending concentric circles, each circle being cusped with a graceful pendant hanging from the apex. The inner sides of the beams are divided into several compartments by means of narrow pilasters. These compartments are filled with the beautiful figures of dancers, drummers, trumpet-bearers and cymbal-beaters. The central ceiling in the mandapa of the main trikuta temple at Nagunuru is the best example.

The roof projecting over the walls of garbhagriha and the porches is a feature of the Kakatiya temples. This feature helps to spread and balance the weight of the roof and the superstructure when it is present. Secondly it protects the walls and exterior sculptures of temples from rain and climatic factors affecting them intensely. In some of the medieval temples, the cornice takes the shape of a wide projecting eave, often curved with a double section, forming not only an artistic but a most useful addition to the temple, serviceable as a protection against the strong light and also as a method of warding off the heavy monsoon rains.[33] Such projecting wide eave cornice all along the roof is arranged in the trikuta temple at Godisala. The prominent eave with exaggerated width has become a characteristic of the Kalyani Chalukyan and Kakatiya temples.

8. The Superstructure

The general English term 'Superstructure' is used here to denote the entire part of the temple rising over the garbhagriha whether it is curvilinear or stepped pyramidal. The other English terms tower and spire are also applied to this part of the temple by the modern writers on temple architecture. The Sanskrit term 'sikhara' is used in the present work for the entire superstructure.

The word sikhara means 'mountain peak'. The sacred snowy peak of the Himalayas is believed to be the abode of Siva. Generally the sikharas of the temples are coated with lime-water to make them glitter white in order to stress their symbolic relationship to the sacred snowcapped peaks of the Himalayas.[34] The attention of a devotee is first drawn to the shinning Kalasas of a temple and from a distance he recognises a temple by its superstructure.

The superstructures of the temples in karimnagar district are mainly of two types curvilinear and stepped pyramidal.

The very name 'curvilinear superstructure' indicates that it is the curve which is the most significant character of it. The curvilinear sikharas are found on the trikuta temples at Raikal, Valgonda and on the single shrine temple of Ramalingesvara at Dharmapuri. Each sikhara has a sukanasa or an ante-fix in front rising over the antarala, which is an early Chalukyan feature found and followed in the Nava Brahma temples at Alampur. The superstructures on the Pulastyesvara temple at Polas and the triple-shrine temple at Chilvakoduru are also curvilinear in form but they do not contain an ante-fix before them.

The curvilinear superstructures of all the above temples in Karimnagar district are more akin to the Chalukyan tradition than Orissan. The curve of these sikharas starts from the beginning of the superstructure like those of the Chalukyan temples at Pattadakal, Aihole and Alampur, whereas this curve begins only at the top of the sikhara in the Orissan tradition. These curvilinear sikharas are crowned by amalakas with Kalasas above them.

The other variety of superstructure is stepped pyramidal form which is acquired from the then Kadamba region, now a part of the Karnataka State.[35]

The superstructure on the Siva temple south of the main trikuta temple and standing just beside the hill consists of diminishing tiers arranged alternate with recesses to form the pyramidal shape. The tiers are decorated with semi-circular stones and the sikhara has an ante-fix in the front. The Narasimha temple at Bejjenki also contains the similar type of stepped pyramidal superstructure.

The stepped pyramidal superstructures of the temples at Chop-padandi and Ramagundam contain a wide tapering band in the centre on all four sides. The temple of Raja Rajesvara at Vemulavada also contained a sikhara in stepped pyramidal form before the recent renovation of the shrine.

The other variety of the stepped pyramidal form is that it consists of diminishing tiers. No recesses enter between them. The steps are vertical edged. Simple and unornamented stepped pyramidal sikharas are found on the Nagaresvara temple at Vemulavada, old Narasimha temple at Dharmapuri, Amaresvara temple at Nandi Mydaram, Western shrine of Gautamesvara temple at Manthani, Western shrine of the ruined trikuta temple at Thimmapur and also on the temples at Vilasagar, Yelgedu, Kasipeta, Nancherla, Neerakulla, Kotilingala, Aravelli, Peddapalli, Sircilla, Karimnagar and most other places. These stepped pyramidal sikharas are generally crowned by a square member flattened at the top with a Kalasa above it.

The superstructures of most of the Kakatiya temples are either ruined or totally lost. The sikharas of the Kakatiya temples at Nagunuru, Kothapalli and Katkuru are ruined beyond recognition of their style and form.

REFERENCES

1. Percy Brown, *Op.Cit.*, p.40.
2. Joanna Gottfried Williams, *The Art of Gupta India*, Plates No. 107, 125, 126, 128, 149, 150, 180, 201, 202.
3. Roy C. Craven, *A Concise History of Indian Art*, p. 131.
4. Percy Brown, *Op.Cit.*, p. 41.
5. V.V. Krishna Sastry, *Op.Cit.*, p.144.
6. *Ibid.*, p.143.
7. Stella Kramrisch, *The Hindu Temple*, Vol.I, p.4.
8. N.V. Mallaya, *Studies in Sanskrit Texts on Temple Architecture*, pp.28, 29.
9. *IAPKD*. Nos. 8 & 11.
10 *Ibid*. No.18, pp.47-49.
11. Abdul Waheed Khan, *An Early Sculpture of Narasimha*, p.1.
12. *IAPKD*. No.25, pp.64-71.
13. M. Rama Rao, *Op. Cit.*, pp.17 & 38.
14. M. Radhakrishna Sarma, *Op.Cit.*, p.173.
15. Ram Raz, *Essay on the Architecture of the Hindus*, p.23.
16. G. Jouveau Dubreuil, *Dravadian Architecture*, p.10.
17. Percy Brown, *Op.Cit.*, p.205.
18. K.R. Srinivasan, "The Pallava Architecture of South India", *Ancient India*, p.129.
19. N.V. Mallaya, *Op.Cit.*, p.176.
20. Stella Kramrisch, *Op.Cit.*, Vol.I, p.146.
21. M Radhakrishna Sarma, *Op.Cit.*, pp.174, 175.
22. N.V. Mallaya, *Op.Cit.*, p.166.
23. M. Radhakrishna Sarma, *Op.Cit.*, p.177.
24. *RE*. 1966, No.305, p.67.
25. M. Radhakrishna Sarma, *Op. Cit.*, p.188.
26. P. Sreenivasachar, (ed), *Op.Cit.*, Plates XXXII to XXXVIII.
27. *EHD*. p.737.
28. Debala Mitra, *Sanchi*, p. 50, Pl.VII.
29. N.V. Mallaya, *Op.Cit.*, p. 260.
30. Debala Mitra, *Panderthan, Avantipur and Martand*, pp.24, 25, Pl.IV B.
31. P. Sreenivasachar (ed), *Op.Cit.*, Pl.XXXVII B.
32. Alexr Rea, *Op.Cit.*, pp.11,12, Pl.XVII.
33. Percy Brown, *Op.Cit.*, p.146.
34. Benjamin Rowland, *The Art and Architecture of India*, pp.167-169.
35. S. Gopalakrishna Murthy, *Jain Vestiges in Andhra*, pp.50, 51.

FIVE

Sculpture

In a message to the book[1] on Indian Sculpture our late Prime Minister Indira Gandhi has expressed the view that our sculpture has evoked great devotion through the ages and our generations have derived great pleasure from its beauty, grace of line and sensuousness. All this work was painstakingly executed not for renown or individual self expression but out of dedication and discipline and pride in one's craftsmanship. The special distinction of our sculpture lies in its ability to capture many layers of spiritual meaning in physical form.

A carved sculpture is that which is cut into shape with tools from a hard material. The process of carved sculpture is just the freeing of the Statue from the enclosing block, cutting away all the material that is not wanted. The term icon or image means a figure representing a deity which is specially meant for worship or which is some way or other associated with the rituals connected with the worship of differnt divinities. A pratima or an idol is the personification of a deity whose qualities and the characteristic form it represents. A pratima always bears the religious sanctity which is granted by installing it into the sanctum sanctorum of a temple according to specified rituals.[2] While it is true that the primary purpose of sacred images is not to give aesthetic enjoyment but to serve as focussing points for the spirit, yet they had their appeal to the people of various mental levels and interests.

There are numerous beautiful sculptures found in the various temples of Karimnagar district. Most of the temples in the district under study are dedicated to Siva. The Siva linga is the principal icon in the main sanctum of these temples. The temples are mostly small in size and do not possess subsidiary shrines as in the case of the south Indian temples. As such the number of icons is small and their variety is much restricted.

There are only a few temples which are richly ornamented with sculpture. Generally speaking, the upapitha, wherever is present, and the adhisthana of some of the temples are carved into various types of mouldings. But in the case of Bhimesvara temple at Vemulavada, a band running along the basement is divided by means of short pilasters into numerous compartments, filled with the figures of the dasavataras of Vishnu, tales from Panchatantra, and the friezes of deer, gajas and Simhas. In general, the walls of the temples are severely plain. But in the case of Kedaresvara temple at Vemulavada, the walls contain rich figure sculpture like those of Ganapati, Brahma, Siva, Vishnu and Saraswati. In the prastara portion the puranic scenes including the churning of the ocean are carved. There is also a sculpture depicting the story of the tortoise from panchatantra. A similar sculpture is found at Alampur on a pilaster on the northern wall of the Visva Brahma temple.[3]

The tall central pillars of the closed mandapa in the Bhimesvara temple at Vemulavada are fashioned in Chitrakhanda form of decoration. They are ornamented with female figures, hamsas, purnaghatas, leaves, animals, creeper and other designs. The four central pillars of the mandapa in the trikuta temple at Raikal are carved with the figures of Kurma, Matsya, Varaha, Gajalakshmi, Kamadhenu and hamsas. A novel feature of the mandapa in the Narasimhha temple at Bejjenki is its exquisitely carved four central pillars. The faces of the square portions of the pillars contain the puranic scenes, the figures of several deities and beautiful female figures in bold relief. Curiously enough the pillars of the mandapa in a Kasipeta temple are sculptured with the scenes of Gopika Vastrapaharanam, beautiful female figures of dancers, huntresses and the friezes of deer, gajas, Simhas and entwined nagas. The pillars in many other temples of Karimnagar district are plain with moulded parts.

The door frames of the Chalukya and Kakatiya temples in the area under study are usually ornamented with a variety of sculpture. The panels beneath the jambs are usually decorated with dvarapalas flanked by chowry-bearers and beautiful female figures. The architraves over the doorways are generally decorated with turrets or as in some Kakatiya temples with a panel of dancing Siva over Apasmarapurusa. The beams and the ceiling slabs of the Navaranga in many Kakatiya temples are carved with the figures of deities, dancers, drummers, floral and creeper designs. The rich collection of sculptures housed in the Karimnagar museum and found in the temples of Vemulavada, Polas and Kalesvaram should have once been decorating the various temples in the area. To these collections one has to add hundreds of sculptural pieces found scattered in the villages of the district.

1. **Ganapati**

Ganapati is worshipped as the popular guardian of house-holds, remover of obstacles, patron of merchants, authors and school boys (for he is the scribe of gods) and god of common sense, who must be invoked before every enterprise and mentioned before any appeal to the divine spirit.[4] Vighnesvara is, as the name indicates, the deity presiding over obstacles; as such he happens to be the god who either puts obstacles in the way or removes them. That he has the capacity for doing both the things is evident from the account of his origin given in the linga purana.[5]

Every village, however small has in it an image of Ganapati with or without a temple to house it. At the entrance of villages and forts, below pipal trees adjoining villages, on the right side of the entrances into Siva shrines, in the niches of Vishnu as well as Siva temples and also in separate shrines especially constructed in Siva temples, the figure of Ganapati is invariably to be seen. One such separate small shrine exclusively dedicated to Ganapati is found in the courtyard of the Ramalingesvara temple at Dharmapuri. However, it is interesting to note that in many of the Brahmanical temples Ganapati has only a subordinate status but nevertheless very important and to be worshipped at first.[6]

Seated images of Ganapati of the early and late medieval periods have been found all over India. Scholars hold that Ganapati begins to appear quite commonly in the Gupta art by about A.D. 400 at such sites as Bhumara, Deogarh etc.[7] An early Gupta relief depicting a seated Ganapati is to be found in the facade of the Chandragupta cave at Udayagiri in Madhya Pradesh.[8] This two armed god is sitting holding modakas in left hand to which his trunk is applied. His vahana mouse is conspicuous by its absence.

The earliest Ganapati concept in sculpture from south India is a gift of the Amaravati sculptor. The seated dwarfish figure of Ganapati with a single pair of arms found at Amaravati on a local lime coping stone is datable to 2nd century B.C.[9] It is this simple Ganapati at Amaravati, that still continues to be content with a single pair of arms in the carvings from Peddamudiyam and Madugula datable to 4th century A.D.[10] An early representation of Ganapati in lime stone with two arms, noticed in the Kapotesvara temple at Chejerla in Guntur district is datable to 5th century A.D.[11] A loose sculpture of Ganapati in the early form found near the linga pavilion in the Vishnu's lotus pond at Mahakut near Badami is datable to about A.D. 600.[12] The archaic form of Ganapati is seen as late as 9th century A.D. in Vengidesa, which can be evidenced by a huge Ganapati now lying in the fields at Biccavolu in East Godavari district. This image has only a single pair of arms. Lack of crown and natural look of the elephant head is striking in this image as well as in other images at Vijayawada and other places.[13]

Several loose images of Vinayaka big and small in archaic mode, continue to be found in Karimnagar district as late as 10th century A.D. These images are distinguished by a natural elephant head without a crown and endowed with single pair of arms. In a few cases the Vahana mouse is present below the seat, while it is absent in some other earlier sculptures datable to 7th-8th century A.D. Loose images of Vinayaka in their early form are noticed at the following places in Karimnagar district.

1. In the temples of Bhimesvara, Nagaresvara and Kedaresvara at Vemulavada.
2. In the mandapa of the old Siva temple at Choppadandi.
3. In a window of the compound wall of Mallannagudi at Potlapalli.

4. In the Siva temple at Mallannapet.
5. In the Amaresvara temple at Nandi Mydaram.
6. Among the loose sculptures now placed outside the Muktisvara temple at Kalesvaram.
7. In the Siva temple at Yelgedu
8. In the Hanuman temple at Thotapalli near Husunabad.
9. In the ruined Siva temple at Dhobiwada in Elkaturti village.
10. In the Hanuman temple beside Jagtial-Karimnagar P.W.D. road near Rajaram.
11. Near Primary School at Gandhinagar in Jagtial town.
12. A big image from Nagunuru village, now placed in Karimnagar museum.

Loose images of Ganapati wearing a short mukuta with single pair of arms are noticed on the tank-bund at Polas and in the old Siva temple at Sircilla. Big images of Ganapati wearing a mukuta and endowed with four hands are noticed in the temples at Dharmapuri, Mutharam, Sanigaram and Jammikunta.

The Ganapati motif adorns the Lalata bimba at the centre of the lintel above the doorway in some of the shrines. Dancing Ganapati is seen in the company of Nataraja and other deities on the architraves over the doorways in the Gautamesvara temple at Manthani, Siva temple at Chandravelli and trikuta temple at Godisala. The figure of Ganapati on one side and the figure of Siva or Virabhadra on the other generally flank the Saptamatrika slabs.

2. **Brahma**

Brahma, one of the gods of the Hindu Trinity, occupies prominent position in the early period of ancient India. He is believed to have born from the lotus that issued from the navel of Vishnu. He is referred to as the creator of universe and the preserver of the world. His importance declined as the other cult gods like Siva and Vishnu grew in prominence. As Brahma appears to have enjoyed no success as a cult god, separate temples for him were built rarely. The Vasantgadh brick temple in Rajputana is as old as the seventh century A.D.[14] The figure in this temple is three faced (the fourth face being the back plate is invisible) and two armed holding an akshamala and Kamandalu. Generally the figures of Brahma show only three faces, as the fourth face being the back-plate of the image cannot be visible. Shrines of Brahma are also noticed at Dudahi and Khajuraho in Madhya Pradesh and Unkal near Hubli in Karnataka State.[15] No temples are dedicated to Brahma for his exclusive worship in Karimnagar district. However his sculptural representations are found in Vishnu and Siva temples, where he is a subsidiary deity.

The most important sculpture of Brahma is found in the mandapa of the old Narasimha temple at Dharmapuri. This is a loose sculpture with a standing figure of 6' height. Brahma is visible with three faces containing a pointed beard for the middle face only. He holds Sruk and Vedas in his upper hands. He keeps his lower left hand in abhaya holding an akshamala while he keeps his lower right hand crossed towards left resting on gada. His Vahana Hamsa is carved to his right at the bottom. His Vahana Hamsa is carved to his right at the bottom. This sculpture resembles the standing figure of Brahma at Sopara in Thana district of Maharashtra State with the similar pointed beard for the middle face alone.[16]

Another standing figure of Brahma is a loose sculpture of 3' height found in the courtyard of the old Siva temple at Karimnagar. He is three faced with four hands. He is adorned with mukuta, graiveyakas, Yajnopavita, Katibandha and Vanamala.

The other sculptural representations of Brahma found in the various temples of this district are:

1. On the southern wall of the Kedaresvara temple at Vemulavada.
2. In the lingodbhava panel on the adhisthana part of Bhimesvara temple at Vemulavada. Three-faced Brahma is seen standing with folded hands to the right while Vishnu is seen on the left side of the linga.
3. In a panel carved on the pillar of the Narasimha temple at Bejjenki, Brahma and Vishnu are seen on either side of Siva who is seated on a pedestal.
4. The figure of Brahma is carved in relief on the wall of the Gautamesvara temple at Manthani.
5. On the architraves over the doorways of the above cited temple, dancing Brahma is seen in the company of Nataraja, Ganapati, Vishnu and devi.

6. On the architrave over the antarala doorway of the Siva temple at Chandravelli.
7. On the architraves over the doorways of the trikuta temple at Godisala.

3. **Vishnu**

In modern popular Hinduism, Vishnu is one of the gods of the Hindu trinity, and is conceived to be responsible for the universal protection as Brahma and Siva, the two another gods are held to be responsible for universal creation and destruction. The images of Vishnu are generally represented in three groups, that is, Sthanaka (standing) Asana (sitting) and Sayana (recumbent). The deities of Vishnu found in this region are in the form of Narasimha, Kesava, Ananta-sayana or Anantapadmanabha, Baḷarama, Venugopala, Goverdhana-Krishna, and Sri Rama.

The temples of the period under study dedicated to the exclusive worship of Vishnu are very few. The Narasimha temples at Dharmapuri, Bejjenki, Sundella and Venugopalaswamy temple at Polas are the chief examples for such temples. But these temples except that of Bejjenki do not contain much of deity sculpture. In face some of the important panels portraying puranic stories about Vishnu are found in the Siva temples. For example the episode of Narasimha tearing out the intestines of the demon Hiranyakasipu is carved on the outer wall of the Gautamesvara temple at Manthani. The ten incarnations of Vishnu are carved on the adhisthana part of the Bhimesvara temple at Vemulavada. One explanation for the presence of sculptures relating to Vishnu in Siva temples is the efforts towards a reapprochement between the different sects. Another explanation seems to lie in the concept of the trinity of Traipurushadeva namely Brahma, Vishnu and Mahesvara. In some cases the trinity is composed of Siva, Vishnu and Aditya (sun god), Brahma being replaced by the Sun god as evident from the three shrines of the trikuta at Raikal dedicated to Siva, Kesava and Suryadeva respectively.

It is a widely known fact that Vishnu possesses Sahsranama or thousand names. Among them twenty four are considered to be the most important and are repeated by many Brahmanas in their daily prayers. Sculptural representations corresponding to these twenty four forms of Vishnu once existed at Nagunuru. The Karimnagar inscription[17] dated A.D. 1171 records that Gangadhara installed twenty four forms of Vishnu in the Vishnu temple at Nagunuru. But neither the Vishnu temple nor the figures of Chaturvimsati-Vishnu are found today at Nagunuru except the remains of a ruined mandapa near Garuda Stambhas.

In Andhradesa, the incarnation of Vishnu in the form of Narasimha had come into vogue during the fourth century A.D. as evident from the panel found at Kondamotu in Guntur district, where theriomorphic form of Narasimha is depicted in the company of Panchaviras.[18] It is only in the later period, prominence was given to human form as seen at Badami and also Kevala and Sthauna Narasimha at Ellora during the Rashtrakuta period. Normal representation of Narasimha during the medieval period shows a human body with a lion's head. These sculptures of Narasimha are found in the Narasimha temples at Dharmapuri, Bejjenki, Sundella, Vellulla, Elgandal, Nandagiri, Nampalli, Nallagonda, Beerpur and Dumpeta.

The incarnation of Vishnu in the form of Matsya in the company of his consort Lakshmi is carved on a big boulder on a hillock at Kothagattu lying south of Karimnagar on the P.W.D. road to Huzurabad. The shrine on the hillock is known as Matsyagiri Swamy temple. It is worth noting that a big fish of 8' length in black granite, considered to be Matsyavatara is lying in the corridor of the temple at Kalesvaram.

On the northern wall of Kedaresvara temple at Vemulavada, a fine figure of Vishnu is carved standing in Samabhanga. At Nagunuru there are two figures of Vishnu of which one is Sridhara and the other is Kesava or Vasudeva as it is difficult to identify in view of the mutilated lower hands. Dasavataras are carved on the Prabhavali of latter sculpture.[19] The sculptures of Vishnu are found at Mutharam, Antakapeta, Aravelli and several other pplaces. Dasavataras are carved on the makaratorana of the Vishnu image at Antakapeta near Husunabad. The deity of Vishnu belonging to the northern shrine of the trikuta temple at Raikal can be identified as Kesava holding Padma in lower right hand, Sankha in upper right hand, chakra in upper left hand and gada in lower left hand as laid down in the silpa texts.[20]

The reclining image of Vishnu is known as Sayanamurti. Vishnu is shown asleep on the coils of the giant multi-hooded serpent. This serpent is called Adisesha or Ananta. So the god who sleeps on Ananta, has the name Anantasayana. Normally the iconographic presentation would show the stalk of a lotus issuing from Vishnu's navel and on its flower Brahma is seated. So the god is also known as Ananta Padmanabha. In this sculpture Lakshmi is found seated near the feet of the Lord. The sculpture of Ananta Padmanabha is found in a separate shrine intended for the deity within the compound of the Raja Rajesvara temple at Vemulavada. A beautiful image of Ananta-Sayana, recovered from Kotilingala is now placed in the Karimnagar museum. An image of Shesha-Sayana is carved on a big boulder on the hillock at Rajaram near Jagtial.

The distinctive emblem of Balarama is plough, consequently he is called Haladhara. The images of Krishna are noticed at Kotilingala, Antakapeta and Nancherla.

It seems that the cult of Sri Rama has come into vogue during twelfth and thirteenth centuries A.D. The temples dedicated to Sri Rama are found at Nancherla, Ramagundam, Illenthakunta and Kasipeta. The seated image of Rama along with his consort seated on his folded left leg is noticed at Nanchberla, Gudem and Kasipeta. The god keeps his right hand in abhaya, while he passes his left hand round the back of the devi. The makara-toranas behind the images are carved with Dasavataras.

4. Siva

Siva is worshipped in the form of Linga and also in a number of anthropomorphic forms. The more common representation is the linga. From a fairly early period the Saivas in general used to place Sivalinga as the principal object of their worship in the main sanctum of the shrines of their god, and the various types of his anthropomorphic figures were carved in the different parts of the temple more or less as accessory figures. Later, in particular, the Virasaivas were not much in favour of worshipping Siva in other types of images than linga.[21]

Siva himself is visibly manifested as the Mahalinga and Sakti in the form of Bhaga (womb) known as Bhagasvarupini.[22] By their union the whole universe comes into being. The two great generative principles of universe, Siva and Sakti or purusha and prakriti, the father and mother of all creations, the energy and matter of the physical scientist, is symbolised briefly in the form of the linga and the yoni. For the past two thousand years, at least, the Hindus, males and females, have been offering worship to this symbol of fatherhood and motherhood of the supreme deity.[23] The lingapurana also states that the altar of the linga is the great goddess and the linga is the true divinity (Mahesvara).[24]

Siva is the prime manifestation of divinity from which all originates and in which all is resolved. He along with Sakti, brings this world into existence and takes it back into himself. The lord, in order to maintain purity of faith assumes numerous forms at different times. The multiplicity of the Saiva figures such as Tripurantaka, Bhairava etc., which are more Tantric in character, must be attributed to the advent of the Kalamukha subsect in Andhradesa.[25]

In Karimnagar district, where almost all the important temples are Saivite, a large number of lingas of various shapes and sizes are found. Devotees establishing Siva in the form of a linga giving it a personal name was a common practice in the Kakatiya period. The Chittapur inscription[26] of the reign of Pratapa Rudradeva records that certain Bairisetti has installed one of the lingas of the trikuta temple after his name as Bairesvara.

A special mention must be made of a Chaturmukha linga found at Kalesvaram. It contains four faces of Siva in anthropomorphic form facing its four quarters. The four faces on the linga are alike. They are two armed and wear Jatamukutas. A similar Chaturmukha linga is found in the fort at Warangal. The mukutas at Kalesvaram are shown to be Jatamukutas conventionally, whereas those at Warangal are more realistic. The ornamentation of the Warnagal figures is pleasant with Naga hara, which is absent at Kalesvaram.[27]

There is a unique icon of Panchamukha linga found at Raikal, which is not in anthropomorphic form but in the form of five lingas emerging from the surface of a single *panavatta* (pedestal). There are four small lingas on the four corners of the panavatta and over them, there is another small linga at the centre.

Another important form of Siva is Lingodbhavamurti, which is a combination of the god's human as well as his columnar form. A panel of Lingodbhavamurti noticed on the adhisthana part of the Bhimesvara temple at Vemulavada is in accordance with the Agama Sastras.[28] The figures of Brahma and Vishnu are sculptured on the right and left respectively of the linga and also facing it with two hands held on the chest in the anjali pose.

Two fine sculptures of Uma Mahesvara are found in the district one at Dharmapuri and the other at Nagunuru. In these sculptures, the left leg of Siva is folded and the right leg is hanging down, slightly bent at the knee. Uma is seated on the left lap of Siva. Siva holds trisula and damaru in his upper hands, while he keeps his lower right hand in abhaya and passes his lower left hand round the waist of Uma. The goddess also passes her right hand round the waist of Siva, while she holds a fruit in her left hand. The Nagunuru sculpture contains Ganapati carved to the right of Siva.

Siva in the form of Nataraja is most beautifully depicted on the architraves over the doorways of the trikuta temple at Godisala. Here Siva is seen dancing on Apasamarapurusa. The absence of Apasmarapurusa in the early Nataraja figures from Alampur is noteworthy, while the later examples of Kalyani Chalukyas and Kakatiyas have Apasmarapurusa. The Nataraja figure at Godisala is a ten-handed variety of Siva. He is accompanied by Vinayaka and Vishnu on his left side, Brahma and Kumara on his right side. This figure is a fine specimen of Kakatiya sculpture. The examples of eight armed Nataraja figures are found on the architraves over the doorways in the temples at Manthani and Chandravelli.

Bhairava is another fierce form of Siva, which received popularity in whole of Andhradesa right from the beginning of the early Chalukyan era. The four hands of Bhairava carry a Khadga, Trisula, damaru and a human skull. The figure of the mount dog is not visible in the early sculptures. In the later sculptures of Bhairava, the dog is very often shown jumping to lick the blood trickling from a human head, which is usually held in the lower left hand of the deity.

The figure of Bhairava is always naked. The Bhairava figures carved on big boulders lying on the hillocks are found at Bejjenki and Nagunuru. Large size loose sculptures of Bhairava are found at Godisala, Sanigaram and Valgonda, while medium size figures are noticed at Vemulavada, Jammikunta, Polas, Mallannapet, Chilvakoduru, Koheda, Peddapalli and Tummenala near Dharmapuri.

5. Surya

The sun god is a very ancient deity found praised in the Vedas. The worship of Sun god for the cure of blindness and leprosy is universal from times immemorial. The myths, legends and a 12th century record mention that Samba one of the sons of Lord Krishna was cured of Leprosy by worshipping Surya and he introduced sun worship by inviting sun priests from Sakadvipa.[29] The earliest image of Surya noticed in the Deccan comes from the Bhaja cave where he is seen riding a chariot flanked by his consorts. This is a Satavahana creation of 2nd century B.C.[30] In the north the Kushanas worshipped sun god in human form wearing full boots, whereas in the south, the early forms of Surya sculpture are found bare-footed. One of the early extant Surya images of the south-Indian variety belongs to the Parasuramesvara temple at Gudimallam near Renigunta. Here Surya stands bare-footed holding two lotus buds in his two upraised hands to the level of his shoulders. This sculpture is of about 7th century A.D.[31]

The solar worship appears to be popular in India during the medieval period, which can be evidenced by the ancient remains of the sun temple belonging to 8th century A.D. at Matan or Martand[32] in Anantnag district of Jammu & Kashmir State, the stupendous Sun temple of 13th century A.D. at Konark[33] in Orissa State and several other temples in various parts of the country. In the extreme south early temples to the sun are rare but in inscriptions of the eighth and ninth centuries Adityagrihas or solar temples in the northern part of the old Madras Presidency are referred to.[34] Surya in limestone panel preserved in the precincts of the Kapotesvara temple[35] at Chejerla in Guntur district and another Surya image preserved in the Agastyesvara temple[36] at Chilamaduru in Cuddapah district are known to be early sculptures in Andhra region. The worship of Surya was also popular in Telingana under the Chalukyas and Kakatiyas.

A good number of icons of Surya found in Karimnagar district, stand testimony to the popularity of solar worship in this region. That Sun worship continued to be popular in this area is evidenced by an epigraph[37] at Vemulavada which records that Peddana, the tantrapala of King Arikesari II built Adityagriha for the Sun god. But this temple is no more extant now except two early images of Surya, one perched behind the gopura in the courtyard of the Raja Rajesvara temple and the other kept loose in the verandah of the Bhimesvara temple. In both the sculptures Surya stands in Samabhanga holding two lotus buds in his two upraised hands crossing the shoulder level as laid down in the Agama Sastras. These sculptures are similar to the Surya images found in the Kolanupaka site museum[38] in Nalgonda district and Alampur museum[39] in Mahaboobnagar district.

References to Sun god can be noticed in the inscriptions of Karimnagar district. The Choppadandi inscription[40] of the reign of Ahavamalladeva dated A.D. 992 refers to Martandadeva, while the Jammikunta inscription[41] dated A.D. 995 records the existence of an Adityagriha, in that village. The latter epigraph mentions the gift of some wet land and two ratanas to the god Aditya by certain Nagiyagavunda of Jammikunta village. But the deities of Surya are not traceable now on the old temple sites in both the villages.

The loose sculptures of Surya in early form standing in Samabhanga, holding lotuses in two upraised hands, ranging from one to two feet in height, are found in the following places of Karimnagar district.

1. In the court-yard of the Mahadeva temple at Koratla.
2. Near Bhimannagudi at Raikal.
3. In the court-yard of the Pulastyesvara temple at Polas.
4. In the southern shrine of the trikuta temple at Chilvakoduru.
5. In the mandapa of the Vishnu temple at Pothgal.
6. In front of the Siva temple at Elkaturti.

The construction of trikuta with three shrines dedicated to Siva, Vishnu and Surya was common during the medieval period. The trinity of Hindu Pantheon got composed of Siva, Vishnu and Aditya (Sun god), Brahma being replaced by the Sun god. The Raikal trikuta has its eastern shrine dedicated to Surya like the Hanumakonda trikuta, which has also its eastern shrine dedicated to Surya.

At Nagunuru an early sculpture of Surya is found carved on a boulder lying between the bus stand and the village. On the walls of one of the shrines of the ruined temple on the road side in the same village, there are sculptures of Surya and this shrine must have been dedicated to Sun god.[42] In Manthani very near to Bhikshesvara temple, an idol of Suryadeva, beautifully carved in black stone was recovered while digging foundations for a house construction.[43]

Among the loose icons found at Kalesvaram, there is a beautiful Surya image of 4'-6" height in basalt. It is a Kakatiyan sculpture as it is well polished and exquisitely ornamented. It has a makara torana behind it and seven horses are carved on its pedestal. After Kakatiyas Sun god as the chief idol of the temple became rare and Harihara became popular while Sun worship completely merged in Vishnu. The position oof Surya remained only as a graha or planet.[44]

6. **Devi**

The Sakti cult was popular even in the early times in Karimnager district. The excavations at Peddabankur and Dhulikatta have yielded the archaic terracotta female figurines of Mother Goddess belonging to the early historical period.[45] A bronze sculpture of Mother Goddess found in the early levels of Dhulikatta, assignable to 2-3rd century B.C. is holding a baby in her left hand. The figure of a mother and the child usually represents the fertility cult.[46]

The cult of Mother Goddess of great anitquity, represented during the medieval period by a nude goddess sitting with legs wide apart showing prominently the genital part probably emphasizing the fertility cult, is evidenced by the figurines carved on the adhisthana part of the temples of Bhimesvara and Kedaresvara at Vemulavada and Narasimha temple at Bejjenki. The issueless ladies probably worshipped these figures to beget children.

The Sakti cult seems to have made greater headway in Andhradesa only during the rule of early Chalukyas of Badami, who attached special significance to Saptamatrikas namely Brahmi,

Mahesvari, Kaumari, Vaishnavi, Varahi, Indrani, and Chamunda. According to Hindu mythology the seven goddesses are stated to have assisted Siva in a fight against Andhakasura. The philosophical interpretation of Saptamatrikas, of course, stands for Atma Vidya (spiritual knowledge) which eradicates andhkara (ignorance) in the form of Andhakasura.[47] The Saptamatrikas are often carved in relief on a rectangular stone slab with the figures of Virabhadra and Vinayaka on either side. The *Rupamandana* says that Virabhadra should be placed first, the mothers in the middle and Vinayaka in the end.[48]

The worship of Saptamatrikas appears to be popular in Karimnagar district in view of the several stone panels found at various places. An early panel carved with seven figures of divine mothers presently lying in the mandapa of the Pulastyesvara temple at Polas shows two armed female figures seated in a row. There are no vahanas or any other distinctive marks to separate them from each other. There is no companion either Siva, Virabhadra or Vinayaka as we find them carved on either side in later representations. The panel no doubt represents earlier iconography of Saptamatrikas as it resembles an early panel of the Chalukyas of Badami which is now lying in front of Yelleswaram Pavilion in the State Museum of Hyderabad.[49] Another broken piece of Saptamatrikas of a later period recovered recently from the foundation in the courtyard of the same temple at Polas contains the four-armed goddesses namely Brahmi, Mahesvari, Kaumari, Vaishnavi and Varahi with their Vahanas, while the remaining piece containing the other two goddesses is not traced out.

The panels flanked by Virabhadra and Vinayaka are found in the Bhimesvara temple at Vemulavada, Ramalingesvara temple at Dharmapuri and the trikuta temple at Katkuru. The panels containing the figure of Ganapati at one end with the absence of Virabhadra at the other end are found in the the Bhimesvara temple at Vemulavada and the old Siva temple at Karimnagar. The broken pieces of Saptamatrika slabs are noticed at Kortla, Sanigaram, Potlapalli, Polas, Mallannapet, Chilvakoduru, Nandi Mydaram and Raikal.

Another goddess, which is so commonly found represented in sculptural art of Karimnagar district is Mahishasuramardini. The icons of the goddess are carved in different poses combating the demon Mahishasura, who is represented either in the form of a buffalo or in human form emerging out of the neck of the slain buffalo. The figure of Mahishasuramardini found in the Vatayana of the north wall of the Bhimesvara temple at Vemulavada is eight armed. The goddess is shown in the stance of combat, trampling the asura. The fluid movement of the combat is well represented by the twist of the body, tilt of the head and grouping of the arms. The tight modelling of the slim figure and the smooth rendering of the surfaces characterise the art. Iconographically the form of Mahishasuramardini has close similarities to the Rashtrakuta examples at Ellora and Alampur.[50] The eight-handed figures of this goddess are found at Nagunuru, Polas and Karimnagar. The figures with mutilated hands can be seen in the Ramalingesvara temple at Dharmapuri and Kedaresvara temple at Vemulavada. The broken pieces of Mahishasuramardini are noticed at Koratla, Sanigaram, Raikal and Chelpur.

The seated devi holding damaru and trisula in upper hands, Khadga and dish of blood in the lower hands is commonly found throughout the district. The attributes of the figure may probably account for its association with goddess Chamunda. But it does not contain the symbol of Jackal or corpse below its seat. The figure of this goddess is found two armed in some villages holding sword in right hand and dish of blood in left hand. The Kakatiyas were mainly responsible for the spread of her worship throughout Andhra Pradesh, though we find her being called under all sorts of names and endowed with odd attributes at some places.[51] The north Indian examples of Chamunda show her in emaciated form, on the contary in south India the goddess is generally portrayed in her more natural form with a lady-like appearance. Her countenance looks more reposeful and calm.[52] In Karimnagar district also this goddess is depicted mostly in pleasing form as found at several places. The figures of this devi are noticed at Polas, Raikal, Nagunuru, Mulkanuru, Vellulla, Aravelli, and Thotapalli near Husunabad.

The figure of Chamunda from Choppadandi, now placed in Karimnagar museum holds damaru and Khatvanga in upper hands, Khadga and bowl in lower hands. She wears a hara of skulls. The two huge figures of the goddess Chamunda in buff-coloured sand stone from Karimnagar district are now exhibited in the Khajana museum building. The youthful charming features, graceful pose and the proportionate modelling of these figures are the distinguishing features of the late Chalukyan art.[53]

A special mention should be made to goddess Annapurna the consort of Visvesvara and giver of food to mortals. The figure of Annapurna is rare in south Indian sculpture. The two-armed goddess at Kalesvaram is seen holding a vessel of food in her left hand and a ladle in her right hand for serving food. Another small figure at the same place obviously a later addition is four-armed holding damaru and trisula in upper hands, vessel and ladle in lower hands. A big sculpture of the four-armed Annapurna goddess now lying on the tank-bund at Polas is quite pleasing and appealing. The figures of Annapurna are also found at Chelpur and Bhushanraopet.

Lakshmi the goddess of wealth and wife of Vishnu is said to have sprung from the Ocean at the time of its being churned for nectar. As elsewhere in India Gajalakshmi is generally found on the lintels of door frames in the temples of Karimnagar district and it is the most popular form of Lakshmi. In the sculptures of the medieval period, Lakshmi is shown invariably seated and attended by elephants pouring out the contents of two jars.

There is a representation of Saraswati, the goddess of learning and the consort of Brahma among the loose sculptures found in the courtyard of the Siva temple at Karimnagar. The four-armed goddess is seen riding on the back of her Vahana Hamsa which is carved in big size.

The Sakti cult was flourishing during the medieval period. Many local cults came into prominence during this age. The cults of Gangamma, Kakati, Ekavira, Irukalamma, Ellamma, etc., are worth mentioning as they are associated with the communities like Gollas, Yadavas, etc.[54]

7. Jain Sculptures

Jainism was in flourishing state during the early medieval period. In Karimnagar district alone the places like Vemulavada, Gangadhara, Repaka, Sanigaram, Potlapalli, Koratla, Polas, Kalesvaram,

Nagunuru, Nampalli, Yelgedu, Mulkanuru, Tangallapalli and Karimnagar have yielded several Jain sculptures and a few important inscriptions.[55]

Vemulavada was a popular centre of Jainism. It is surprising to notice as many as a dozen figures of Jain Thirthankaras scattered in all its temples. There are now in Vemulavada five Parsvanatha figures three Vardhamanas, a Gomatesvara and four other Tirthankaras not identifiable for want of their characteristic symbols below their seats. The figures range from early Rashtrakuta period to the late western Chalukyan period.[56]

The most interesting pieces of Vemulavada are the Chaumukhas and Chauvisa-Tirthankaras. These are four and show by their number that Vemulavada had been a very big Jain centre during the period of the Rashtrakutas. The chamukha looks more tall than broad compared to the Danavulapadu one in Cuddapah district and like that one was used exclusively for the abhisheka festival being mounted on a *panavatta* or pedestal. The carving of a chaumukha or Sarvatobhadra-pratima is an early tradition, which had been practised at Mathura, Ellora and other centres.[57] It seems to have been introduced in Karimnagar region during the rule of the Chalukyas of Vemulavada, as is evident from the extant Jain remains.

The Chauvisa-Tirthankara or a carved stone panel showing twenty four Tirthankaras is modelled on the same lines as the Chamukha, but is shaped as a miniature temple. At the rate of six on each face, twenty four Jinas are carved on the two floors of the Chauvisa temple.

A beautiful figure of Chakresvari, the Yakshini of Vrishabha and the standing figures of Adyanta Tirthankaras Vrishabha and Vardhamana are carved on a big boulder with plain surface lying on Bommalagutta, a hillock near Gangadhara. The inscription[58] carved below these figures reveals the date round about A.D. 945.

The figures of Jain Tirthankaras are found either in standing or sitting postures. The standing figures invariably show the meditating (Kayotsarga) pose, youthful body, long arms extending upto knees, elongated ears and nudity. The standing Jina figures are carved on the surfaces of the big boulders lying on the hillocks at Gangadhara, Sanigaram, Nampalli and Nagunuru.

Another very interesting device to beautify the statues of the Tirthankaras is the profusely carved background. The coiling of a snake several times behind a standing Jina seems to be a very popular motif which was started at Vemulavada in the ninith century A.D. and was perfected at Patancheru during the reign of the Kalyani Chalukyas.[59] The hoods of a serpent are spread above to form a canopy over the head of a Tirthankara image. This variety of loose sculptures of Parsvanatha are noticed at Vemulavada, Koratla and Karimnagar.

The seated images of Tirthankaras are shown in full Padmasana with both legs folded and intercrossed keeping the soles of the feet upward. The seated figures are found at Vemulavada, Potlapalli and Polas.

REFERENCES

1. C. Sivaramamurti, "Message by Smt. Indira Gandhi". *An Album of Indian Sculpture*.
2. M.L. Nigam, *Op.Cit.*, p.1.
3. M. Radhakrishna Sarma, *Op.Cit.*, p.129. Pl.131.
4. E.B. Havell, *Op.Cit.*, p.66.
5. *EHI*. Vol.I, Part I, p. 35.
6. I.K. Sarma, "A Unique Ushnisha from Amaravati". *JAHRS*. Vol.XXXV. p.284.
7. *Ibid*. p.281.
8. Late Jitendranath Banerjea, *Op.Cit.*, p.359. Pl.XV. Fig.1.
9. C. Sivaramamurti, *Early Andhra Art and Iconography*. p.3. Fig.12.
10. *Ibid*. Fig. 11 & 13.
11. B. Rajendra Prasad, *Op.Cit.*, p.70.
12. Stella Kramrisch, *The Art of India*, p.203, Pl.57.
13. B. Rajendra Prasad, *Temple Sculpture of Andhra Pradesh*, p.15.
14. Late Jitendranath Banerjea, *Op.Cit.*, pp.514-518.
15. M. Radhakrishna Sarma, *Op.Cit.*, p.223.
16. *EHI* Vol.II, p.508, Pl.CXLV.
17. *IAPKD*. No.25, pp.64-71.
18. Abdul Waheed Khan, *Op.Cit.*, pp.1, 2.
19. M. Radhakrishna Sarma, *Op.Cit.*, p.227.
20. *EHI*. Vol.I, Part I, p.228.
21. Late Jitendranath Banerjea, *Op.cit.*, p.454.
22. Vidya Dehejia, *Early Stone Temples of Orissa*. p.195.
23. *EHI*. Vol.II, Part I, pp.69, 70.
24. Danielou Alain, *Hindu Polytheism*, p. 452.

25. M.L. Nigam, *Op.Cit.*, pp.38 & 46.
26. *IAPKD*. No.38, pp.106-111.
27. S. Gopalakrishna Murthy, *The Sculpture of the Kakatiyas*, Fig. 31 & 32.
28. *EHI*. Vol.II, Part I, p. 108.
29. G.R. Varma, "Surya-Vishnu Worship in Andhra", *JAHRS*, Vol.XXIX, Parts I & II, pp.69-72.
30. C. Sivaramamurti, *Op.cit.*, p.2, Pl.3.
31. Late Jitendranath Banerjea, *Op.Cit.*, p. 440.
32. Debala Mitra, *Op.Cit.*, pp.6 & 79. Pl.XV A&B
33. Debala Mitra, *Konark*, p.6.
34. H.D. Bhattacharya, "Religion and Philosophy", Chapter XI, *The History and Culture of the Indian People*, Bharatiya Vidya Bhavan, Vol.IV, pp.334, 335.
35. M. Rama Rao, *Select Andhra Temples*, p.9.
36. B. Rajendra Prasad, *Op.Cit.*, p.35, Fig.19.
37. *Telangana Sasanamulu* (Telugu), No.21, pp.173-177.
38. S. Ramakantham, *Op.Cit.*, pp.14-16.
39. M. Radhakrishna Sarma, *Op. Cit.*, pp.51-56. Plates 99 and 100.
40. *IAPKD*. No.8, p.23.
41. *Ibid*. No.9, p.25.
42. M. Radhakrishna Sarma, *Op.cit.*, pp.131 & 241.
43. T. Vedantam (ed), *Op.Cit.*, p.161.
44. R.S. Gupte, *Iconography of Hindus, Buddhists And Jains*, p.52.
45. V.V. Krishna Sastry, *Op.Cit.*, pp.223, 224, Plates 93, 94, 95.
46. *Ibid.*, p.223, Pl.82.
47. M.L. Nigam, *Op.Cit.*, pp.54, 55.
48. Late Jitendranath Banerjea, *Op.cit.*, p.505.
49. M.L. Nigam, *Op.Cit.*, p.55.
50. B. Rajendra Prasad, *Op.Cit.* p.42.
51. S. Gopala Krishna Murthy, *Op.Cit.*, p.5.
52. M.L. Nigam, *Op.Cit.*, p.56.
53. *Ibid.*, p.92.
54. B. Rajendra Prasad, *Art of South India*, p.171.
55. *IAPKD*. Nos. 3,4,5,14,17.
56. S. Gopala Krishna Murthy, *Jain Vestiges in Andhra*, p.44.
57. M.L. Nigam, *Op.Cit.*, p.62.
58. *EA*. Vol.II, pp.21-28.
59. M.L. Nigam, *Op.Cit.*, p.99.

SIX

Temple and Religion

Early medieval era of the Indian history brings forth a dramatic change in the social outlook, religious concepts and mythology, which has given a new life to Indian art and architecture. The Mahabharata, Ramayana and the various Puranas received greater attention and admiration of the people at large. The Bhakti cult which emphasized the concept of personal devotion of individual gods and goddesses received greater impetus, wherein the lay Hindu worshipper had liberty to choose his own deity, Aradhyadeva, for selfless devotion and worship. The religious concepts of the people developed the idea of building up lofty and majestic temples for enshrining the idols of Hindu divinity.

In the sphere of religion people of Karimnagar region followed Buddhism, Jainism and Hinduism, a study of which is necessary from the point of view of art and architecture.

Buddhism

The rise of Buddhism and Jainism during 6th century B.C. in Gangetic valley and former's phenomenal success in Andhradesa is of great importance. Although Ashoka had introduced Buddhism in the Deccan, yet the real chamions who imported the high artistic traditions, religion and language of the north into south India were the Satavahana monarchs.[1] Buddhism commanded a large following during the Satavahana period in Andhradesa. The Karimnagar region also, which was a nucleus of political activity for the

Satavahana rulers, contains Buddhist centres at Dhulikatta and Pashigaon.

The archaeological excavations at Dhulikatta near Sultanabad in Karimnagar district clearly demonstrate that the people welcomed Buddhism. It may be surmised that the Buddhist religion was rather more organised than the Brahmanical among the common folk as evidenced by the discovery of a Buddhist stupa, a kilometre north of Dhulikatta mud fort. The label inscription in early Brahmi script found on the ayaka slab of Muchilinda Naga is datable to 2nd century B.C.[2] It is built with bricks entirely. Atop the dome the *harmika* and *chatra* must have been the crowning members, remnants of which are found in the excavations. On the north-west of stupa and just two metres away are a series of square monastic cells each measuring 3.30 x 3.50 m. Certain well-known decorative motifs such as half blown lotuses and other sculptural representations like Muchilinda Naga of this place bear a close resemblance to those of Amaravati and Nagarjunakonda.[3] The effulgence of the Amaravati art, which gave birth to several prolific art centres such as Nagarjunakonda, Kesanapalli, Phanigiri, Chandavaram etc., might have also influenced the art of Dhulikatta. It is not unlikely that some of the Buddhist acharyas and trained craftsmen, who had executed the decor of the Amaravati and Nagarjuna stupas had joined in the beautification of the stupa at Dhulikatta also.

On a hillock at Pashigaon village near Stambhampalli a small stupa can be noticed by a traveller on the road leading from Karimnagar to Lakshettipt. The remains of a big monastery in rectangular shape with the layers of Satavahana bricks are found quite adjacent to the south of stupa.

Having enjoyed glory and grandeur for centuries Buddhism slowly ceased to exist by 10th and 11th centuries in Andhradesa. The famous aramas of Buddhism became Hindu shrines which attained great celebrity and attracted vast crowds of pilgrims. It is interesting to note that Buddha himself had, by this time, been recognised by the Hindu faith as an incarnation of Lord Vidhnu. Buddhism and Hinduism thus became amalgamated and the former was slowly absorbed into the latter. However stray references to Buddhism can be noticed in the epigraphs. one such epigraph[4] from Karimnagar pertainingto the Kakatiya minister Gangadhara dated A.D. 1171 refers to the installation of Buddha at Pattashala by him. The verses in the epigraph denote that Lord Vishnu manifested himself in the form of Buddha to deceive the asuras or demons. Thus even the followers of other faith believed the Buddha as one of the avatars of Vishnu.

2. **Jainism**

The entry of Jainism into Andhra may be ascribed to 4th century B.C. Maurya Chandragupta's sojourn in his last days as a Jain at Sravanabelagola and the town named after Chandragupta-Pattana opposite Srisailam is worth recalling in the context. However Jainism took a few centuries more to make its presence felt in this region.[5] The Jaina faith existed in Deccan from very early times but flourished especially during the period of the ninth to eleventh centuries A.D.[6] Jainism enjoyed royal patronage under the Rashtrakutas. In Telingana, particularly the Chalukyas of Vemulavada extended full patronage to that religion as evidenced by their monuments and literary works like *Adipurana* and *Yasastilaka champu* written by their court poets Pampa and Somadeva respectively.

In Karimnager district Vemulavada, Gangdhara, Repaka, Nampalli, Sanigaram, Potlapalli, Koratla, Polas, Kalesvaram, Nagunuru, Yelgedu, Mulkanuru, Thangallapalli and Karimnager were once important centres of Jain worship as evidenced by the existing Jain vestiges. An inscription of Vemulavada[7] records the construction of Subhadhama Jinalaya by the King Baddega I for favour of the famous Jain scholar Somadeva. The Repaka inscription[8] records that a chief named Srimat Vujaya Gavunda made gifts of lands to a Jinalaya built by Arikesari-III. In the damaged epigraph, after the omission of the first letter of the name of Jinalaya, which is not identifiable, it can be read now as Khalivuttu Jinalaya. The Kurkiyala inscription[9] records the installation of the images of first and last Jaina Tirthankaras and the construction of a basadi called Tribhuvanatilaka by Jinavallabha, the brother of Pampa. The Sanigaram inscription[10] dated A.D. 1051 records the renovation of Duddhamalla Jinalaya, which as the name indicates, was probably builit by Yuddhamalla, one of the rulers of the Chalukyas of Vemulavada. The Koratla inscription[11] records the name of Rattamartanda Jinalaya probably built by a Rashtrakuta Chief.

Subhadhama Jinalaya of Vemulavada, Khalivuttu Jinalaya of Repaka, Tribhuvanatilaka basadi of Gangadhara, Duddhamalla Jinalaya of Sanigaram and Rattamartanda Jinalaya of Koratla undoubtedly played an important role for the propagation of Jainism in the Karimnagar region. But unfortunately none of these Jain temples is extant today. A great havoc was wrought through the rivalry of contemporary faiths and there is epigraphic evidence to prove that some Jaina shrines were burnt and razed to the ground. Such acts of vandalism seem to have been perpetuated at Patancheru and Kulpak (Kolanupaka) where the Archaeological Department has dug out from the ground and also collected from the surface a large number of Jaina images.[12] Probably the same thing might have happened with the Jinalayas of Karimnagar region, which is not very far away from the above mentioned places.

The Jain image recovered recently from Polas stirs our imagination to believe that there might have been a Jinalaya at Polas also, which was the capital of the Polavasa Chiefs, the patrons of Jainism. There is an epigraphic evidence[13] that Medaraja I has built Virakamala Jinalaya at Banajipet in Narsampet taluk which was under his sway. According to the Padmakshi temple inscription[14] of Hanumakonda dated A.D. 1117 Medaraja II of Polavasa made gifts of lands to Kadalalaya-basadi lying on the top of the hill. The above acts reveal that the Polavasa Chiefs patronised Jainism and one can infer that their capital Polas was also a popular Jain centre during their times.

The worship of Parsvanatha was popular in Karimnagar district. People believed that Parsvanatha would bless the devotees with progeny, which can be evidenced by the small figure of a lady with her child carved beside the Parsvanatha images at Vemulavada and Sanigaram. Another popular figure of worship was Gomata, whose sculptures are generally found in South India. He is entirely a South India's hero and a Digambara in affiliation.[15] The figure of Gomata at Vemulavada is impressive. Gomata is not considered to be a Tirthankara but only a Siddha, a monk who has attained the highest knowledge about reality. He must have been famous at first only in Bodhan, which was particularly endearing to the Jains as the capital of Bahubali, the younger son of their first Tirthankara. Bodhan had numerous Jain temples and shrines. It is believed that Bodhan had contained at one time a colossal figure of Bahubali even taller than that of Sravanabelagola. An inscription at Sravanabelagola reveals that Chamunda Raya tried to instal an equally imposing Gomata like that of Bodhan on the Indragiri hill at Sravanabelagola but could have a smaller Gomata only.[16] It is unfortunate that the huge figure of Bodhan installed earlier to that of Sravanabelagola is now no more extant. Bodhan had close political ties with Vemulavada. Figures of Gomata were made in profusion at Bodhan and these found their way to the several Jain centres near Bodhan probably including Vemulavada and Koratla in Karimnagar district. It is interesting to note that Jain Chamukhas and Chauvisa-Tirthankaras of early tradition are unique pieces of art found at Vemulavada.

A good number of gifts appear to have been made to the Jain temples and Jaina basadis as gleaned from the inscriptions of Karimnagar district. Jaina basadis were the religious centres like the temples of Hindus. They carried on not only religous propagation but also worked for the spiritual and temporal development of the Society. Jaina ascetics imparted education to their Shishyas or disciples. Tribhuvanatilaka figures as an important Jaina basadi at Gangadhara, where the famous Jain scholar Somadeva Suri stayed for some time and composed his most popular work *Yasastilaka Champu* in A.D. 959. Besides the kings and their subordinates, the common people embraced Jainism. Like Hindus, Jains also observed caste system, i.e. Brahmanas, Kshatriyas etc. In those days conversion from one religion to the other was easy as one retained his caste although he converted himself to Jainism from Hinduism or vice versa. The change in religion did not mar the caste system and therefore the conversion did not break the unity of the Society.[17]

The Karimnagar region had profound influence of Jainism during the early medieval period. However it started declining during the Kakatiya period. It is generally said that there was bitter persecution of the Jains and that their temples were totally destroyed during the Kakatiya period. The *Basava-Purana* and the *Panditaradhya-Charitra* are cited in proof of this statement.

9. Saivism

The famous Siva linga at Gudimallam ascribable to first century B.C. suggests that Saivism was fully in vogue in Telugu country right from the ancient times. However it is during early medieval period that the Saivism emerges as a widely accepted religion amongst the people of the region. During the period form A.D. 600 to 900, Andhradesa witnessed the erection of large number of shrines dedicated to Siva. The Chalukyas of Vemulavada, who were the patrons of Saivism erected good number of Siva temples in their capital Vemulavada. There were several schools of Saivism like the Kalamukha, Aradhya-Saiva, Vira-Saiva and Kapalika which had influence during the early medieval period over Andhradesa including the Karimnagar region.

The Kalamukha Sect:

In the history of Andhradesa, ninth and tenth centuries witnessed the emergence of Kalamukha Sect of Saivism. This trend is noticed at Vemulavada also. The King Arikesari I is said to have gifted the village of Belmoga to the Saiva ascetic named Mugdhasivacharya, the head of the Kalamukha matha at Elesvaram as Vidyadana or gift for imparting education.[18] The Vemulavada inscription[19] of Arikesari II mentions the names of few Saiva ascetics Mallikarjuna, Vyaktalingi, Vidyarasi and Vyakhyani Bhattaraka as eye witnesses, when the King made some gifts to local gods. Another inscription[20] at the same place belonging to the reign of the Western Chalukyan King Ahavamalla Taila II refers to certain subordinate officer, who made some gift to Saiva ascetic Mahesvara-Sakti-Pandita for feeding the ascetics.

The Kalamukhas enjoyed royal patronage and their mathas served not only as educational centres but also initiated several social welfare activities. Each Kalamukha matha or monastery maintained an education centre, where free education, lodging and boarding facilities were provided both to the teachers and the taught. One such inscription[21] at Vemulavada records that Mahamandalesvara Rajaditya made some gifts of land and a village to the local deity and for feeding the students and their teachers. The Kalamukha school was at its zenith during the rule of the Western

Chalukyas of Kalyani particularly from the time of Somesvara I onwards if not from a still earlier period.[22] Vemulavada which was under the sway of the Western Chalukyas certainly had profound influence of Kalamukha sect of Saivism.

The early Kakatiya rulers patronised the Kalamukha school of Saivism. The Sanigaram inscriptions[23] reveal that Prola I, Beta II and Prola II were Parama-Mahesvaras. Beta-II and Prola II were the disciples of Ramesvara Pandita, the head of the Mallikarjuna-Sila-matha at Sriparvata or Srisaila in Kurnool district. Ramesvara Pandita was an authority of Lukulesvara-agama which means that he was a Kalamukha, for Lakulesvara is a common name of the head of a matha of the Kalamukhas. Beta II gifted him a village called Sivapura, built to the south-west of Hanumakonda.[24]

Ramesvara Deekshita or Pandita and Mahendra, the renowned scholars of Saivagamas are said to have settled at Kalesvaram on the banks of Godavari in Karimnagar district. Ramesvara the religious preceptor of Prola II constructed several temples and Saivite establishments. The Kalesvaram shrine was perhaps founded by him.[25] It is noticed that upto the end of twelfth century Kalamukha Saivism spread throughout Andhradesa not only in temples and mathas but also at the royal court.

The Pasupata Sect:

The reign of Ganapatideva is a memorable period in the history of the Saiva religion of the Kakatiya period. The advent of the Saiva teachers of Pasupata school in the Andhra country brought about a change in the fortunes of the Kalamukha Sect. The three fundamental concepts of Saivism are pati, pasu and pasa. Pati was Siva himself, Lord of the pasus, the creatures who are bound by the pasas or fetters. The followers of the Pasupata sect consider Pasupati as the supreme cause of all creations. The pasu (soul) is released from the pasa (Bondage) of the Samsara only by the grace of pati (Siva).

During the reign of Ganapatideva the pasupata Saivas belonging to the Golaki-matha of Devakipuram in the Chedi or Dahala country on the bank of Narmada, gained popularity among the masses as well as the rulers. Out of the three famous Acharyas Vimala Siva,

Dharma Siva and Visvesvara Siva, the latter Visvesvara Siva was the diksha-guru or religious preceptor of Ganapatideva and his daughter Rudramadevi. He established a large monastery at Mandaram on the banks of the river Krishna.[26]

Visvesvara Siva or Sambhu has played an important role in the religious life of the people of Karimnagar district as evidenced by the inscriptions at Kalesvaram and Khammampalli.[27] He founded a stone monastery called upala-matha at Kalesvaram and granted to it as a perpetual fief the Brahmana village of Ponnagrama, which he himself has founded.[28] He is said to have established temples or mathas at Kalesvaram, Ponnagramamu, Mathanavati (Manthani), Utupalli, Chandravelli, Khammampalli and other places.

Mostly the Sivacharyas of Golaki-matha were the sthanadhipatis of the temples constructed on the various sites and exerted much influence not only on their own disciples and students but also on the common folk on neighbouring communities. Visvesvara Sambhu and other Sivacharyas of the Golaki-matha were celibates and Vaidikas. Pasupata Saivism of the Golaki-matha of this pattern appears to have flourished almost upto the end of the reign of Prataparudra, the last Kakatiya monarch of Warangal, who was himself a Parama-Mahesvara.

Aradhya Saivism:

There is another school of Srauta Saiva in the Telugu country known as Aradhya Saivism. Although the Kakatiya Kings did not extend patronage to this creed, nevertheless it gained momentum during this period. The three Acharyas popularly known as Panditatraya namely Sripati Pandita, Mallikarjuna Pandita and Manchana Pandita flourished in this period and preached Saivism throughout Andhra. Those Brahmanas, who followed these Acharyas are called Aradhyas or Lingadharis because they bear the lingas on their body. Their adherents even now form a distinct sect among the Brahmanas of the Andhra country. They strictly observe caste distinctions upto the present times.

Mallikarjuna Pandita was a contemporary of the Velanati Choda King of Chandavolu in Guntur district, who ruled from A.D. 1162 to

1181.[29] Palkuriki Somanatha, a contemporary of King Prataparudradeva, composed a biography of Mallikarjuna Pandita in Telugu in the Dvipada metre and thus immortalized him in his famous work *Panditaradhya-Charitra*. He states that Mallikarjuna Pandita greatly admired and respected Basava, the minister of Kalachuri Bijjala and the protagonist of Vira-Saivism in Karnataka.

The present day Aradhyas have some features in common with the Vira-Saivas. The custom of wearing a Linga on the body and the custom of burying their dead instead of burning them are common, but they are essentially different from the Vira-Saivas and observe most of the Brahmanical rites. The Aradhya families are noticed today in large numbers at Warangal and a few at Vemulavada. These Ardhyas undertake religious tours periodically to several villages and conduct the initiation ceremonies by giving *upadeshamu* or religious preaching to their disciples reaffirming the faith in Saivism. People of Karimnagar region receive their religious Aradhya gurus from Warangal even today to get *Upadeshamu* or initiation from them.

Vira-Saivism:

Basava, although not the founder of the faith is said to be the most potential force for popularising the Vira-Saivism means the Saivism of the stalwarts or heroic Saivism. Each Vira-Saiva man or woman carries a linga about his person usually in a silver or wooden reliquary suspended from the neck. Hence the Vira-Saivas are also called lingayats. It is curious enough to notice that this sect did not make a headway in the Telugu country under the Kakatiyas. However its representation in Andhra was found in Palkuriki Somanatha, who became a Vira-Saiva and advocated the teachings of Basava in his famous *Basava-purana* and other works.

The Kapalikas:

The Kapalikas had many practices similar to those of the Kalamukhas except that they believed in human sacrifices and laid more emphasis on erotic rituals. They lived in cremation ground, besmeared the body with the ashes of the dead, ate food in a human skull and drank liquor from skull cups. The religious devotion of this sect was reserved for the horrid god Bhairava wearing a garland of human skulls and requiring human sacrifices and offering of wine for his propitiation.[30] Both tne sects Kapalikas and Kalamukhas worshipped Bhairava, the fierce form of Siva. The worship of Bhairava was popular from the early Western Chalukyan period as evidenced by several sculptures of Bhairava found at various places in Karimnagar district.

The Kakatiyas who patronised Saivism were great temple builders. Many Siva temples of this period at Nagunuru, Kothapalli, Manthani, Chandravelli, Katkuru, Godisala and several other places are still extant either in half ruined condition or in a good state of preservation.

Sakti cult was also popular during the medieval period. Uma, the wife of Lord Siva, was a popular goddess. Her popularity can be suggested from her so many names such as Parvati, Ambika, Bhavani, Gauri, Nagendra, Kanya, Mahesvari etc.[31] *Kreedabhiramamu,* the famous Telugu work of Vallabharaya states various forms of Durga as Kakati, Ekavira, Jagadamba, Girijanandana, Uma, Parvati and Adisakti.[32] The village and family deities such as Ekavira, Mahuramma were very popular and their worship was general throughout the Kakatiya period. It is interesting to notice that Polavasa, once an abode of Ekavira[33] is now treated as a popular centre of worship for Ellamma. Polavasa and Vellulla for Ellamma and Aravelli for Nayakuralu are famous centres of Devi worship for the common folk even today.

4. Vaishnavism

Vishnu was a sun deity of the Rigveda, but in the classical age, he commanded supreme power and importance in religious life of the day. Vishnu was no more considered a part of Surya, but an all powerful god and the puranic incarnations of Vishnu were Rama, Krishna and Buddha. Vishnu is found reclining on the couch formed by the thousand-hooded serpent, his feet rest on the lap of Lakshmi sitting on a lotus, his body is covered by silk garments. He wears on his chest Kaustubha gem and is awaited by the humble Garuda. He is the creator, preserver and destroyer of the universe. Three Gunas viz. Satva, Rajas and Tamas emanated from him.[34]

The temples of the medieval period under study in Karimnagar district dedicated to Vishnu are very few. The Narasimha temples at Dharmapuri, Bejjenki, Sundella and Venugopalaswamy temple at Polas are some of the important temples dedicated to Vishnu.

Installation of Hari as a component deity in most of the trikuta temples became common as evidenced by the deities found in the trikuta temples at Raikal, Valgonda and Chilvakoduru. People worshipped Vishnu as Vasudeva, Kesava, Venugopala and in several other forms.

During the Kakatiya period Vaishnavism is known to us chiefly from the records of the construction of temples to the god Vishnu in his different aspects and from references to his worship. Very little is infact known about the type of Vaishnavism prevailing in this period. No religious Vaishnavacharya is mentioned in any one of the inscriptions of the Kakatiya princes and there is no evidence to show that there was any rivalry between Saivism and Vaishnavism in the Kakatiya Kingdom in general.

In spite of their preference to Saivism, the Kakatiya rulers and their chiefs were the worshippers of Vishnu also. The society was in general divided into two important religious groups namely the Saivas and Vaishnavas. Vellaki Gangadhara, the minister of Kakati Rudra installed the figures of *Chaturvimsati-Vishnu,* the twenty four forms of Vishnu in the Vishnu temple at Nagunuru as described in his Karimnagar inscription dated A.D. 1171.[35] The same minister Gangadhara and the ruler of Nagunuru had installed the image of Buddha at Pattashala treating him to be an incarnation of god Vishnu.[36] The Manthani inscription[37] of the reign of Kakati Ganapatideva records the installation of a temple to the god Kesavadeva and the gift of a garden to the god Gopijanavallabha of Mantrakuta or Manthani. Prataparudra's queen Lakumadevi is noticed in an epigraph[38] dated A.D. 1301 at Yelgedu granting some gifts to the god Ramanathadeva of that place.

The Velama chiefs patronised Vaishnavism in Telingana during Prataparudra's time. After the fall of the Kakatiyas the Velamas of Karimnagar region patronised Vaishnavism and made certain constructions and additions for the pleasure of the Narasimha deity. The names of certain important families like Juvvadi, Inumaganti, Jupalli, Jupudi of Velama or Padmanayaka caste appear in the inscriptions of Karimnagar district. An inscription[39] at Vellulla dated A.D. 1613 records that certain Juvvadi Dhala-patiraya of the Velama caste, a devotee of Vellulla Narasimha deity, constructed the sluice of the Nagula tank for the pleasure of the said god. Another inscription[40] at Dharmapuri dated A.D. 1644 records that Jupalli Dharmaraya of Velama caste constructed the platform of the present Bhoga mandapa in the centre of the holy tank known as Brahma Pushkarani. He is also stated to have built the steps on all four sides of the Brahma Pushkarani. The above philanthropic works confirm that the Velamas or Padmanayakas of this region were the followers of Vaishnavism. Their successors form generations together even to this day are the devotees of local Narasimha deities.

The Buddhist, Hindu and Jain establishments were the main centres to promote learning and fine arts. The construction of divine edifices was considered as a meritorious act of the highest rank. The motives underlying the construction and establishment of temples are mainly religious, though vanity might have played its own part in conditioning the size of the temple and its endowement. The Kings, queens, nobles, guilds of traders and craftsmen got the magnificent structures built to glorify their respective creeds. Even the repairs and additions to the existing shrines were deemed to be the pious deeds of religious significance. The religious motives proved as the biggest incentive for the art and architecture to develop in varied forms. The different sects flourished side by side without interfering into the field of each other and this type of social and religious harmony created a very congenial and conducive atmosphere for an all round development of art and architecture in this region.

REFERENCES

1. M.L. Nigam, *OP.Cit.*, pp.12, 13.
2. V.V. Krishna Sastry, *Op.Cit.*, pp.144, 145.
3. C. Sivaramamurti, *Op.Cit.*, Plates 14 & 22.
4. *IAPKD* No.25, p.69.
5. B. Rajendra Prasad, *Op.Cit.*, p.4.
6. *EHD.* p.757.
7. *RE.* 1966, nO.169, P.42.
8. *IAPKD.* No.5, p.12.
9. *EA.* Vol.II, pp.21-28.

10. *Ibid*. Vol.IV, p.68.
11. *IAPKD*. No.17, pp.44-47.
12. *EHD*. p.757.
13. *IAPWD*. No.14, pp.26-30.
14. *Ibid*. No.22, pp.55-60.
15. S. Gopalakrishna Murthy, *Op.Cit*., p.41.
16. *Ibid*.
17. N. Venkataramanayya, *Pallavulu-Chaiukyulu* (Telugu), p.234.
18. N. Venkataramanayya, *The Chalukyas of Vemulavada*, pp.43, 44.
19. *Ibid*., p.43.
20. *IAPKD*. No.6, p.17.
21. *Ibid*., No.18, p.47.
22. *EHD*. p.706.
23. *EA*. Vol.IV, pp.70-89.
24. *IAPWD*. No.15, pp.30-35.
25. S. Gopalakrishna Murthy, *The Sculpture of the Kakatiyas*, p.7.
26. *Corpus*, Part I, p.20.
27. *IAPKD*. Nos. 32 & 34.
28. *EHD*. p.710.
29. *Ibid*. p.711.
30. R.C. Majumdar, "Saivism", *History And Culture of the Indian People*, Chapter XVI, Bharatiya Vidya Bhavan, Vol.V, p. 458.
31. Schindra Kumar Maity, *The Imperial Guptas And their Times*, p.101.
32. *Kreedabhiramamu* (Telugu), verse 127.
33. *Ibid*. verse 128.
34. Sachindra Kumar Maity, *Op.Cit*., p.176.
35. *IAPKD*. No.25, pp.64-71.
36. *Ibid*.
37. *Ibid*. No.28, pp.75-80.
38. *Ibid*. No.37, pp.104-106.
39. *Ibid*. No.48, pp.119, 120.
40. *Ibid*., No.49, pp.120-122.

SEVEN

Temple As a Socio-Cultural Institution

General aspects of the Society:

The Society in Andhra during the Chalukya and Kakatiya period was basically divided into four main castes, the Brahmanas, Kshatriyas, Vaisyas and Sudras, as in other parts of the country. But there were several sub-sects in each of these castes based on regions. In civil life the Brahmanas occupied a highly respected position. They played a very predominant role in the day to day maintenance and administration of the temple. They lived on voluntary gifts from all classes of people from the King downwards.

In fact the institution of caste with all its social and economic implications was accepted almost universally and the upholding of the social order organised on its basis was held to be the primary duty of the ruler. This accounts at once for the prevalence of much social exclusiveness in matters of food and marriages among different sections of the people, and for the readiness with which they came together and cooperated on matters of common concern like the management of a temple and its adjuncts, the regulation of land and irrigation rights in the village and the administration of local affairs generally. Both in towns and villages the castes tended to live in separate quarters of their own and followed their own peculiar customs and habits. The out-castes who tilled the land and did menial work, lived in hamlets at distance from the village proper. There is no proper evidence to prove whether the out-castes were allowed for the entry into the temple or not.[1]

The vast majority of the population lived in villages and agriculture was their main occupation. Great prestige was attached to ownership of land, and every one, whatever his occupation, aimed at having a small plot, he could call his own. The Brahmanas and others, who were employed in the temple enjoyed deva-vritti or temple lands gifted by various officials, nobles and merchants. The landless labourers, an agrarian proletariat assisted in the operations of cultivation and shared the proceeds of agriculture. They had less to do with the management of temple and local affaris than the land owners. Day labour was usually paid for in grain and even the small peasant was ready to hire himself out in his spare time.[2]

The Brahamanas played an important part in the educational life of the country. They were the custodians of learning and princes and people alike honoured them by gifts of land and other forms of wealth. They were placed above want so that they could devote their time solely to the advancement of learning, morality and religion. There is no evidence to determine the state of literacy at that time. A knowledge of dharma or law in its secular and non secular aspects, a clear conviction about the fundamental principles of religion and a general sense of culture was attained by the common man without the necessity of reading and writing. The temple, the matha and the most ancient order of wandering monk, contributed to educate the populace in all branches of learning and culture.[3] The existence of schools for imparting instruction, and the provision of various facilities, such as food and clothing to students, is testified by the temple inscription[4] of Vemulavada dated A.D. 1083, which records some gifts of land and a village to the deity and for feeding the students and their teachers.

The position of women:

The temple sculpture sheds welcome light on the position of women in that age. Women were not debarred from playing an important part in social life. There are a number of panels which give us an idea of the dress, ornaments, coiffure, cosmetics, amusements and pastimes of the ladies of those times. They were well versed in various arts, archery and hunting. The figures of women as dancers, drummers, trumpet-blowers, cymbal-beaters and huntresses holding bows and arrows are found in most of the Kakatiya temples. It is interesting to note that women have always been particular of beautifying themselves. They dressed well and decked themselves with fine jewels and ornaments and their long hair tied into side-knots decorated with beautiful flowers enhanced their naturally bewitching beauty. Sometimes their dark and pendant tresses adorned with Jasmine buds and parted in the centre, their dark eyes like petals of blue lotuses, their big and high breasts added to the charm of their slim bodies decked with necklaces and pearl-garlands of which they were so very fond. The beauty of women as gleaned from the sculptures was a notweorthy feature of certain places like Vemulavada, Polavasa, Nagunuru and Manthani which were once capital cities with plenty of wealth, many temples and beautiful women.

Dress and ornaments:

The dress of women according to our sculptures, generally consists of a lower garment, such as sari and upper garment includes scarf or bodice. Most of the female images both divine and human are shown without an upper garment. The portion above the waist is often seen undraped. Modern scholars have different opinions about the bareness of the upper part of the women and they differ in their conclusions. Cunningham thought that nudity conveyed no sense of indecency in India prior to the advent of Muslims. So women in sculptures and paintings naturally appear to be scantily dressed.[5] Charles Fabri states that any one with eyes can see that in the whole history of Indian art from the earliest times to approximately the twelfth century A.D. women are invariably shown as wearing no garment to cover their breasts. It appears that women of all classes went about bare from the waist upwards for many hundreds of years.Further Charles Fabri opines that the undress is so much more natural, especially as in ancient India, no woman ever wore any upper garment and a dancing pose of grace and elegance comes so easily to a people, to whom dance is of tremendous importance in daily life, in its religious ceremonies and festivities.[6]

Cholika was one of the most important garments of women and they used to put it on for covering their chest region. *Yasastilaka champu* also refers to the Cholika, a cloth for covering the breasts of women.[7] The breast garment called Kanchuki covers the breasts only. It is a small piece of cloth which just covers the middle portion of the breasts, while the abdomen and waist are left bare. The sari was the most important and popular item of the dress of women. It was almost as it is worn in modern times. The sculptures reveal that the ladies who belonged to the upper class of society always wore the sari reaching down to their feet. On the other hand the sari of the poorer sections of the community reached either upto the knees or slightly below the knees. It was usually fastened round the waist, a part of it was converted into graceful pleats and tucked in front and the other end dangling downwards and finally thrown over the shoulders to wrap the upper part of the body.

The male dress generally consisted of a turban, an upper garment and a dhoti which covered the loins. Since man conceives the sculptures after his own image, we may regard the costumes of the images also as similar to those times. Male figures are shown wearing a dhoti worn in different styles. Sometimes dhoti is worn tightly and it clings to the legs. The sculptures of soldiers generally reveal this fashion. It helps them in their swift movements. The ascetics are noticed putting on a Kaupina or a small piece of cloth in the middle.

The sculptures reveal profuse ornamentation in male and female figures of both divine and human. It appears that the people of those times were very much fond of wearing ornaments. The common ornaments worn by women were necklaces, ear-rings, pendants, haras, keyuras, armlets, wristlets, waistlets, anklets, nupuras, girdles, jewelled belts with loops and hanging tassels. Men also wore haras, armlets, wristlets, anklets and finger-rings.

Food and Drinks:

The actual living conditions of the ordinary people in those days are not known from inscriptions. A few general points about the sort of dinner they had may be gleaned from the contemporary Pilalamarri inscription. The food served in a choultry was well cooked, rich in good pulses and ghee. Vegetables were the inevitable subsidiary course while butter-milk or curds were invariably the last item.[8] Fruits were an important article of food and fruit gardens and groves are referred to in the inscriptions of Karimnagar and Godisala.[9] Mangoes, madiphala are a few of the important varieties of fruit grown. Fruits like mangoes and grapes are delineated in certain sculptures. Sweet meats must have also been popular in those days as they are today, but the sculptures portray only modakas placed in a dish or a bowl held by lord Ganapati in one of his hands. Being worshippers of Chamunda, people also consumed meat in those days.

Flowers were evidently in great demand and the laying out of gardens and the planting of flower shrubs is referred to in the inscriptions[10] of Karimnagar and Vemulavada. Growing of flower gardens is commonly found for the purpose of worship in a temple. The Vemulavada inscription mentions certain Machiganga, the garland maker of the garden.

Temple as Nucleus in Socio-Cultural Life:

Hindu temple was the pivot round which the life in India in the past revolved. Of all the constructional activities of the early medieval society in India, temple-building was the foremost. The money, the energy, the skill and the art of land were exhibited in this singular religious activity. Our surviving monuments are temples alone and they bear ample testimony to the fact that the medieval society was predominantly religious and its medium of expression was the temple. The society in the Chalukya and Kakatiya kingdoms was no exception in this regard.

The temple became a symbolic representation of the various socio-cultural activities in the medieval history of the Deccan. For a modern researcher it is the largest repository, where not only the religious, but also the political, social and cultural aspects of history are preserved on stones, often found mutilated. There was hardly any village without a temple. When new villages were constructed, the architects invariably made provision for a temple by leaving proper site for it. The Manthani inscription[11] dated A.D. 1199 of the reign of Kakati Ganapatideva records that the King's priest Manchibhattopadhyaya founded a village, excavated a tank and installed temples for Kesavadeva and Mahadeva and gave a garden to the god Gopijanavallabha of Mantrakuta or Manthena. Installation of temples in those days was considered as one of the seven acts of righteousness known as Sapta-santanas namely one's own son, adopted son, literary work, an agrahara, a garden, a tank and a temple as mentioned in the inscription dated A.D. 1171 on a stone pillar lying in the Collector's Bunglaw at Karimnagar.[12] Several inscriptions of Chalukyas and Kakatiyas reveal that the nobles, officials, merchants and rich people used to spend their hoards of money and other resources on the construction of temples and tanks. The temples at Vemulavada, Kalesvaram, Nagunuru, Kothapalli, Manthani, Chandravelli, Katkuru and Godisala are important Saiva temples. The temples at Dharmapuri, Bejjenki and Sundella are a few important Vaishnava temples of Karimnagar district. The epigraphic evidences show that these temples were endowed with lands and several other gifts in cash and kind.

In the early medieval period the temple played a very significant role as an institution of varied activities. Professor K.A. Nilakanta Sastri illustrated the role of the temple in the following words.

"The temple was not merely a place of worship; it filled a large place in the cultural and economic life of the people. Its construction and maintenance offered employment to number of architects and crafstmen who vied with one another in bold planning and skilful execution. The making of icons in stone and metal gave scope to the talents of the best sculptors of the country. The daily routine, especially of the larger temples gave constant employment to number of priests, choristers, musicians, dancing girls, florists, cooks and many other classes of servants. The periodical festivals were occasions marked by fairs, contests of learning, wrestling-matches and every other form of popular entertainment. Schools and hospitals were often located in the temple precincts and it also served often as the town-hall, where people assembled to consider local affairs or to hear the exposition of the sacred literature. The large endowments in land and cash bestowed on each temple by successive generations of pious donors tended to make it at once a generous landlord and a banker, whose aid was always available to those that needed it. The practice of decorating images particularly those used during processions with numerous jewels set with precious stones encouraged the jeweller's art to a considerable extent. And it is no exaggeration to say that the temple gathered round itself all that was best in the arts of civilized existence and regularised them with the humaneness born of the spirit of Dharma. As an agency of social well-being, the medieval temple has few parallels".[13]

The reason for the above position is due to the temple being a Devalaya or the house of god. It is essential to discuss the significant role of the temple as an institution of multifarious activities.

Temple as a religious centre:

The temple held a place of supreme importance in the socio-religous life of the people. It continued to be the main centre of public worship among the Hindus. Deities worshipped in them were puranic gods, like Siva, Surya, Narasimha, Kesava, Vanugopala, Balarama, Krishna and Sri Rama etc. The records show that temple worship was then more or less similar to what it is now. Musk and sandalwood paste were used, flowers and garlands were offered, fragrant perfumes were burnt and lamps and camphor censors were slowly swung in ritual cadence. The construction of a temple and a tank is considered as an act of religious merit. A number of temples were constructed out of religious zeal and numerous gifts were endowed in cash and kind to the temples with the same spirit. The young and the old, man and women, kings and common people visit the temple, offer their prayers and worship the deities.

The temple was more a popular resort for rest and entertainment than a heaven of peace and tranquillity. Naturally worship in temples was elaborate and ostentatious. It was roughly of two kinds namely *anga-bhoga* and *Rangabhoga*. *Anga-bhoga* was probably the daily routine of worship associated with the main deity of the *sanctum sanctorum* or worship on special occasions festive and non-festive. *Anga-bhoga* also included the provision of all princely comforts and luxuries to the deity. The best food, fine clothes, costly ornaments, music and dance at intervals followed by the chanting of vedic hymns, in fact every conceivable source of pleasure for a human being was amply provided for the god. *Rangabhoga* was probably worship associated with processions and other functions, that took place on several days in the year, outside the *sanctum sanctorum,* as for example the Kalyanotsava or the marriage ceremony that was celebrated annually in the rangamandapa or Kalyana-mandapa. For such a purpose a different image was used, generally made of metal, because the main image fixed in the *sanctum sanctorum* should never be moved and it was impossible to celebrate a grand festival like the marriage ceremony in the confined precincts of a sanctum sanctorum.[14] One such beautiful festival in the tank arranged for god Vishnu by Gangadhara an officer of Kakati Rudra is recorded in the Karimnagar inscription.[15] It was the duty of devotees, princes or peasants to contribute their best to ensure proper worship to the deity and strive to enhance the splendour of the temple. This was done by grants of taxes, land and entire villages with all their annual income. The inscriptions[16] of Vemulavada, Godisala, Dharmapuri, Khammampalli and Chittapur record such grants for the worship, *Anga-bhoga* and *Ranga-bhoga* of the deities.

During the Kakatiya period the performance of various religious acts such as *vratams* attained much importance. Some of these *vratams* like Laxminarayana Vrata, Anant-Arundhati vrata and Jalasayana-vrata etc. described in the Kalpa texts are mentioned in the Kakatiya inscriptions. The performance of vrata was an act from which the performer acquired much merit.[17] Generally temple was the centre of these religious acts. Pilgrimages were also undertaken often with the same object of religious merit. A fragmentary epigraph[18] at Hanumakonda records that the minister Gangadhara performed pilgrimages to Varanasi and Gaya with an object of earning religious merit. Those who were unable to go on a pilgrimage used to perform these vratas preferably in temples.

Vemulavada, Dharmapuri and Kalesvaram are very popular pilgrimage centres in Telingana. People from Karnataka and Maharashtra areas also visit these places with a faith that their desires will be fulfilled.

The temples continued to be the most important centres of philanthropic activities. Many of them maintained rest houses where free meals were available for the destitute. They maintained choultries or *Dharmasalas* for feeding the ascetics and pilgrims. The inscription[19] of Arikesari II at Vemulavada bears an evidence to the same. Another epigraph[20] at the same place records that flower gardens were endowed in Vemulavada agrahara with religious devotion for the offerings and worship of the god Arikesvaradeva and for the Achari who worshipped that god. The village Illimdikunta was gifted by Maha-Mandalesvara Jagaddevarasa of Pavarakula to the same deity for feeding the ascetics. Thus the temple exerted much benevolent influence on the religious life of the village.

Temple as an educational centre:

The temple developed into a great religious as well as an educational institution. The recitation of the Puranas which spread Hindu doctrine and culture among both literates and illiterates continued to be a special feature of temple activities. Adult education was provided through out the country by endowments in temples for the recitation and exposition of the Epics and Puranas. An intelligent and popular expositor seldom confined himself to the words of his text, but at once instructed and amused his audience by ranging over a variety of topics including shrewd comments on current affairs. This form of popular instruction is in vogue even at the present day. The singing of devotional hymns in temples by choirs regularly maintained for that purpose and the training of young men for the same purpose in schools generally attached to mathas is another side of education that deserves notice. Besides Mathas, Jain Pallis and Buddhist Viharas played a part in educating the people wherever they existed and they had large libraries of books in all branches of learning which were being copied from time to time.[21] The 'Three Rs' were taught in village schools which met under the shade of a tree or in the verandahs of temples. The big temples used to maintain Vidhya-mandapas, where efficient teachers were employed and free boarding was provided for students.

The Mathas were not merely the abodes of the monks, who devoted themselves to ascetic practices and contemplation. They had usually a *Satra* or feeding house and a hospital attached to them, where the poor and the destitute were fed and the sick and suffering were given free medical aid. The Mathas were also seats of learning, where pupils were taught the arts and sciences. Gifts of land and money were made to them frequently for the purpose of imparting education.[22] Monasteries in fact played an important part in the promotion of education and morality in the country and as might be expected, Saiva institutions of this character were more numerous than the rest. The Saiva Mathas attached to the temple were also educational institutions. They maintained teachers who taught Vedas, Sastras, Agamas, Puranas, Itihasas, Kavyas, dramas and the various arts and the Saiva philosophy to their disciples. Such Kalamukha Saiva Mathas did exist in Vemulavada, where eminent teachers were employed to impart instruction freely to their disciples.[23] The kings and nobles made liberal grants of land and villages to these monasteries for the support of the customary rites and festivals in temples and for the education of students. Each of these Saiva monasteries had a *Satra* or feeding house attached to it, where free meals were available to both the teachers and the taught. The Vemulavada inscription[24] dated A.D. 1083 confirms that Mahamandalesvara Rajaditya made some gifts of land and a village to the deity and for feeding the students and their teachers.

Hindu temples of the early medieval period had become the centres of the diffusion of Hindu culture. People flocked to them not only to worship, but also to listen to religious sermons, which instructed them regarding the principles of Hindu religion, ethics and philosophy. The epigraphic evidences reveal that Vemulavada, Dharmapuri, Polas, Gangadhara, Nagunuru and Manthena were once great centres of learning in Karimnagar district.

Temple as a Cultural Centre:

As a cultural centre, the temple witnessed the evolution of different schools of art, architecture, sculpture, painting, music and dance in different parts of the country, which brought out a variety of systems in plastic and performing arts, although all of them stemmed from the same spiritual stock. Cultural activities ranging from music and bhajans to theatre and dramas have taken place in the temple precincts. The temples had also provided inspiration to a number of poets, composers and artists who have richly contributed to the Bhakti literature, music and dance. The ranga-sila in the central part of the mandapa, as its name would imply, has provided venue for dancing.

The temple continued to be the most important centre of religious and cultural activities. Religion is the substance of culture; culture is the form of religion. In order to express itself religion has to make use of cultural forms and every religious act is formed by the particular culture of a country.[25] Therefore the temple which is a religious centre represents the culture of the people of that land.

There are ranga-mandapas in big temples, where ranga-bhoga is to be conducted before the god. On festive occasions special programmes are generally arranged. If any drama or music party or Harikatha is to be conducted in the village, the venue would be naturally the temple which serves as a theatre.

A temple festival was an occasion of great social rejoice. The rich and the poor alike had the benefit of these entertainments. During the festivities pilgrims were given free food and lodging in the rest houses and in the choultries attached to the temples.[26]

The temple cult also helped art and architecture by employing a large number of artists and artisans to build their noble fanes and to carve their beautiful sculptures. Dancing and music also received their share of temple patronage, for dancing girls were often employed to give musical performances at the times of worship. Temples were able to undertake these various activities because of rich endowments both by state and by private persons as gleaned from the various temple epigraphs of Karimnagar district.

The temple had its own services for conducting *anga-bhoga* and *ranga-bhoga* of the god installed therein. The big temples had the establishment of devadasis, who were engaged in performing dances on both daily and special occasions. They maintained their own pipers, drummers, conch-blowers, musicians, choristers and dancing girls for the daily routine as well as for the temple festivals. The gifts of land for conducting *anga-bhoga* and *ranga-bhoga* to the deities are noticed in the inscriptions of Vemulavada, Dharmapuri and other places.

The temple was the main prop of the fine arts which are indispensable for it. As seen from the various temple sculptures, one can infer that the temples at Nagunuru and Godisala once maintained their own establishment of dancers, drummers, pipers and cymbal-beaters etc. The temple was the common venue, where the jesters, readers of Panegyrics, actors, dancers, humorists, general speakers, voice-entertainers, persons proficient in gestures, musicians, debators, orators, and poets could exhibit their talents in their respective fields. The patronage given by the temple and the ruling class was the sole factor in the advancement of these arts. Riding was an art and the control of vicious horses was a special qualification. Dommaraja of Nagunuru was noted for his skilful riding. Archery was equally important and Rudra is stated to have driven away Dommaraja by hundreds of his shining arrows as Arjuna did to Karna.[27]

The annual and periodical festivals were occasions marked by temple fairs or Jatras. Devotees at these places manifested their feelings more through gymnastics and other daring feats than by prayer and penance. The existence of Hero-worship seems to have been prevalent as a number of Hero-stones are found at Nagunuru, the capital of Dommaraja. Folk songs and folk plays were two important factors in educating the masses. The annual temple festivals of Raja Rajesvara Swamy at Vemulavada on Mahasivaratri and of Narasimha Swamy at Dharmapuri of Kamudu-purnima i.e., Phalguna Suddha purnima are very important occasions marked by temple fairs and Jatras attracting thousands of pilgrims from far off places. The festivals are marked by numerous cultural activities, contests, in learning, music and dramas. The deities are taken in procession with great pomp and show. These temple festivals do reflect the culture of the society with various types of gatherings at the temple.

Temple as Museum:

It is an undeniable fact that a temple is a modern museum with best art pieces. The making of icons in stone and metal gave scope to the talents of the best sculptors of the land. Bhimesvara, Raja Rajesvara and Kedaresvara temples at Vemulavada exhibit the art of the Chalukyas of Vemulavada and serve as museums to the local people and the pilgrims. The temples of Polas, Mallannapet, Nandi Mydaram, and Raikal represent the late Chalukya art. The temples at Nagunuru, Godisala, Manthani and Chandravelli are all art museums which attract visitors in thousands. They are the galleries of the Kakatiya art.

Temple as a place of Assembly:

Temple served often as the town-hall, where people assembled to consider local affairs or to hear the exposition of sacred literature. Marriages are celebrated in temples. They were also the meeting grounds for the learned and vedic scholars. Important religious texts, treatises and epics covering various aspects of human life and mythology ranging from education and art to renunciation and god-realization were discussed here by the specialists in the fields. The kings and nobles in those days used to meet the citizens in temple. Even coronations and victory celebrations of the kings were performed in temples. Whatever deed people considered noble and sacred, they used to execute it in the presence of god.

The temples were also the centres of service activities. Hospitals were often located in the temple precincts. The Mathas or monasteries attached to temples were almost centres of selfless service. The monks fed the poor, tended the sick and the suffering, consoled the afflicted and set up schools for educating children and young people.

The temple festivals were marked by wrestling matches, cock and ram flights, sports and pastimes and every other form of popular entertainment for all classes of people.

In short the medieval temple was not only a place of worship, but also the venue, where the very socio-cultural life is reflected. In a word the temple was the nucleus of the village or town life.

Literature

The temple epigraphs throw considerable light on the scholars, poets and the literary works of those times. Places in Karimnagar district such as Vemulavada, Dharmapuri, Manthani and Polas were the well-known centres of ancient learning. They were the home of great vedic and Sanskrit scholars, who taught large number of pupils the Vedas, Sastras and Sanskrit literature.[28]

The Chalukyas of Vemulavada patronised Sanskrit, Kannada and Telugu. Pampa was a great Kannada court-poet of Arikesari II. The Kirkiyala inscription[29] records that the ancestors of Pampa belonged to Kamme-Brahmana caste and hailed from Vangiparru in Venginadu. Pampa was the author of *Kannada Bharata* or *Vikramarjuna Vijaya* and *Adipurana,* a Jaina religious work.

Pampa's *Bharata,* a work conceived in the spirit of Jainism, is universally regarded as a masterpiece of art. It has set the norm for epic poetry in Kannada. Graceful and dignified in its diction, the work has a charm rarely met with elsewhere in Kannada literature. As a model of sweet mellifluous and elegant verse, it remains unrivalled.

Pampa is said to have been born in A.D. 902 and his *Adipurana* is said to have been written in A.D. 941. His *Vikramarjuna Vijaya* is considered to be a still later work.[30] Arikesari II having been pleased with *Vikramarjuna Vijaya* gave him Dharmapuramu (Dharmapuri) village as a gift.[31] Pampa had a brother named Jinavallabha, who was also a great scholar and was responsible for engraving the inscription of Kurkiyala on a hillock named Bommalagutta.

An epigraph[32] engraved on the pedestal of a Jaina image refers to the celebrated poet and Jain scholar Somadeva Suri, the head of Gauda-Sangha and the author of his famous work *yasastilaka-Champu.* In his honour Subhadhama Jinalaya was constructed by King Baddega II. He composed his work *Yasastilaka-Champu* in the Saka year 881 corresponding to A.D.959. Nemideva was his guru. Nemideva had many pupils of great excellence of whom the most famous was Somadeva, the abode of learning, the seat of fame, whose beauty was matched by his high character. His other works are *Nitivakyamrita, Yasodhara-Charita,* and *Syadvadopanishad.*[33] He was patronised by Vagaraja and Arikesari III. Pampa and Somadeva both Jains, two of the greatest names in medieval Indian literature, shed their luster on the court of the Chalukyas of Vemulavada. There was another scholar by name Peddanabhatta in the court of Arikesari III.

An inscription[34] of Ahavamalladeva at Vemulavada refers to certain Mahesvara Sakati Pandita a religious scholar, while the Sanigaram epigraphs[35] of the Western Chalukyas refer to the famous scribes like Senabova Jakkanamayya, Donayyam, Damarasana baraha etc., who engraved these inscriptions.

The Kakatiyas patronised Sanskrit and Telugu. Gangadhara, the ruler of Nagunuru and the minister of Kakati Rudradeva appears to be a scholar of great eminence. The beautiful verses in Telugu which the Karimnagar inscription contains, are believed to have been composed in A.D.1171 by minister Gangadhara himself.[36] Visvesvara Siva the religious preceptor of Kakati Ganapatideva is believed to have been the author of the epigraphs at Kalesvaram and Chandravelli.[37] The Manthani epigraph[38] refers to great scholars like Mallikarjuna, Kesavasuri, Pratyangabharan, and Gopalasuri. Ramanandatripada was a great astrologer at Manthena.

Madiki Singana is said to have lived in Ramagiri fort and completed his *Padmapurana* in A.D. 1342. Koravi Goparaju was a great Telugu poet of this region during the 14th century A.D.[39] Veligandula Naraya was a great Telugu poet of Elgandal. He is said to have completed the lapses found in *Andhramaha-Bhagavata* of Potanamatya. Poet Sarabhanka was the author of *Chennabasavapuranamu,* and *Sarabhankalingasatakamu.* He lived in Vemulavada during the 14th century A.D. During the 16th and 17th centuries great scholars like Charigonda Dharmaya, Charigonda Honnaya and Seshachaladasu lived in Dharmapuri. Charigonda Dharmaya wrote *Chitra Bharatamu,* while Honnaya was the author of *Jyotisharatnakaramu. Nrisimha Sataka* was written by Seshachaladasu, a great devotee of Lord Narasimha of Dharmapuri.[40]

The temples and the deities were the source of spiritual and devotional inspiration for the poets, scholars and writers to produce the works of high standard in Sanskrit, Kannada and Telugu, which helped to strengthen the religious, moral, spiritual and ethical valued among the monarchs and the masses.

REFERENCES

1. K.A. Nilakanta Sastri, *A History of South India*, p.319.
2. *Ibid.*, p.327.
3. Corpus, Part I, pp.32, 33.
4. *IAPKD*. No.18, p.47.
5. Asha Kalia, *Art of Orissan Temples*, p.19.
6. Charles Fabri, *Discovering Indian Sculpture*, p.62.
7. Asha Kalia, *Op.Cit.*, p.20.
8. *Corpus*. Part I, p.34.
9. *IAPKD*. Nos. 25 & 30.
10. *Ibid.*, Nos. 7 & 20.
11. *Ibid.*, No.28, p.75.
12. *Ibid*. No.25, p.71.

13. K.A. Nilakanta Sastri, *Op.Cit.*, pp.324-326.
14. *Corpus*, Part I, p.25.
15. *IAPKD*. No.25, pp.64-71.
16. *Ibid*. Nos. 21, 30, 31, 34, & 38.
17. *EHD*. p.713.
18. *JAHRS*. Vol.XXXVI, Part I, p.58.
19. *Telangana Sasanamulu* (Telugu), Vol.I, No.21, pp.73-177.
20. *Ibid*., No.13, p.116.
21. K.A. Nilakanta Sastri, *Op.Cit.*, pp.321, 322.
22. N. Venkataramanayya, *Op.Cit.*, pp.43, 44.
23. N. Venkataramanayya, *Pallavulu-Chalukyalu* (Telugu), pp.233, 234.
24. *Telangana Sasanamulu* (Telugu), Vol.I, No.19, pp.120-122.
25. John C.B. Webster (ed), *History And contemporary India*, p.26.
26. T.V. Sairam, *Indian Temple-Forms And Foundations*, p.32.
27. *IAPWD*. No.36, pp.94-100.
28. *APGKD*. 1974, p.195.
29. *EA*. Vol.II, pp.21-30.
30. N. Venkataramanayya, *Op.Cit.*, p.278.
31. *Ibid*. p.260.
32. *IAPKD*. No.4, p.12.
33. *EHD*. pp.511-512.
34. *IAPKD*. No.6, p.17.
35. *EA*. Vol.IV, pp.67-89.
36. P.V.Parabrahma Sastry, *Kakatiya Sasana Sahityamu* (Telugu), p.106.
37. *Ibid*., p.53.
38. *IAPKD*. No.28, pp.75-80.
39. *Karimnagara Mandala Charitra* (Telugu), pp. 12, 13.
40. *Ibid*., p.14.

EIGHT

Temple As An Economic Institution

1. The Economic Functions of the Temple:

The inscriptions of the Chalukyas of Vemulavadaa, Western Chalukyas and Kakatiyas in Karimnagar district throw ample light on the manifold and multifarious activities of the temple which played a dynamic and vital role in the economic life of the people. The growth of massive Hindu temples and religious establishments in South India coincides with the increasing popularity of donating land and other objects without which their maintenance would have been impossible.[1] in view of the liberal endowments of lands made by the rulers, their chiefs and feudatories, the temples were considered as the landed magnates in the early medieval period. The land grants to temples on large scale gave them feudal dimensions.[2] There are several instances noticed in the epigraphs of South India which record the lease of temple lands to individuals or institutions on certain conditions. Such evidence of the lease of temple lands leads us to infer that the lease system was probably of importance among the various systems of land tenure prevailing in the medieval period.[3]

Grants of lands and villages converted the temple or monastery into a land owner, which gave it economic and political control in the rural areas like a feudal Lord. The larger monasteries were so richly endowed that they had to employ labourers and slaves for the routine work of the monasteries and for cultivating the lands with which the monastery attached to the temple had been endowed.[4] The large endowments in land and cash, cattle and corn bestowed on the temple by successive generations of the pious donors tended to make it once a generous landlord and a banker, whose aid was always available to those who needed it.[5] Cash endowments which amounted to several thousands were loaned to numerous village assemblies at rates of interest fixed in kind or cash and generally about 12 per cent per annum. This sort of loaning system was in vogue in South India.[6] Several tenth century endowments from Tamilnadu country under the Cholas suggest 15 per cent as the annual rate of interest.[7] On the whole the laws regarding interest seem to favour the creditors in early medieval times.[8]

The gifts of Ratanas:

The gifts of ratanas to the deities formed a source of income to the temples. Drawing water by means of *Etamu* or *Mota* was in vogue in olden days. Bullocks were generally used to lift the water from deep wells. Reference to ratanas that is lifting water by pulley device is very common in the inscriptions. There are instances where ratanas with necessary wood and bullocks were gifted to the temples. The Jammikunta inscription[9] dated A.D. 995 records that Nagiyagavunda gifted two ratanas to the god Aditya. The gifts of ratanas also figure in the epigraphs of Potlapalli and Koratla. The five epigraphs[10] of the early Kakatiyas, the subordinates of the Western Chalukyas at Sanigaram dated successively A.D. 1051, 1053, 1107, 1128 and 1149 record the gifts of ratanas to the local deities. It seems that these ratanas were let out for the rent by the temples and individuals, who were the owners of the wells for supplying water to those who did not possess wells for agriculture. These and other references clearly indicate that the money or grain collected towards the cost of the water supplied by means of ratanas was given as gift to the temples.

Thus there is ample epigraphic evidence in Karimnagar district to say that a good number of ratanas were presented to the temples with necessary wood and bullocks. The same age-old tradition of gifting bullocks and calves to temples seems to have continued till today. A large number of he-calves are donated to the temple of Raja Rajesvara at Vemulavada even in the present days and the amount derived out of the sales of these he-calves forms the major source of income to the temple.

The gifts of Ganuvus or Oil-Mills:

The oilman and the weaver are the common small scale industrialists who often figure in the inscriptions as tax payers. Generally the gifts in the shape of ganuvus or oil-mills were made for the regular supply of oil to the perpetual lamps in the temples. There are references of ganuvus gifted to the temples in Karimnagar district. The Sanigaram inscription[11] dated A.D. 1128 records that Repola Kuruvaraja the *Savadora of Sabbi-Sahasramu* or Sabbi-one thousand (Karimnagar region) and a subordinate of Prola II gifted an oil-mill for burning a lamp to the god Kommesvaradeva. Another inscription[12] at the same place dated A.D. 1149 records that Mandaparasar, the *dandanayaka* or general of Repola Kuruvarasar gifted an oil-mill for burning a perpetual lamp to the god Parthesvaradeva. It appears that these ganuvus or oil-mills were given to the oil-millers, who in turn supplied oil to the temples for burning the perpetual lamps. The miller was also supposed to earn his livelihood from the gift mill itself. So he had necessarily to produce some additional quantity of oil than that is required for the temple and sell it in the market to earn his livelihood. On such sales probably he was exempted from the taxes. The Durgi inscription[13] in Guntur district of the reign of Rudramadevi dated A.D. 1269 while registering the gift of a ganuvu to the god, records the remission of certain taxes namely Ari, Sunkamu, Pannu and kanika on the mill as meras or privileges of Sarvamanya nature.

The medieval period in the history of Andhra witnessed a remarkable religious activity. Members belonging to different sections of the community donated the temples to the best of their ability in cash, cattle, jewellery and land, constructed new temples and added new elements.[14] The provision of the renovation and the general repair of temples was by no means unusual and often in such cases the donor simply made a grant of land leaving the execution of the actual work to the temple authorities.[15]

A gift to a temple was always recorded on a special stone pillar usually set up in the court-yard of the temple. Almost all the inscriptions in Karimnagar district are set up in the court-yards of the temples and mostly they are of the nature of gifts made to the deities. Grants were usually made on special occasions such as the solar or lunar eclipse and on the chief festival days or on suitable auspicious days. Generally at the beginning of an inscription the invoking verses praise the rulers and at the end the imprecatory verses record that any one, who declines and obstructs the gift, was declared a Sivadrohi or traitor to Siva incurring the sin of having pierced a cow and a Brahmana on the banks of the holy river Ganges. As such it appears that the temples faced no obstruction in enjoying the gifts which were a perennial source of income to them.

The epigraphs of Chalukyas and Kakatiyas in Karimnagar district often record the gifts to the deities for their *Anga-ranga-Vaibhogamu* and *Dhoopa, Deepa, Naivedyamu.* (All types of ritualistic performances with flowers, burning incense, sandal paste, musk, camphor, lamps and offerings etc., observed at the time of worship together with dance and music). The Chittapur inscription[16] states that Bairisetti made gifts of lands and tolls to the temples for *Gandha, Pushpa, Dhoopa, Deepa, Naivedya, Tambula* and *anga-ranga-bhogamu* of the deities.

Thus the temples endowed as they were with so much of property were very rich and occupied an important place in the economic life of the community. The medieval temple was not only a place of worship but also the venue where the very social and economic life is reflected. Hence it is essential to study the various economic functions of the temple.

Temple as land holder:

The temples were endowed liberally by those who constructed them and by kings, nobles, rich merchants and land owners with grants of lands either wet or dry or both and of villages, whose rents and produce were devoted to the upkeep of religious institutions. The temple lands are known as deva-vrittis commonly exempted from all kinds of taxes otherwise called Sarvamanya. In some cases only nominal taxes were collected.

The epigraphs of Karimnagar district record the grants of lands, gardens, flower-gardens, fruit-gardens and villages. King Arikesari II made a gift of hundred Nivartanas of Bhu-kshetra or dry land and eight Nivartanas of Paniyakshetra or wet land to the temples of Vemulavada.[17] There are instances where whole villages were granted as gifts for maintenance of religious institutions. For example the Vemulavada inscription[18] dated A.D. 1108 registers the gift of whole village Illimdikunta to god Harikesvaradeva.

During the period of Kakatiyas Visvesvara Sambhu, the religious preceptor of Ganapatideva granted the village of Ponna-grama, which he himself had founded as a perpetual fief to the temples and upala-matha monastery at Kalesvaram.[19] Another epigraph at Godisala[20] dated A.D. 1236 records that Kataya an officer of Ganapatideva granted the whole village Pincharapalli to the local Siva temples.

The grants to the temples included the flower-gardens and fruit-gardens also. An inscription at Karimnagar[21] dated A.D. 992 records the gift of a flower garden and some wet land to the temple of Mallikarjunadeva by certain army commander of Ahavamalladeva. Another inscription at Vemulavada[22] dated A.D. 1106 records the gift of a flower-garden for the Achari or priest who worshipped that god. It also mentions certain Machiganga the garland maker of the garden. The Godisala[23] epigraph dated A.D. 1236 records the gifts of fruit gardens like Mango-garden, Tamarind-garden and a garden with Palm trees. All the deva-vritti lands and villages were practically granted with all immunities otherswise called Sarvamanya. This was the nature of the landlordship of the temple in those days.

Black land and red land are mentioned in the epigraphs besides the usual wet land, dry land, garden-land and waste land. Betal and areca-nuts, ginger and turmeric, fresh fruits and flowers were the chief items of garden produce.[24] Besides cultivating food grains and pulses on both wet and dry land, intensive flower and vegetable growing was also practised on *Tomta-bhumi* or garden land. Flower gardens were largely grown where there were temples.

Closely allied to agriculture was cattle raising and dairy farming and land was set apart for pasture. This industry might have been wide spread at all times but in inscriptions we hear more of the cattle belonging to temples, of the cow-herds incharge of them and of the obligations they owed to the temple. The cow-herds and shepherds were bound to supply ghee for the temple. Ghee was not only an important item of food among the upper classes, but was used in considerable quantities for burning in lamps in the larger temples.[25]

The limited available data may imply that the temples which received grants of land practically enjoyed it at will. Temples which became rich land-owning institutions in course of time could not have cultivated all their lands directly, which perhaps led to the practice of leasing them to tenants. It is obvious that the temples must have neded a good number of people to work their land in cases where the whole villages were granted to them. Thus it would not be unreasonable to hold that the grant of fiscal privileges with land or village to the temples might have caused greater economic subjection of the peasants.[26]

Temple as Employer:

The construction of temple and its maintenance offered employment to numbers of architects and craftsmen who vied with each other in bold planning and skilful execution. Generally the big temples gave constant employment to numbers of priests, choristers, musicians, dancing girls, florists, cooks and many other classes of servants. Its establishment included the Sthanadhipati and Srikarana, who was the accountant incharge of the temple treasury. The temple services included Sanis (devadasis), pipers, drummers, umbrella-bearers, bodyguards, torch-bearers, conch-blowers and *nibandhakaralu* or menial servants.

The temple originally conceived as an embodiment of faith to serve the religious and spiritual needs of the community came to be associated with various social, cultural and economic activities as well. Mundane economic functions such as providing employment for workers, masons, artisans, artists, engineers, priests, scholars, teachers etc. for constructing and maintaining the religious institutions, achieving redistribution by receiving donations from the rich people, functioning as the money-lending institution at the hours of crisis such as drought, inundations etc. Organising trade fairs etc. could be cited as the most common examples of its economic and financial functions.[27]

The governing body of the temple is called Sthana. The head of the body is called Sthanadhipati or Sthanapati. The Sthanadhipati is a vritti holder appointed to look after the temple administration. The term Deva-Sthana is in vogue even today to denote the administrative office of a temple. The status of Pujaris in the temple administration was not equal to Sthanapati. The Sthanapatis were generally provided with lands as vrittis towards remuneration like other employees of the temple. The Vemulavada inscription[28] of Arikesar II mentions Mallikarjuna, Vyaktilingi, Vidyarasi and Vyakhyani Bhattaraka as the Sthanadhipatis of four principal temples of Rajesvara, Adityagriha, Baddegesvara and Nagaresvara respectively at Vemulavada.

The second class employees of the temple are the officers like Pujari, Kottaruvu or Store-keeper, Bhandari or treasurer, Srikaranamu or accountant, who come under the category of *Manulu* or *Manyulu* or respected persons. The third variety of employees in a temple are *Sanis*. This word is derived from the Sanskrit word *Swamini*. These Swaminis were donated to the temple by the devotees for the purpose of conducting dance during the time of daily *ranga-bhoga* performed in the ranga-mandapa. The *Sanis* are not ordinary prostitutes as generally mistaken. The last category of employees are *Nibandhakaras* or menial servants who included cooks, watermen, sweepers, watchmen, masons and other artisans.[29]

The Pauranikas and Haridasus, goldsmiths and sculptors were also included among the temple employees. Thus the temple in those days employed a large number of people only next to royal palace both on regular salaries in kind and coin and on vrittis in the form of lands.[30] The growth in the economic resources of the temple led to a corresponding increase in the number of employees, whose services were required by it. Thus the role of the early medieval temple as an employer has rightly been emphasized.[31] But in the absence of adequate statistical data relating to different temples it is difficult to form a correct idea of the employment opportunities which they may have afforded.

Temple as consumer of Goods and Services:

Out of devotion the valuable products of the land first go to the temple in various forms like grain, fruit jaggery, sheep, cows, oxen and even *Sanulu* or devadasis. The Raja Rajesvara temple at Vemulavada is a good example, where farmers and other devotees even now offer to the god several oxen and he-calves which form the main source of income to the temple. The temple consumed large quantities of grain and other provisions next only to the royal palace. One can easily understand all that huge consumption ultimately goes to the villagers because the daily offerings were distributed among the temple servants and the poor.

About the services also, any unemployed person could seek shelter, do some work and make his livelihood as temple had enormous resources to feed the helpless poor. The persons like the Boyas, shepherds, oil-mongers and petty merfhants, who supply ghee or oil and other provisions regularly to the temple on behalf of the donors were also to be considered among the servants, although they were not regular employees.

Temple as Bank:

In South India temple managements dominated by priests and Brahmanas did invest gold with the village assemblies and others and received interest thereon for the maintenance of worship, burning of perpetual lamp and similar other purposes. All this was done on religious grounds.[32] The South Indian epigraphs suggest 12 to 15 per cent as usual rate of interest per annum.[33]

Financiers both individual bankers and trade guilds profited from trade. Money was not to be kept idle. Usury was a legitimate economic activity. The sources mention 15 per cent per annum as the normal rate of interest on money lent for trading purposes and this figure remained constant over many centuries.[34]

Temples in those days used to give loans on interest. The monetary donations were generally lent and interest on it alone was used for burning the perpetual lamps or for other intended purpose. Thus the temple was indeed a peculiar bank.

Temple as a Commercial Centre:

Temple was the nucleus around which villages, towns and commerce flourished. Temple indirectly helps for the promotion of trade and commerce in the village. Generally temples are surrounded by numerous shops selling various articles needed to pilgrims and for the worship of the deity. On the occasion of festivals and fairs, the temple attracts thousands of pilgrims and consequently the enormous increase in the sales will benefit the trading community. Generally *samtas* or weekly-fairs are conducted around the temple. In certain cases the Sthanadhipati or pontiff, who was the administrative head of the temple estate as well as the town or village also accorded permission by issuing licences of trade in Addas or pemtas (Samta or market). The Warangal epigraph[35] of Ganapatideva mentions several groups of merchants and their articles of trade and allocation of respective places in the market-yard.

Usually the wholesale or retail trade is conducted in the vicinity of the temple at select places called *pemta* or *adda* or *Samta,* the former two terms are no longer in usage, whereas the word *Samta* or fair or weekly-bazar is still in vogue in the present times. The duty collected on sales effected in the *Peta* or market-place on articles of trade was called *pemta-sunkamu* or *magama* and sometimes is was bestowed as a gift for charitable and religious purposes such as the setting up of lights before god in temples.[36] The Koccherlakota[37] inscription of the Kakatiya general Devarinayaka dated A.D. 1310 describes the nature of a public fair or pemta or Samta and states that the Bacchus or Komatis, who collect *Mudra-Sunkamu* or registration tax should remit the same to the temple as Sarvamanya. The duties collected in market places, in places of pilgrimage and in the precincts of shrines and temples of acknowledged repute, were generally gifted to the temple. The Godisala epigraph[38] in Karimnagar district dated A.D. 1236 records that a Kakatiya Chief named Kataya gifted *amgadi-Sunkamu* or the duty levied in the market place for the worship and offerings to the gods of local temples.

Besides shops a number of hawkers or street vendors carry the commodities on heads, in baskets or bags and *Kavadis* or shoulder rods with two equal loads hanging at either end of it and sell the articles. This system is still in vogue in the places of pilgrimage. Some villages even today organise *pemtas* or *Samtas*. Vemulavada, Dharmapuri, Manthani which are the age-old towns organise *Samta* or weekly-bazar even in the present times. It is believed that most of the village or town names ending with *Peta* are derived from the word *pemta* in the Telugu and Karnataka regions, where formerly business fairs were organised once in a week. Mallannapeta, where there is Mallanna (Siva) temple of Chalukya period might have derived the ending name with *peta* in the same and similar manner.

The Warangal fort inscription[39] of Ganapatideva dated A.D. 1228 records in detail about the several articles of trade brought to the market-place like salt, minerals, aromatics, pepper, ginger, cloves, areca-nuts, gingili, betel-leaves, nili or indigo, cloth, fruits, wheat, paddy, gram, millet, oils, tin, copper and lead metals, sandal wood, camphor, musk and other perfumes. The duties levied on these articles were granted for conducting the *anga* and *ranga bhoga* of god Virabhadresvara. All these articles are sold even today in a temple fair or festival known as Jatra celebrated annually at several places in Karimnagar district like the temple Jatras celebrated in other regions. The jatras celebrated annually at Vemulavada, Dharmapuri, Beerpur, Mallannapet, Konpur and Kothakonda are very famous and popular in Karimnagar district. The common articles of trade include not only foodstuffs and eatables but also several other industrial and general articles. The Velpuru inscription[40] dated A.D. 1247 mentions horse, ox, sheep, cart, ropes as items of trade. It suggests that there were separate *Samtas* for animals as organized at present. Thus the temple gives scope to turn the village into a good commercial centre.

2. General Economic Aspects of the Temple and Sources of Income:

Agriculture:

The Godavari Valley which formed a part of Dandakaranya of Ramayana was sparesely populated in the ancient and medieval times due to its rocky nature of soil and inadequate rainfall. Villages were founded where there were water resources and the rest of the country was left uninhabited and covered with vegetation like shrubs. The ancient sites at Kotilingala, Peddabunkur and Dhulikatta indicate the Satavahana occupation of the Karimnagar region. Similarly the records of Badami Chalukyas and Vishnukundins throw some light on the early history of Tilingana.

The temple epigraphs reveal that the Chalukyas of Vemulavada and the Western Chalukyas of Kalyani made efforts for the reclamation of vast areas of forests into arable lands. They caused the tanks to be dug for the settlement of the people. The Kurkiyala inscription[41] of the reign of Arikesari II datable to A.D. 945 records that Jinavallabha constructed a tank called Kavitagunarnava near Gangadhara. The Choppadandi epigraph[42] of the reign of Ahavamalladeva records the construction of a tank called Achebbe-Samudra.

The Kakatiya rulers had a tough task before them in cutting down the forests for cultivation with the co-operation of the people. The Kakatiyas being the native rulers of the land for generations strove hard for its development and brought large tracts of fresh terrritory under plough. A large number of villages were founded either by themselves or by their subordinates. Most of the present villages in the forest tracts of Dharmapuri, Manthena, Narsampet, Kalesvaram and Chennuru were founded during the Kakatiya regime as evidenced by the temple epigraphs. The Manthani inscription[43] of Ganapatideva dated A.D. 1199 records that the priest Manchibhattopadhyaya founded a new village and excavated a tank in the land gifted to him. Mahadevpur village near Kalesvaram was probably founded after the name of King Mahadeva and Pratapagiri fort was constructed after the name of King Prataparudradeva.

Most of the tanks in Karimnagar district appear to have been constructed alongwith the erection of temples during the Kakatiya period. Gangadhara, the minister of Kakati Rudra erected a trikuta temple and excavated a tank named *Vilasattatakamu* as evidenced by the Karimnagar inscription dated A.D. 1171.[44] The other temple inscriptions of the reign of Ganapatideva at Katkuru, Godisala and Chittapur also record the construction of new tanks.[45] To establish a village in those days, was a pious deed. Similar was the sanctity attached to the digging of a tank. Divine prosperity is always there in Hindu ethics attached to the construction of tanks which in several codes is mentioned as one of the *Saptasantanas* or seven acts of righteousness which would perpetuate the name of the doer and establish his fame permanently in the world. The Karimnagar epigraph[46] of minister Gangadhara dated A.D. 1171 and other records allude to *Saptasantanas* namely one's own son, adopted son, literary work, an agrahara, a garden, a tank and a temple. Tank digging was generally preceded by installation of Varuna, the Lord of waters in order to ensure good supply of water by his grace.

Before the new settlement, the presiding deity was installed in a temple and a festival called *Urumu* was held in his or her honour. Then the houses for the new settlers were erected. The *Ayagars* (Twelve village officers) were appointed. The cultivable land was plotted among the settlers. With the construction of tank, the formation of a village was finally completed.[47] Along the course of a rivulet or a stream a point was to be chosen, where it passed between the two mounds or hillocks and a bund connecting the two hillocks had to be constructed with mud and stone so as to form a big tank or a reservior. The tanks at Sanigaram, Polas and Nandi-Mydaram appear to have been constructed in the same manner and the temples stand either on the tank-bund or beside the tanks. There is hardly a village today without a tank in Karimnagar district and several other villages have more than one tank. Storing up the rain water for irrigation purpose by constructing tanks at proper places along the streams proved to be a successful endeavour for the promotion of agriculture which in turn resulted in the economic prosperity of the kingdom in general and the temple in particular.

Besides tanks the canals also formed another important source of irrigation. Reference is made in a copper plate record[48] dated A.D. 1246 to *Gonugu Kaluva* about which a dispute arose between Chamanpalli and other surounding villages in Karimnagar district. In an unpublished inscription at Raikal dated A.D. 1305, reference is made to *Donula-Kaluva* where five *marturs* of land was gifted by certain Rudradevani to the local gods. *Martur* or *mattar* is a land measure, the exact value of which is yet to be known. Methods of agriculture were almost the same as we find them till recent days before the introduction of mechanized farming. The indigenous tools and bullocks were used.

As gleaned from the temple inscriptions, one can notice that the cultivated land was divided as at present into dry land (Veli-Volamu) or Veli-chenu or Veli-Bhumi) wet land (Paniya-Kshetra of Niru-nela) and the garden-land (Tomta-Bhumi) which were generally granted to the temples by various people on different occasions. The above terms figure in the temple epigraphs[49] at Vemulavada, Repaka, Jammikunta, Sanigaram, Godisala, Regonda and other places in Karimnagar district.

The cultivators used to make festivities on *Eruvakapunnama* or the full moon day of the month of Jyeshtha (in the month of June) when the South-West monsoon sets in and the season becomes suitable for sowing the seeds. This is the main festival for the cultivators to begin the new agricultural year. On that day they used to perform certain worship at a common place like tank-bund, a hill or a temple. The Godisala epigraph[50] dated A.D. 1236 mentions a hill named Eruvaka-Gubbali, the hillock where the villagers perform the Eruvaka worship. They come there with their bullocks, decorated ploughs and seeds and worship the deity and proceed to the fields to sow the seeds. Similarly they perform some worship at the time of harvest. But this festival is merged with the Uttarayana-Sankranti generally ceremonised as festival on every fourteenth of January in the Telugu country. However a nominal worship is done on the harvesting days.

Taxes and Temple gifts:

There is no direct evidence to know the exact value of the levies, particularly the land taxes. They are to be inferred only from the remissions or gifts of such taxes on Brahmana-Vrittis and temple lands. Even the Brahmana agraharas and deva-vrittis or temple lands which come under Sarvamanya tenures were also subjected to a concessional rate of tax. However the holders of agraharas and the temple lands possessed more privileges than other land owners.

The term *Siddhaya* in the early medieval period used to denote taxes both cash and kind. During the period of the Chalukyas of Vemulavada the term *Siddhaya* figures in the Karimnagar epigraph[51] dated A.D. 946. The other temple inscription[52] at Vemulavada records that the *Siddhaya* of the gifted lands to the local temples by King Arikesari II was fixed at twelve drammas. The epigraphs[53] of the reign of the Western Chalukyas at Kadaparti dated A.D. 1005 and Vemulavada dated A.D. 1033 also record *Siddhaya* as gift to the temples and in the latter inscription it figures in drammas. But coming to the Kakatiya period this term is exclusively used for levy in cash alone and not in kind on lands as per the Matedu inscription dated A.D. 1310 in Warangal district.

The tax which was collected from wet land was called *para* and that from dry land *Pangamu, Pangamu*, according to the Telugu dictionaries means one-fourth part of the rent and *para* meant probably one-eighth part. Even this minimum tax was remitted in case of deva-vrittis or temple lands. A general term for land tax was *Ari* and those ryots who were subjected to it were called *Arigapulu.*[54] The gift inscriptions generally contain various terms denoting land taxes like *pannu,* Panga or Pangamu, Pangatappu, Pangasumkamu, Vennu-pannu or Ennu-pannu, Kanika, Darisanamu etc., which were remitted to those who cultivated deva-vrittis or tomple lands. The Telugu word *Panga* means a branch and it seems to convey the meaning of a share of the produce. The tax *Kanika* was a tribute payable to the king because the proprietorship of the land primarily lies with the king. As a mark of their submission, the cultivators had to pay tribute to the king or his representative. *Vennu-pannu* or *Ennu-pannu* is a tax levied on the crops when they are ready for harvest, the amount being assessed on the appearance of corn (Vennu). If there is a good crop, the cultivator is liable to a levy of additional tax apart from what is stipulated originally. The tax by name *Darisanamu* was exempted to the temple lands which was levied on the ryot who went to see the King of chief. Even if he did not go to see the king the payment was made compulsory.[55] A number of inscriptions record the remission of *Kanika, Vennu-pannu* or *Ennu-pannu* on deva vritti lands. The terms *Vennu-Pannu, Kanika, Katnamu* and *Kani* occur in the Yelgedu inscription[56] of Lakmadevi, the queen of Prataparudradeva. The epigraph is dated A.D. 1301 and records her gift of the above taxes to the local god Ramanathadeva. According to Noboru Karashima the tax *Kani* means the right of *atchi, parru,* and *Ulavu* which mean *holding, acquiring* and *cultivation* respectively and the tax *Kanika* may be a right of holding land.[57]

There are epigraphic evidences showing that temple lands were exempted from additional taxes like *Niru-vidi* and *Bamtela-ayamu. Niruvidi* or *Nirudi* is an additional tax towards the cost of water drawn from a tank or well or streams by ratanas and canals.

Bamtela-ayamu was also one of the remissions granted to the temple lands. As indicated by the word *Bamtela,* it was probably a levy intended for the maintenance of *Bamtus* or warriors.[58] The Kakatiya epigraph of Hasanabad[59] records certain gift made by the *ekkatis* or warriors to the god Rudresvara. The gift includes four puttis of paddy.

There are some lands where the King is entitled for two-thirds share of produce. The Chittapur inscription[60] of the reign of Prataparudradeva records that certain Bairisetti constructed a tank known as Sakalasamudra and donated one-third of the produce in the irrigated land to the local gods Bairesvara, Sakalesvara and Nagesvara leaving two-thirds to the King because the whole land belonged to the King.

The information regarding taxes is mostly drawn from the records, where remissions of taxes were granted as gifts to temples. The two important taxes, which occur frequently in the epigraphs are *Illari* and *Pullari. Illari* is a compound word consisting of *Illu* (house) and *ari* (Tax). The tax levied on house is called *Illari*. Some of the local chiefs granted *Illari* or house-taxes of the village to the temples. *Pullari* is a tax levied on the cattle-breeders for grazing the sheep, goats, oxen, cows, buffaloes, and other domestic animals in the pasture lands and forests, the proprietory rights of which rest with the King. *Pullu* means grass and *ari* means tax. There are instances where the tax *Pullari* is granted to the temples. The Yelgedu inscription[61] dated A.D. 1301 records the remission of *Pullari* on milch animals as *vritti* or gift to the god Ramanathadeva. Levying tax on various professions is also noticed in the Kakatiya records. Thje Mogalutla copper plates[62] dated A.D. 1219 in Guntur district record that Ganapatideva granted to certain Rudrapareddy the taxes payable by the village communities namely Takshaka (Carpenter), Ayawskara (blacksmith), Kumbhakara (potter), Suvaranakara (goldsmith), Rajaka (Washerman), Napita (barber), Chandala (sweeper), Ardha-Siri (cultivator paying half produce) and Adi (and the like etc.). In certain cases the village with all its income was granted to the local temple.

The Akunuru epigraph[63] of Rudradeva dated A.D. 1172 records that the King has granted to the temple certain levies due to him from industries like ratanas and professionals.

1. Owners of ratanas	5 Madas
2. Garden ratanas	3 Sinnas
3. Tammadi	8 gadyas
4. Gollavaru	2 gadyas
5. Anamiklu (Miscellaneous)	4 gadyas
6. Potters	1 gadya
7. Barber	5 rukas
8. Vasadi (dwellers (Jains)	5 rukas
9. Garland makers	5 rukas
10. Cattle-sheds	2 rukas.

As Akunuru is in Warangal district quite adjacent to Karimnagar district, it can be generalised that all the above taxes were levied in the Karimnager region also during the Kakatiya period.

The Chalukyan administration had toll collection on all kinds of merchandise. It was called *Vaddaravula Sumka* which formed a major source of revenue. During the Kakatiya period the term *Vaddaravula* was replaced by the Telugu term *Adda-vattu* or simply *adda* or Majili, where business transaction is conducted. The word *adda* seems to be a derivative of the Sanskrit word *hatta* which means *Addavattu* or *adda-pattu* denoting the place, where market is organised. Only from gifts made to gods out of the tolls collected in a market place, we have to infer the nature of these taxes. *Mudra-Sumka* (Registration fee) was also collected in a *pemta* or *adda* or market place. Miscellaneous taxes like Burra-Sumkamu (tax on pots used for measuring oils) PeruSumkamu (levied on the occasion of naming the child), marriage tax, Gamdi-Sumkamu, Ravu-Sumkamu (levy on ferry) and Alamu (levy on vegetables) appear to have been donated to local gods in various inscriptions of the Kakatiya period. *Sumkas* or tolls or duties with varying designations such as ammubadi-Samkamu, ammu-kada-Sumkamu, Peruka edla-Sumkamu, and Uppu-perika-Sumkamu etc., find mention in the records of the Kakatiyas.[64]

Traders and Temple:

Evidence of gifts and donations to religious institutions by mercantile people is available from as early as the Satavahana period, when merchants individually as well as collectively seem to have financed the Buddhist stupas and monasteries. There are favourable references to Setti-gahapatis and the merchants in Buddhist literature who rendered financial assistance to the stupas.[65] One such instance of assistance by a Ganapati is noticed on one of the ayaka slabs of Buddhist stupa at Dhulikatta with a Brahmi label inscription which reads as *GAHAPATINO PATHALASA MATHUYA DANAM.* The similar mercantile groups and merchants indeed in later centuries financed the Hindu temples.

During the Chalukya and Kakatiya periods trade was conducted by well organised merchant guilds. The epigraphic sources reveal that several kinds of merchant guilds used to carry on the commercial operations in the kingdom. The temple building activity particularly in stone gained momentum as a sequel to the economic prosperity. The merchant guilds like Ayyavolu guild, Nakaramu, Komatis or Vaisyas supported the temple building activity and made gifts to them. The Polas inscription[66] dated A.D. 1108 records that the Virabalanja community (The brave merchants) consisting of Ayyavali-five-hundred swamis, Mummuridandas and Ubhayananadesis (Itinerant merchants) made some gifts to the god Pulastyesvara of that place.

The *komatis* or the Vaisyas as the trading class were a flourishing community, whose benefactions to temples and other religious and charitable foundations often figure in the inscriptions. The Vaisyas (merchant class) of Sanigaram village in Karimnagar district made certain gifts to the Jain temple of Parsva Jinesvara at Govindapuram, which was then included in the principality of Polavasa Chiefs.[67] The epigraph of Govindapuram is dated A.D. 1122 and now the village is in Warangal district. It can be deduced from the above epigraph that there were close trade ties between Sanigaram and Govindapuram. It is interesting to note that Sanigaram was also a Jain centre in those days. The horse dealers made a gift of one pair of clothes per each horse to the same god. The same epigraph records that Toppa-Sresthin, a Vaisya (merchant) is said to have constructed a big tank at Govindapuram which is called even today as *Komaticheruvu* or the tank of the Vaisyas.

Although the trade guilds consisted of the members of various castes, the Vaisya community dominated the trade in medieval India. A Vasya, is also termed as *Komati,* a term derived from Jain god Gomatesvara as some of these people followed Jainism in their religious persuastion.[68] These *Komatis* are otherwise called *settis* or setthis (Sreshthins) and chettis. The importance of a Komati in the economic life of the medieval Deccan is attested by the twelfth century Telugu work *Sumati-Sataka* supposed to be of Baddena, the author of *Nitisastra-Muktavali.* He says that Komati was the life of a town like the trunk to an elephant and water to the paddy crop. Even today in remote villages the small scale Komati meets all the daily requirements of the people. In short he was the main agency through which the economy of the country was distributed in its nook and corner.

The Sreshthins or Setthis appear to have been very popular and powerful as seen from the Vemulavada inscription which mentions about the nine merchants, Chandra Sreshthin and others as witnesses when the King Arikesari II made grants of lands to the four local temples.[69] The names of setthis also figure in the epigraphs as the patrons and donors of the temples. The Nagunuru[70] inscription dated A.D. 1228 on a stone lying near the images in front of the Sakti temple outside the village records that Nijaramgala Malli-Setti and his son Venni-Setti established temples of Siva and made gifts to them. Another inscription at Chittapur[71] records that certain Bairisetti of the Virabalanja community installed temples to Siva and made gifts of lands and tolls levied on the articles sold in Peddapariyala village.

The trade guilds or the individual merchants had to purchase trade licence for conducting the business in a particular *adda* or *Samta* or fair. The numerous records which register gifts to the temples bear testimony to this fact. The Chittapur inscription of the reign of Prataparudradeva records that certain Bairisetti excavated a tank and donated 1/3 of the yield from the irrigated land to the temple, the remaining 2/3 being left over to the King. It seems that the merchant purchased the trade licence from the King or state and the cost of which he paid by digging the tank. Besides obtaining trade licence, he could donate 1/3 yield to god and acquire religious merit. The transaction reveals the business-cum-religious motive and merit of merchant.[72]

Important Routes of the Region:

There were no regular roads and means of communication in this region. Traffic was through cultivated fields in the beginning. Several parts of this region were impracticable for wheeled traffic, the roads being mere tracks. Travenier, the French Jewel merchant, who travelled in India during 1641-1648, was of the opinion that the roads in South India were not so good as the Mughal roads in the north. However, he felt that travelling in India was more commodious than in France or Italy. In those days it took forty days to journey from Surat to Golconda. The traveller did not use horses or asses but either rode on an ox or was carried in a coach or Palanquin.[73] Travellers who could afford might go in a Palanquin mostly carried by six men, three at each end. The bearers of Palanquin ran so swiftly that travelling in the peninsula was more easy and rapid than in any other part of India.[74] Little coaches drawn by two oxen generally carrying not more than two persons were used by the rich and the poor had to travel only on foot from one place to the other. Bullock carts and pack animals were the chief means of conveyance through mere tracks and this system continued in Karimnagar district like other parts of Tilingana till the first quarter of the twentieth century, when Nawab Mir Osman Ali Khan, the Nizam VII started laying down the Kaccha Morrum roads or rough mud roads connecting the district headquarters with the capital Hyderabad.

From the above facts it can be inferred that the transportation of merchandise during the early medieval period was very difficult and more particularly in the rainy season. However, there was hardly any vilage which was not connected by a cart-track. These cart-tracks, which are slightly better than the foot-tracks, are still extant in the rural areas besides the recently laid down Zilla Parishad and Panchayat Samithi roads.

The important trade centres of the Karimnagar region during the early medieval period were Vemulavada, Polavasa, Nagunuru, Mantrakuta, Dharmapuri, Kotilingala, Kalesvaram, Koravattu (Koratla), Chittapur, Godisala and Sanigaram. The famous Ayyavali merchant guilds used to transport their trade goods on asses, horses, oxen and carts along certain routes which were also used by military personal known as *Dandu-bata* or military route. Hired means of transport was comon for the transportation of merchandice in olden days as at present. Individual merchants and guilds might have also maintained their own carts, oxen, horses and the like to a certain limit but that was not always adequate to meet the needs of their trade. In all the market centres, therefore, there used to be some people who maintained carts, oxen, horses, asses and the like for hire and made their livelihood like the lorry owners of the present day. The oxen of the Kampus or Kapus, who owned them for hiring purpose, were called *Perika-edlu.* The tax on *perika-edlu* or pack-oxen laden with sacks containing articles of trade, was called *perika-edla-Sumkamu.* Tolls were collected not only on the sale of all goods but also on the possession of many other commodities such as carriages (bandi), slaves (banisa) and horses (gurramu).[75] It seems that the oxen used to carry free of hire all the commodities required for the temple. As these perika-varutransported the temple goods freely, they were exempted from Sumka like the professional tax and property tax. Both the temple and perika-varu were the beneficiaries and such was the role played by the temples in the medieval ages.

Vemulavada, the capital of the Chalukyas of Vemulavada was a big trade centre having trade ties with Podana (Bodhan), Nagaruru (Nagunuru), Polavasa (Polas), Mantrakuta (Manthani), Sanagara (Sanigaram), Orugallu (Warangal), Kollipake (Kolanupaka) and Pottalakere (Patancheru).

Polavasa, the capital of Medaraja, Nagaruru the capital of Dommaraja, Mantrakuta the capital of Gundaraja were also important trade centres. The Virabalanja merchant community and Ayyavali merchant guilds figure in the temple epigraphs[76] of Polavasa and Chittapur.

Dharmapuri, a holy place from ancient times, might have been a trade centre on the banks of Godavari, where, besides ordinary ferry, transportation of commercial goods also continued on the river. Wherever the boats used to load or unload the merchandise, the owners had to pay *revu-Sunkamu* (levy on ferry) which was usually collected during the Kakatiya period. Perhaps the small leather boats locally known in Telugu as *puttis* might have been in use for transportation of men and material throughout the year except the rainy season in Ashada, Shravana and Bhadrapada maonths. The same mode of transportation is still continuing for crossing the Godavari in the rural areas where there are no bridges over the river.

Keeping in view the above trade centres, the following ancient routes can be drawn connecting the capital cities and pilgrim centres of this region taking into consideration the nearest possible cart-tracks which existed till the formation of the recent roads.

1. Vemulavada - Rudrangi - Koravattu (Koratla) - Chittapur - Mallapur - Valgonda.
2. Vemulavada - Potuganti (Pothgal) - Siddipet - Duddeda - Cherial - Kollipake (Kolanupaka).
3. Vemulavada - Nampalli - Elgandal - Nagunuru - Choppadandi - Kotilingala.
4. Polavasa (Polas) - Mallannapeta - Chilvakoduru - Ambaripeta - Nandi - Mydaram - Peddapalli - Mantrakuta - Kalesvaram.
5. Polavasa - Rajaram - Cheppyala - Nallagonda - Vemulavada.
6. Polavasa - Mothey - Bathikapalli - Pegadapalli - Gundi - Gumlapur - Choppadandi.
7. Polavasa - Rajaram - Kurkiyala - Kothapalli - Vannaram - Nagunuru.
8. Sanigaram - Koheda - Husnabad - Elkaturthi - Hanumakonda - Warangar.
9. Polavasa - Rajaram - Cheppyala - Nallagonda - Vemulavada - Potuganti (Pothgal) - Dubbaka - Miridoddi - Alwal - Golconda - Pottalakere (Patancheru).
10. Polavasa - Rajaram - Gangadhara - Kothapalli - Manakonduru - Huzurabad - Elkaturthi - Anumakonda - Orugallu (Warangal).
11. Vemulavada - Boinapalli - Garisekurthi - Velisala - Kothapalli - Nagunuru.
12. Polavasa - Koravattu (Koratla) - Armuru - Induru (Nizamabad) - Podana (Bodhan).

All the above places had trade routes of cart-track and the merchandise was transported mainly by carts drawn by oxen.

Coins:

The temple epigraphs throw some light on the coinage of the Chalykyas and Kakatiyas. The coins by name *drammas* were in circulation during the reign of the Chalukyas of Vemulavada and the Western Chalukyas of Kalyani. The Vemulavada inscription[77] of Arikesari II records that the *Siddhaya* of the gifted lands by the King was fixed as twelve *drammas*. The Choppadandi epigraph of Ahavamalladeva dated A D. 992 and the Vemulavada epigaraph of Jayasimhadeva dated A.D. 1033 also make a mention of the *drammas*.[78] One Kanheri Rashtrakuta inscription refers to a golden *dramma* and distinguishes it from ordinary *drammas* which were probably silver pieces.[79] It is difficult to know whether the *drammas* mentioned in the epigraphs of Karimnagar district were of gold or silver. However the exact value of a *dramma* is difficult to be fixed.

The titles of Gaja-Kesari are attributed to the Kakatiya rulers. The Raya-Gaja-Kesari motif represents Rudramadevi and Daya-Gaja-Kesari motif represents Prataparudradeva. The coins which bear the image of Varaha and the legend either Raya-Gaja-Kesari or Daya-Gaja-Kesari can be safely ascribed to the Kakatiya rulers.[80] The hoard recently found at Suddala, near Sircilla in Karimnagar district contains 52 coins and out of which 51 bearing legend Daya-Gaja-Kesari can be surely ,and safely ascribed to Kakti Prataparudradeva.[81] The crest of the Kakatiya dynasty was a boar or varaha. The Kakatiyas were, however, devotees of Siva and there is, therefore, nothing improbable in the theory that they adopted the Bull (Nandi) as the main motif on their coinage.[82] Daya-Gaja-Kesari coin contains boar, bull, sword, sun, moon and an inscription in oiTelugu script as *Daya-Gaja-Kesari*.

It is found from the Kakatiya inscriptions that Kesari-gadyana, Kesari-mada and Nishka are synonymous names of a single denomination of ten rukas.[83] A ruka is similar to the present one rupee. *Adduga* is half-ruka and *Padika* is one-fourth of a ruka. Paraka is one-eighth of a ruka and one *Visamu* is 1/16 of a ruka similar to that of an *anna* which was in use till recent days before the introduction of the present metric system. The standard coin is *ruka*. Visa, Paraka, Padika and Adduga are denoted by the following symbols in the temple inscriptions.

Symbol

One visa or Visamu	One horizontal stroke
One Paraka or Byada	Two horizontal strokes
One Padika or chukka or Pavula	One vertical stroke
One adduga or ardha	Two vertical strokes.

The following table gives the relative values of a ruka.

1. Visa	=	1/2	paraka	1/16 Ruka
2. Visas	=	1	paraka	1/8 Ruka
2. Parakas	=	1	Padia or chukka	1/4 Ruka
2. Padikas	=	1	Adduga or Ardha	1/2 Ruka
2 Addugas	=	1	Ruka	
10 Rukas	=	1	Mada or Gadyana or Nishka	

The coin *Mada* is mentioned in the Chittapur epigraph.[84] The denomination lower than the visa coin is yet to be known. Other terms like *Dabbu, Kasu, Kani* are also of inconsistent values in various regions and times. Therefore, any conclusion in assessing the exact value of these coins may not be better than a conjecture.[85]

Measures:

The standards of Kakatiya measures and weights were named with prefix *Kesari* like Kesari-putti, Kesari-tumu, Kesari-Manika, Kesari-Kunchamu etc. The Kesari measurements were first introduced by the Kakatiyas in the Telugu country. Formerly there were Gandhahasti-Madas, Birudu-Gadyas, Tribhuvanankusa-Manikas during the periods of Western Chalukyas, Velanti Chodas and Eastern Chalukyas respectively. Kesari measures, weights and coins were decidedly of the Kakatiya origin.[86] For the purpose of land measures rods of standardised lengths called *Ghadas* were used. A study of the Kakatiya inscriptions reveals that there were regional variations in the standard length of the pole in different parts of the Kakatiya empire. The land was surveyed by means of a bamboo pole (gada or damdaka or Kola) usually of thirty two *Jenas* in length.[87] Two *Jenas* are equivalent to one *mura* or cubit. For instance poles of eight and twenty four cubits in length for measuring house-sites and fields respectively are referred to in an inscription at Penumali in Guntur district.[88] A line of standard *mura* is a cubit and two *muras* make one yard.

It was customary that the wet land should be measured in *Martur* or *Mattar*, and its sub-divisions, while dry land was reckoned in *Khanduva*, *Khanduka* or *Putti* and its component parts. It is clear that the former comprised a comparatively smaller area than the latter. The measures of lands gifted to the temples are recorded in *marturs* or *mattars* in the epigraphs of the Chalukyas of Vemulavada, Western Chalukyas of Kalyani and Kakatiyas.[89] The stone inscription[90] of Arikesari II dated A.D. 946 now lying in Karimnagar museum records that the King made a gift of fifty *mattars* of wet land to a Brahmana named Dharapayya. Another inscription[91] of the same ruler at Vemulavada states the measures of land in *nivartanas*. Arikesari II made a gift of hundred nivartanas bhu-Kshetra (dry land) and eight nivartanas of Paniya Kshetra (wet land) to the local temples. It is interesting to notice that both dry land and wet land are in measures of *nivartanas*. It is clear from the epigraphs that the land was measured in *nivartanas* and *marturs* or *mattars* but we have no knowledge of their exact value.

With regard to the volumetric measures of the Kakatiya period, *Gidda* was the lowest denomination and *putti* the highest. The following table gives the relative values of these measures.[92]

4 Giddas	=	1 Sola
2 Solas	=	1 Tavva
2 Tavvas	=	1 Manika
2 Manikas	=	1 Adda
2 Addas	=	1 Kuncha
2 Kunchas	=	1 Irsa
2 Irsas	=	1 Tumu (denoted by letter Na)
2 Tumus	=	1 Iddumu (equivalent to one Tumupalla)
2 Iddumus	=	1 Nalthumu
5 Tumus	=	1 Eddumu
10 Tumus	=	1 Pandumu
20 Tumus	=	1 Putti (denoted by letter Kha)

All the above terms occur in the inscriptions. *Tumus* and *puttis* are the basic measures, whereas the remaining units are their fractions or multiples. The measures such as Soledu (1 Sola) Manedu (1 Manika), and Tumedu (1 Tumu) figure in the Chittapur epigraph[93] of the reign of Kakati Prataparudradeva. The Hasanabad epigraph[94] of the Kakatiyas records four *puttis* of paddy and the Mallannapet epigraph[95] of the Velama chiefs mentions twelve *Kunchas* of paddy gifted to the local temples.

Most of the above measures are still in vogue in the rural areas of Karimnagar district even after the introduction of the present metric system. But some variations are found locally in these volumetric measures. On enquiry, the following measures are noticed, which are still in vogue in the Metapalli and Koratla areas.

2 Pavedulu	=	1 Arasola
2 Arasolas	=	1 Chittedu
2 Chittedulu	=	1 Attedu
2 Attedulu	=	1 Tavva
2 Tavvas	=	1 Manika
2 Manikas	=	1 Kuncha
8 Kunchas (or 16 Manikas)	=	1 Tumu
20 Tumus	=	1 Putti

The measure *Manika* of Jagtial area differs from that of Metpalli area. Four solas form one *Manika* at Jagtial whereas five solas form one *Manika* at Metpalli. Five Solas of Jagtial are equivalent to four Attedulu of Metpalli. Thus there are variations in measures from place to place.

Weights:

The inscriptions mention the gravimetric units like *tula, pala,* and *visa*. For weighing fold and precious stones *Guriginja* a seed is the lowest unit. The following table gives the relative values of these weights.[96]

4 Guriginjas	=	1 Sinna or Chinna
30 Sinnas	=	1 Tula

3 Tulas	=	1 Pala
40 Palas	=	1 Visa (or Takkedu)
2 Visas	=	1 Ettu
8 Visas or 4 Ettus	=	1 Manugu (or Tumu)
20 Manugus	=	1 Putti (or Khanduka)

The above units were in vogue in the Telugu country before the present metric system was introduced.

Thus the temple, though deemed to be a place of religious worship, gave new dimensions to the social, cultural and economic life of the people.

REFERENCES

1. D.N. Jha, *Studies in Early Indian Economic History*, p.74.
2. *Ibid.*, p.76.
3. Noboru Karashima, *South Indian History and Society*, p.159.
4. Romila Nilakanta Sastri, *Op.Cit.*, p.41.
5. K.A. Nilakanta Sastri, *Op.Cit.*, p.324.
6. *Ibid.*, p.325.
7. Ram Saran Sharma, *Light on Early Indian Society and Economy*, p.123.
8. *Ibid.*, p.144.
9. *EA.*, Vol.II, pp.36-38.
10. *Ibid.* Vol.IV. pp.67-89.
11. *Ibid.*, pp.81-84.
12. *Ibid.*, pp.84-89.
13. *SII.* Vol.X, p.422.
14. Alladi Vaidehi Krishnamurthy, "Temple Endowments in Medieval Andhra", *JAHRS*, Vol.XXVI, p.163.
15. *Corpus*, Part I, p.26.
16. *IAPKD.* No.38, pp.106-111.
17. *Telangana Sasanamulu* (Telugu), Vol.I, No.21, pp.173-177.
18. *Ibid.*, No.13, p.116.
19. *EHD.* p.710
20. *IAPKD.* No.30, pp.88-93.
21. *Ibid.*, No.7, pp.19-21.
22. *Ibid.* No.20, pp.52-54.
23. *Ibid.* No. 30, pp.88-93.
24. K.A. Nilakanta Sastri, *Op.Cit.*, p.328.
25. *Ibid.*, p.329.
26. D.N. Jha, *Op.Cit.*, pp.82-85.
27. T.V. Sairam, *Op.Cit.*, p.31.
28. N. Vemlataramanayya, *Chalukya of Vemulavada*.pp.43 & 84.
29. P.V. Parabrahma Sastry, *The Kakatiyas of Warangal*, pp.284-286.
30. *Ibid.*, p.287.
31. D.N. Jha, *Op.Cit.*, pp. 76 & 77.
32. Ram Saran Sharma, *Op.Cit.*, p.120.

33. *Ibid.*, p.123.
34. Romila Thapar, *Op.Cit.*, p.41.
35. *IAPWD*. No.63.
36. *EHD*. p.684.
37. *Nellore District Inscriptions*, p.340.
38. *IAPKD*. No.30, pp.88-93.
39. *IAPWD*. No.63.
40. *SII*. Vol.X, p.314.
41. *EA*. Vol.II, pp.21-30.
42. *IAPKD*. No.8, pp.21-24.
43. *Ibid.*, No.28, pp.75-80.
44. *Ibid.* No.25, pp.64-71.
45. *Ibid.* Nos. 29, 30, 38.
46. *Ibid.* No.25, pp.64-71.
47. *EHD*. pp.681, 682.
48. *JAHRS*.Vol.XXXV, pp. 183-188.
49. *IAPKD*. Nos. 2, 5, 9, 24, 30, 39.
50. *Ibid.* No.30, pp.88-93.
51. *Ibid.*, No.1. pp.1-5.
52. *Ibid.*, No.2, pp.5-10.
53. *Ibid.*, Nos. 10, 13.
54. *EHD*. p.684.
55. P.V. Parabrahma Sastry, *Op.Cit.*, pp.214-220.
56. *IAPKD*. No.37.
57. Noboru Karashima, *Op.Cit.*, p.162.
58. P.V. Parabrahma Sastry, *Op.Cit.*, pp.220, 221.
59. *IAPKD*. No.36, pp.103, 104.
60. *Ibid.* No.38, pp.106-111.
61. M. Somasekhara Sarma (ed), *Op.Cit.*, No.38, p.84.
62. *EA*. Vol.IV, pp.93-102.
63. *IAPWD*. No.37.
64. *EHD*. p.685.
65. Romila Thapar, *Op.Cit.*, p.42.
66. *IAPKD*. No.75. pp.139-141.
67. *JAHRS*. Vol.XXXVI, Part I, pp. 33-47.
68. P.B. Desai, *Jainism in South India*, pp.13, 14.
69. N. Venkataramanayya, *Op.Cit.*, p.84.
70. *Corpus*. Part III, p.2.
71. *IAPKD*. No.38, pp.106-111.
72. P.V. Parabrahma Sastry, *Op.Cit.*, p.245.
73. Y. Vittal Rao, "Socio-Economic Conditions in Andhra till 1858", *JAHRS*. Vol.XXXVI, p.64.
74. *Ibid.*
75. *EHD*. pp.685, 686.
76. *IAPKD*. Nos. 75, 38.
77. *Ibid.* No2, pp.5-10.
78. *Ibid.* Nos. 8, 13.
79. *EHD*. p.802.
80. P.V. Parabrahma Sastry, *Kakatiya Coins and Measures*, p.9.
81. *Ibid.*, p.10.
82. *EHD*. p.806.
83. P.V. Parabrahma Sastry, *Op.Cit.*, p.11.
84. *IAPKD*. No.38, pp.106-111.

85. P.V. Parabrahma Sastry, *Op.Cit.*, p.14.
86. *Ibid.*, p.18.
87. *EHD*. P.683.
88. *Ibid.*
89. *IAPKD*. Nos. 1, 5, 7, 9, 15, 38.
90. *Ibid.* No.1, pp. 1-5.
91. *Ibid.* No.2, pp.5-10.
92. P.V. Parabrahma Sastry, *Op.Cit.*, p.19.
93. *IAPKD*. No. 38, pp.106-111.
94. *Ibid.* No.36, pp.103, 104.
95. *Ibid.* No.53. pp.125, 126.
96. P.V. Parabrahma Sastry, *The Kakatiyas of Warangal*, p.269.

BIBLIOGRAPHY

Altekar A.S.: *The Rashtrakutas and Their Times,* Poona, 1954.

Anand, Mulk Raj: *Hindu View of Art,* Asia Publishing House, Bombay,1957.

— : *Ajanta,* Marg Publications, Bombay, 1971.

Anne-Marie Gaston : *Siva in Dance, Myth and Iconography,* Oxford University Press, Delhi,1982.

Asha Kalia : *Art of Osian Temples,* Abhinav Publications, New Delhi, 1982.

Avadhani,V.V.S. : *Guide Book to Victoria Jubilee Museum, Vijayawada,* Hyderabad, 1976.

Bawa, V.K. (ed) : *Aspects of Deccan History,* Institute of Asian Studies, Hyderabad, 1975.

Benjamin, Rowland : *The Art and Architecture of India,* Penguin Books, Baltimore, USA, 1971.

Bhattacharya, B.C.: *The Jaina Iconography,* Motilal Banarsidas, Delhi, 1947

Bhattacharya, H.D. : 'Religion and Philosophy', *The History and Culture of Indian People'*Chapter XI, Bharatiya Vidya Bhavan, Vol,IV, Bombay.

Brown, Percy : *Indian Architecture* (Fifth edition), Bombay, 1965.

Casale, A. : *A Cultural History of India,* The Macmillan Company of India, Madras, 1973.

Charles, Fabri : *Discovering Indian Sculpture,* New Delhi,1970.

— : *A History of Indian Dress,* Orient Longmans, 1961.

Cousens Henry : *The Chalukyan Architecture,* Archaeological Survey of India, 1926.

Danielou, Alain : *Hindu Polytheism,* London, 1964.

Dasgupta, S.N. : *Fundamentals of Indian Art*, India, New Delhi, 1978.

Debala Mitra : *Sanchi*, Archaeological Survey of India, New Delhi, 1978.

— : *Panderthan, Avantipur and Martand*, Archaeological Survey of India, New Delhi, 1977.

— : *Konark*, Archaeological Survey of India, New Delhi, 1976.

— :*Udayagiri and Khandagiri*, Archaeological Survey of India, New Delhi, 1975.

— : *Ajanta*, Archaeological Survey of India, New Delhi, 1980.

Desai, P.B. :*Select Stone Inscriptions of Andhra Pradesh*, Hyderabad, 1962.

—: *Jainism in South India*, Sholapur, 1957.

Devasthali, G.V. : 'Sanskrit Literature', *The History and Culture of Indian People*, Chapter IX, Bharatiya Vidya Bhavan, Vol.IV, Bombay.

Dipakranjan Das : *Temples of Orissa*, Agamkala Prakashan, Delhi, 1982.

Dubreuil, G. Jouveau : *Iconography of Southern India*, Bharatiya Publishing House, Varanasi, 1978.

— : *Dravadian Architecture*, Madras, 1917.

Fergusson James : *History of Indian and Eastern Architecture*(Second Indian edition) New Delhi, 1972.

Francesco Abbate (ed) : *Indian Art and the Art of Ceylon, Central and South East Asia*, Peerage Books, London, 1972.

Ganguli, D.C. : 'Later Chalukyas and Kalachuris of Kalyana', *The History and Culture of Indian People*, Chapter VI, Bharatiya Vidya Bhavan, Vol. IV, Bombay.

Gopala Krishna Murthy, S. :*Jain Vestiges in Andhra*, Hyderabad, 1963.

— : *The Sculpture of the Kakatiyas*, Hyderabad, 1964.

— : *The Art of Lepakshi*, Hyderabad 1970.

Gopinatha Rao, T.A. : *Elements of Hindu Iconography*, Vol.I (Parts I & II), Vol.II (Parts I &II), Indological Book House, Varanasi, 1971.

Goverdhan Singh, Mian: *Art and Architecture of Himachal Pradesh*, B.R. Publishing Corporation, Delhi, 1983.

Gupte, R.S. : *Iconography of Hindus, Buddhists, and Jains*, Bombay 1972.

— : *The Art and Architecture of Aihole*, Bombay, 1967.

Havell, E.B. : *Indian Architecture through Ages,* Asian Publication Services, New Delhi, 1972.

— : *Indian Sculpture and Painting,* Cosmo Publication, New Delhi, 1980.

— : *A Hand Book of Indian Art,* Indic Academy, Varanasi, 1972.

— : *The Ancient and Medieval Architecture of India*(Reprint), New Delhi, 1972.

Hingorani ,R.P. (ed) : *Digambara Jaina Iconography,* Ashutosh Prakashan Sansthan, Varanasi, 1979.

Iswara Dutt, Kunduri : *Prachinandhra Charitraka Bhugolamu,* Andhra Pradesh Sahitya Akademy, Hyderabad, 1963 (Telugu)

Iswari Prasad : *History of Medieval India,* Allahabad, 1950.

Jha, D.N. : *Studies in Early Indian Economic History,* Delhi, 1980.

Jitendranath, Banerjea : *The Development of Hindu Iconography,* Delhi, 1974.

Joanna Gottfried Williams : *The Art of Gupta India,* Delhi, 1983.

Karashima,Noboru : *South Indian History and Society,* Oxford University Press, Delhi, 1984.

Kramrisch, Stella : *The Hindu Temple,* two volumes University of Calcutta, 1946.

— : *The Art of India* (Third edition), The Phaidon Press, London, 1965.

Krishnadeva and Nayal, B.S. : *Guide to Khajuraho Museum,* Archaeological Survey of India, New Delhi,1980.

Krishna Sastry, V.V. : *The Proto and Early Historical Cultures of Andhra Pradesh,* Hyderabad, 1983.

— : 'Terracottas from Peddabankur and Dhulikatta', *The Andhra Pradesh Journal of Archaeology,* Vol.I, Hyderabad, 1979.

— (ed) : *Annual Report of the Department of Archaeolcgy, 1976-1977,* Hyderabad, 1978.

—(ed) : *Annual Report of the Department of Archaeology and Museums, 1977-1978,*

Lakshimiranjanam, K. : *Spot Lights on Telugu,* Hyderabad, 1968.

Majumdar, R.C. : 'Rise and Fall of the Pratihara Empire', *The History and Culture of Indian People,* Chapter II, Bharatiya Vidya Bhavan, Vol.V, Bombay.

'Saivism',*The History and Culture of Indian People*, chapter XVI, Bharatiya Vidya Bhawan, Vol. V. Bombay.

Mallaya, N.V. :*Studies in Sanskrit Texts on Temple Architecture,* Annamalai University, 1949.

Munn, L. (ed) : *Annual Report of the Archaeological Department of H.E.H.the Nizam's Dominions,* Hyderabad,1925-1926.

Nigam, M.L. : *Sculptural Art of Andhra,* Sundeep Prakashan, Delhi,1980.

Nilakanta Sastri, K.A. : *A History of South India,* Oxford University Press, Delhi, 1966.

Nilakanta Sastri, K.A. and Sreenivasachary, G : *Advanced History of India*(Reprint), 1982.

Parabrahma Sastry P.V. :*The Kakatiyas of Warangal,* Hyderabad, 1978.

— : *Kakatiya Coins and Measures,* Hyderabad, 1975.

— : *Siddodvaha of Narasimha,* Hyderabad, 1968.

— : *Kakatiya Charitra,*Hyderabad, 1977 (Telugu)

— : *Kakatiya Sasana Sahityamu,* Andhra Saraswatha Parishad, Hyderabad, 1981 (Telugu).

— : 'Sanigaram Epigrahs of the Early Kakatiyas',*Epigraphia Andhrica,* Vol.IV, Hyderabad, 1975.

— (ed) : *Inscriptions of Andhra Pradesh - Karimnagar District,* Hyderabad, 1974.

— (ed) : *Select Epigraphs of Andhra Pradesh,* Hyderabad, 1965.

— (ed) : *Annual Report on Epigraphy, 1967,* Hyderabad, 1975.

— (ed) : *A Catalogue of Inscriptions Copied Upto 1964,*Hyderabad, 1965.

Parameshwarilal Gupta : *Punch-Marked Coins in the Andhra Pradesh Government Museum,* Hyderabad, 1960.

Paul, G. Hiebert : 'A Brief History of Patancheru or Pottalakere', *The Journal of Andhra Historical Research Society,* vol.XXXVI (2-4 parts), Hyderabad, 1975-1976.

Phanindranath Bose : *Principles of Indian Silpasastra,*Bharatiya Publishing House, Delhi,1972.

Radhakrishna Sarma, M : *Temples of Tilingana,* Hyderabad,1972.

Radhakamal Mukerjee : *The Cosmic Art of India,* Allied Publishers, Bombay, 1965.

Rajaram Singh Thakur : 'Prehistoric and Early Historic Sites in Karimnagar Region, Andhra Pradesh', *Journal of Archaeology in Andhra Pradesh,* Hyderabad

Rajendra Prasad, B. : *Art of South India, Andhra Pradesh,* Sundeep Prakashan, Delhi,1980.

— : *Temple Sculpture of Andhra Pradesh,* Hyderabad, 1978.

Raj Reddy, D and Suryanarayana Reddy,P : *Uninscribed Coins of Andhra,* The Numismatic Society of Hyderabad, 1984.

Ramachandra Murthy N.S. : 'Art and Architecture of Karimnagar District', *Proceedings of Andhra Pradesh History Congress*, Sec.II, Warangal, 1983.

Ramachandra Murthy, S.S. : *A Study of Telugu Place-Names,* Delhi, 1985.

Ramakantham, S. : *Guide Book to Kolanupaka Site Museum,* Hyderabad, 1976.

— : *State Museum, Hyderabad,* Hyderabad, 1976.

Ramakrishna Sarma, G : *Tilangana Sasanamulu,* Vol.II, The Lakshmanaraya Parishodhaka Mandali, Hyderabad, 1960 (Telugu)

Rama Rao, M. : *Eastern Chalukyan Temples of Andhra Desa,* Hyderabad, 1964.

— : *Andhra Through Ages,* Guntur, 1958.

— : *Select Andhra Temples,* Hyderabad, 1970.

— : *Early Chalukyan Temples of Andhra Desa,* Hyderabad, 1965.

— : *Satavahana Coins in Andhra Pradesh Government Museum,* Hyderabad,1961.

Rama Swami, N.S. : *Monograph on Temples of Mukhalingam,* Hyderabad, 1976.

— : *Temples of Tadpatri,* Hyderabad, 1976.

Ramesan, N (ed) : *Copper Plate Inscriptions of Andhra Pradesh Government Museum,* Vol.I,Hyderabad, 1962.

Ram Raz : *Essay on the Architecture of the Hindus,* Indological Book House, Varanasi, 1972.

Ram Saran Sharma : *Light on Early Indian Society and Economy,* Bombay, 1966.

Rea Alexr : *Chalukyan Architecture,* Indological Book House Delhi,1970.

Romila Thapar : *The Past and Prejudice,* National Book Trust India, Delhi, 1975.

Roy C. Craven : *A Concise History of Indian Art,* New York, 1976.

Sachindra Kumar Maity :*The Imperial Guptas and Their Times,* Munshiram Manoharlal Publishers, New Delhi, 1975.

Sadasiva Sastry, K. : *Dharmapuri Kshetra Mahatmyamu,* Dharmapuri, 1957 (Telugu)

Sairam, T.V. : *Indian Temple, Forms and Foundations,* Agamakala Prakashan, Delhi, 1982.

Sankar Prasad Ghosh :*Hindu Religious Art and Architecture,* D.K.Publications, Delhi,1982.

Sarkar,H. : *Monuments of Kerala,* Archaeological Survey of India, New Delhi, 1973.

Sarkar, H. and Mitra, B.N. : *Nagarjunakonda,* Archaeological Survey of India, New Delhi, 1966.

Sarkar, H. and Nainar,S.P. : *Amaravati,* Archaeological Survey of India, New Delhi,1980.

Sharma, R.S. : *Survey of Research in Economic and Social History of India,* Indian Council of Social Science Research, Delhi, 1986.

Sharma, T.R. : *Personal and Geographical Names in the Gupta Inscriptions,* Delhi,1978.

Sherwani, H.K. : *History of the Qutub Shahi Dynasty,* Delhi, 1974.

— : *Mohammad Quli Qutub Shah,* Asia Publishing House, New Delhi, 1967.

Shyam Sundara Sastry (ed) : *Trisati* (Financed by Government of A.P.), Dharmapuri, 1979 (Telugu)

Sinha, S.K.: *Medieval History of the Deccan,* Vol.I, Hyderabad, 1964.

Sircar, D.C. : 'The Eastern Chalukyas', *The History and Culture of Indian People,* Chapter VI, Bharatiya Vidya Bhavan, Vol.IV, Bombay.

Sivaramamurti, C. :*Early Andhra Art and Iconography,* Hyderabad, 1979.

— : *An Album of Indian Sculpture,* National Book Trust India. New Delhi, 1975.

— : *Indian Sculpture,*Allied Publishers, New Delhi, 1961.

— : *The Chola Temples,*Archaeological Survey of India, New Delhi, 1978.

Somasekhara Sarma, Mallampalli : *Corpus of Telingana Inscriptions,* Part IV, Hyderabad, 1973.

— : *Andhra Samskriti Tarangini,* Hyderabad, 1976 (Telugu)

Soundara Rajan, K.V. : *Architecture of the Early Hindu Temples of Andhra Pradesh,* Hyderabad, 1965.

— : *Art of South India - Deccan,* Delhi, 1980.

— : *The Art of South India - Tamilnadu and Kerala,*Sundeep Prakashan, Delhi, 1978.

Sreenivasachar, P. (ed) : *The Archaeological Bulletin,* No.II, Hyderabad, 1963.

— (ed) : *A Corpus of Inscriptions in Tilingana Districts of H.e,H. Nizam's Dominions,*Part I, Hyderabad, 1942.

—)ed) : *A Corpus of Inscriptions in Telingana Districts of Andhra Pradesh,* Part III, Hyderabad, 1956.

Srinivasa Iyengar, K.R. : 'Kannada Literature', *The History and Culture of Indian People,* Chapter IX, Bharatiya Vidya Bhavan, Vol. IV, Bombay.

Subrahmanyam, R. : *Ashokuni Erragudi Sasanamulu,* Hyderabad, 1975 (Telugu).

Urmila, Agarwal : *Khajuraho Sculptures and Their Significance,* S.Chand & Co. Delhi, 1964.

Vaidehi Krishnamurthy, Alladi : 'Temple Endowmenets in Medieval Andhra', *The Journal of Andhra Historical Research Society,* Vol.XXVI, Hyderabad, 1960-61.

Valladharaya : *Kreedahiramamu* (Verses 127, 128), (Telugu)

Varma, G.R. : 'Surya-Vishnu Worship in Andhra', *The Journal of Andhra Historical Research Society,* Vol.XXIX, Parts 1 & 2, Hyderabad, 1963-1964.

Vedantam, T.V. (ed) : 'Town Study of Manthani', *Census of India, Andhra Pradesh, 1971.*

Venkataramanayya, N. : *Chalukyas of Vemulavada,* Hyderabad, 1953.

— : *Pallavulu-Chalukyulu,* Madras, 1969, (Telugu)

— (ed) : *Inscriptions of Andhra Pradesh, Warangal District,* Hyderabad,1974.

— (ed) : *Report on Epigraphy for 1965,* Hyderabad, 1968.

— (ed) : *Report on Epigraphy for 1966,* Hyderabad.

— (ed) : *Epigraphia Andhrica,* vol. I,

— : 'The Kurkiyala Inscription of Jinavallabha', *Epigraphia Andhrica,* Vol.II, pp.21-39, Hyderabad, 1974.

Venkat Krishna Rao, Bhavaraju : *History of Eastern Chalukyas of Vengi,* Andhra Pradesh Sahitya Akademy, Hyderabad, 1973.

Vidya Dehejia : *Early Stone Temples of Orissa,* Vikas Publishing House, New Delhi, 1979.

Vidhya Prakash : *Khajuraho,* Bombay, 1967.

Vittal Rao, Y. : 'Socio-Economic Conditions in Andhra Till 1858', *The Journal of Andhra Historical Research Society,* Vol.XXXVI. (2-4 parts), Hyderabad, 1975-1976.

Vincent Smith, A. :*The Oxford History of India,* (Fourth edition), New Delhi, 1986.

Waheed Khan, Md.Abdul : *Qutub Shahi Coins in Andhra Pradesh Museum* Hyderabad, 1961.

— : *An Early Sculpture of Narasimha,* Hyderabad, 1964.

— : *The Discovery of Mural Paintings of Kalyana Chalukyas at Aladurg,* Hyderabad, 1968.

Webester, C.B.John (ed) : *History and Contemporary India,* Asia Publishing House, Bombay, 1971.

Yazdani, G. (ed) : *The Early History of the Deccan,* Two Volumes, Oxford University Press, London, 1960.

Book on Epigraphy and Miscellaneous Publications

Andhra Pradesh Gazetteer, Karimnagar District, 1974.

Census Hand Book, Karimnagar District, 1961. (Chapters I & XII)

Census of India, Administrative Atlas Andhra Pradesh, 1971, (p.453).

Imperial gazetteer of India Volumes XIII, p.377. XIV, P.305, XV, p.399.

Epigraphia Andhrica Volumes, I,II,III & IV.

South Indian Inscriptions, VI & X.

Nellore District Inscriptions

Annual Report on Epigraphy, 1967., Hyderabad, 1975.

Tilingana Sasanamulu (Telugu), Lakshmanaraya Parishodhaka Mandali, Hyderabad, 1935.

Journals of Andhra Historical Research Society, Hyderabad, Vol.XXXII (parts I-IV), 1971-1972, Vol.XXXIV (Parts 1-4), 1974-1975, Vol.XXXV, 1975-1976, Vol.XXXVI (Part I), 1975-1976, VOl.XXXVI (parts 2-4), 1975-1976, and Vol.XXXVII, 1978.

Indian Art and Architecture in Ancient and Medieval Periods, Director of Publications, Delhi, 1981.

Proceedings of Indian History Congress, Annamalai University, 1984.

Guide to Ajanta-Ellora, Published by H.E.H. Nizam's Government, Hyderabad.

Karimnagara Mandala Charitra (Telugu), Sri Tyagaraja Lalitakala Parishad Publications, Karimnagar, 1981.

Raja Rajesvara Kshetra Mahatmyamu (Telugu), Vemulavada Devasthanamu Publication,1970.

Vemulavada Charitra (Telugu), by C. Chandra Mouli, Vemulavada.

Ramagiri Charitra (Telugu), by late Yarabati Babu Rao, Ramagiri Devasthanamu Publication, Ramagiri, 1982.

'Rajesvara shrine at Vemulavada', by P. Srinivasa Rao, in *The Hindu,* daily newspaper, Sunday, dated 24-1-1965.

'Dharmapuri Kshetra Mahatmyamu, by Rotte Visvanatha Sastry, *Andhra Prabha,* Telugu weekly, dated 19.6.1963.

'Roman Coins at Nagarappad, Khamman District', *Eenadu* Telugu daily, Wednesday dated 13.4.1983 (columns 2 & 3, p.2)

Articles by Thakur Rajaram Singh, on 'Prehistoric and Early historic Cultures in Karimnagar Region'.

Samgraha Andhra Vijnana Kosamu, Volumes II to VIII.

Andhra Desa Charitra Bhugola Sarvasvamu, Volumes I to III.

The History and Culture of Indian People, Volumes III to V, Bharatiya Vidya Bhavan,Bombay.

Glossary

Abhisheka	: Sacred anointing, Lavation
Acchu-Kattu Lands	: Lands brought under plough
Adhisthana	: Socle of a temple
Akshamala	: Rosary, a string of beads
Alamu-Sumkamu	: Tax on Vegetables
Amalaka	: Flattened cogged stone
Ankusa	: Goad
Antarala	: Vestibule
Ardhaya	: Half of the total produce as tax
Ari	: Property tax in coin
Astasrakumuda	: Eight sided moulding of the Adhisthana
Asura	: Demon
Avatara	: Incarnation
Aya	: Tax
Bamtela-ayamu	: Levy for the maintenance of Bamtus or Warriors
Bhitti	: Wall
Bhuvangama	: Sill, underneath part of door Jamb
Burra-Sumkamu	: Perhaps tax on pots used for measuring oils
Chakra	: Disc, Wheel
Chandrasila	: Moon stone in front of the door sill
Chitrakhanda	: A variety of pillar
Chitra-torana	: A variety of torana decorated with flowers, creepers etc.
Damaru	: Small drum held by deity
Darisanamu	: Tax to be paid on seeing the King

Deepa	: Lamp
Devakostha	: A niche on the wall
Deva-vrittis	: Temple lands
Dhupa	: Incense burning
Dvara	: Doorway
Dvarapala	: Door-keeper of Temple
Dvitala	: Two storeyed
Gada	: Mace, Club
Gadya	: Ten rukas
Gaja	: Elephant
Gala	: Neck
Ganuvu	: Oil-mill
Garbhagriha	: Sanctum
Ghata	: Vase
Gudhamandapa	: Closed hall in front of antarala
Hamsa	: Swan
Hara	: Garland, Necklace
Illari	: House Tax
Jagati	: The vertical moulding above the upana in the socle.
Jala	: Lattice
Jala Vatayana	: Lattice Window
Jatra	: Temple fair
Kadalikakarana	: Triangular slabs placed one above the other in two or three tiers cornerwise forming hollow in middle
Kakshasana	: Seats with back rest
Kalasa	: A vase shaped finial
Kalyana Mandapa	: A hall where ceremonial wedding takes place
Kamandulu	: Water vessel held by deity
Kampa	: Fillet
Kanika	: Tax payable towards the proprietorship of land by the King
Kapala	: Skull-cup
Kapota	: Over hanging eave cornice
Khadga	: Sword
Khatvanga	: Club with a human skull mounted on the handle
Kolagaru	: Officers of weights and measures

Kostha	: Niche
Kudyastambha	: Pilaster
Kumbha	: A flat and bulbous moulding in the pillar capital
Kumuda	: An important moulding of the socle. It may be either tripatta, three faceted or vritta, circular.
Kund or Kundamu	: Tank
Lalatabimba	: A small ritual carved tablet located in the centre or the lintel of the cella door.
Latapatra	: Creeper and foliage
Mada	: Ten rukas
Madiga-Sumkamu	: Tax on shop
Mahamandapa	: An open or closed hall in front of the vestibule
Makara	: Crocodile motif
Makara-torana	: A decorative motif with crocodile at either end supporting the garland
Mukuta	: Crown on head gear of image
Mandapa	: Hall
Matha	: Monastery
Meras	: Privileges
Mudra-Sumkamu	: Registration Tax
Mukhamandapa	: Pillared hall in front of vestibule
Naivedya	: Oblation, offering of food to the deity
Nakaramu	: Swadeshi merchant guilds
Natyamandapa	: Dancing hall
Niru-nela	: West land
Niru-vidi	: Tax for additional water supplied to the lands.
Nishka	: Ten rukas
Padma	: Lotus
Panchasakha	: Lotus
Panchasakha	: Five jambed as in a doorway
Pangamu	: A share of tax in produce from dry land.
Panga-tappu	: Levy in kind
Paniya-Kshetra	: Wet land
Pannu	: Tax
Para	: A share of tax in produce on wet land
Parasu	: Axe held by an image

Parivara-alayas	: Subsidiary shrines
Pasa	: Noose
Patta	: A band in the socle
Pemta	: Market
Phaladaru	: Tax assessor
Phalaka	: Abacus. A member of the pillar capital.
Pitha	: Base, socle
Potika	: Bracket for a pillar
Prabha-mandali	: halo or nimbus
Pradakshinapatha	: Circumambulatory path
Prakara	: Enclosure Wall
Pranala	: Provision made for discharge of abhisheka water.
Prastara	: Entablature
Prati	: The top most moulding of the socle
Pullari	: Tax on pastures
Pustaka	: Scripture held by an image
Puttu-peru-Sumkamu	: Tax on the occasion of naming the child.
Rangamandapa	: An open hall used for theatrical purposes.
Ratana	: Lifting water by pulley device
Revu-Sumkamu	: Tax on ferry
Sakha	: Jamb
Samabhanga	; Even posture of legs
Samaya	: Guild
Samta	: Weekly bazaar
Samudra-mathana	: The churning of the Ocean
Sandhara	: Temple with inner ambulatory
Sankha	: Conch
Siddhaya	: Tax both in cash and kind
Sikhara	: Superstructure, spire
Sopana	: Flight of steps
Stambha	: Pillar
Sthapati	: Architect
Stupi	: Finial of Vimana or Sikhara
Sukanasa	: An ante-fix which projects from the base of the spire and rises over the vestibule
Sula	: Lance
Sumkamu	: Toll, duty, tax
Sumkari	: Tax collector

Talari	: Watchman
Tambula-sarva	: Exchange of betel leaves
Tantrapala	: Minister of army
Teliki-vevuru	: Oilmen's association
Tirtha	: Place of pilgrimage
Tomta-bhumi	: Garden land
Torana	: An arch, A gateway
Trasu-Nyayagandru	: Those who collect tax on weighed articles
Tribhanga	: Body moulded in three curves
Trikuta	: Triple shrine
Trisakha	: Triple Jambed
Trisula	: Trident
Tamu-Nyayagandru	: Those who collect levy on measurable articles.
Udhaya-nanadesis	: Itinerant Merchants
Upana	: The lower most moulding of the socle
Upapitha	: The Sub-base
Vahana	: Vehicle or mount of deity
Vatayana	: Window
Vedi or Vedika	: A railing like moulding in between Kapota and bhitti
Veli-Volamu or Veli-Chenu, Bhumi	: Dry land
Vennu-Pannu	: Levy on crops when they are ready for harvest
Vina	: Lute, Lyre
Vratas	: Religious vows
Vyalamala	: A frieze of Leonine form.

Appendix 'A'

Nagunuru

(Karimnagar Taluk)

Unpublished Inscription on a broken stone near Ramalingalagudi

Undated

Kakatiya

Rudradeva or Rudramadevi.

This inscription records the gift of certain wet land near Brahmanagadda in the village Nagaruru towards the salaries of the garland makers to the god Ramanathadeva by Mahamandalesvara Kakati Rudradeva or Rudramadevi. The names of certain tanks are mentioned. This is an undated and incomplete inscription. It mentions the name of the village as Nagaruru, which is now known as Nagunuru.

Text of the Nagunuru Inscription

Svasti Srimanu maha
Mandalesvara Kakati
Vya Rudradeva maha
rajula dharmamu tadari

Ramanathuni puman (di)
Sese Malakarula Ji
talaku Nagarurina (ga) ra
mu Brahmana gadda Vritti
Vilichi itchina Polumu
Chintala Cherna rombache
la Ramesvani paddevari
de adda andamuda chera
gundali adda : anda aa
tota atithivamgu podu
gu___________________
Brahmala davi cherna ba

Appendix 'B'

Raikal

(Jagtial Taluk)

Unpublished Inscription on a broken stone near the Trikuta temple

S. 1227, Visvavasu, Sravana, Bahula 12, Vaddavara (A.D. 1305)

Kakatiya

Prataparudradeva

This Pillar inscription surmounted by Nandi is of the reign of Kakati Prataparudradeva noticed in the court-yard of the trikuta temple. It is carved on three sides in Telugu script, the Second side contains the symbol of lingam, while the third side contains the sun and crescent. This pillar inscription is found broken into two pieces. When these two broken pieces are properly placed one over the other, the matter can be read out except at the place, where the stone is broken.

It records that certain Rudradevani son of some Reddy (name is missing at the broken place) has made a gift of five marturs of land near Donula Kaluva and another five marturs of land near Budumulagatu, total ten marturs of land for angabhoga and rangabhoga, to the gods Ramanathadevara and Lakhumesvaradevara of village Ravikanti on Sravana Bahula, 12 dvadasi, Vaddavara, in Visvavasu year S. 1227 corresponding to A.D. 1305, when the Kind Prataparudradeva was ruling the country happily and peacefully. Komatis (Vaisyas) and ashtadasapraja are also mentioned. It is interesting to notice the name of the village as Ravikanti, which is now known as Raikal.

Text of the Raikal Inscription Text

Svasti Sri Sakavarushalu
1127 Svasti Sri
Manmaha Mandalesvara
Kakatiya Pratapa
Rudradeva maha
Rajulu Sukha Samga
Tavinodana prithvi
Rajyamu Cheyu
Chundaganu Visvavasu
Samvatsara Sravana
Bahula 12 vaddava
Rana Svasti Srimatu
.......toli
redi koduku Rudra
Devanigaru Ravikam
ti Ramantha de
Varaku

Lakhumesva
ra devaraku
Nu angabho
ganakunu
rangabhogana
kunu donula
Kaluva Ma.5
budimala
gatulo 5
Verisi padi
marturunu
daraposi svasti Srimatu
Bejagangule (Stone broken)

Kagarunu ra
Vikamti (Prolu)

(--------) Komatlaku
mani----ashtadasa (Prajalu)
ku-------laku
devaralu yaja ma
angabhodanaku deva
yamu madapa (duka)
Lekha nu daraposiri
Svadattam dvigunam punyam
Paradattanu palanam pa
radattapa harena svada
ttam nishphalam bhavetu (stone broken)
Shashtirvarsha saha
Srani vishtayam Ja
Yate Krimi: 11

Appendix 'C'

Additional List of old Temple Sites

1.	Nandagiri (near Mallial)	: Narasimha temple on the hill
2.	Nampalli	: Narasimha temple on the hill
3.	Nallagonda (near Vemulavada)	: Narasimha temple on the hill
4.	Beerpur (near Dharmapuri)	: Narasimha temple on the hill
5.	Elgandal	: Narasimha temple on the hill
6.	Dumpeta (near Koratla)	: Narasimha temple on the hill
7.	Odela (via Sultanabad)	: Mallikarjuna temple
8.	Kothakonda	: Virabhadraswamy temple
9.	Akkannapet (near Husunabad)	: Siva temple
10.	Chelpur (near Huzurabad)	: Siva temple in the fields Narasimha temple in the village.
11.	Kothagattu	: Matsyagiriswamy temple
12.	Ramagiri fort	: Sri Raka temple
13.	Deevakonda (via Mallial)	: Ruins of old temple
14.	Thotapalli (near Husunabad)	: Siva temple, Hanuman temple, Ruined single shrine temple.
15.	Gariskurthi (via Kurkiyal)	: Vaishnava temple
16.	Thangallapalli (near Koheda)	: Siva temple, Venugopalaswamy temple.
17.	Varkolu (via Husunabad)	: Siva temple

18.	Anpur (near Nampalli)	: Siva temple
19.	Ramancha	: Sri Rama temple
20.	Uppal (via Huzurabad)	: Ruins of old temples
21.	Illenthakunta (near Jammikunta)	: Sri Rama temple
22.	Kamalapur (via Huzurabad)	: Sri Rama temple
23.	Medipalli (near Jammikunta)	: Sri Rama temple, Venugopalaswamy temple
24.	Illenthakunta (via Sircilla)	: Saiva and Vaishnava temples
25.	Kallepalli (near Bejjenki)	: Venugopalaswamy temple
26.	Sanigaram (near Huzurabad)	: Ruined temple
27.	Jangapalli (near Bejjenki)	: Old temples
28.	Galepalli	: Old temples
29.	Molanguru	: Siva temple, Virabhadra Swamy temple
30.	Vempalli (near Raikal via Jagtial)	: Ruined Bhimesvara temple
31.	Mallapuram (via Metpalli)	: Somesvara temple on the hill
32.	Sundaragiri (near Husunabad)	: Venkatesvara temple on the hill
33.	Kodmial	: Ruined Siva temple in the fields beside vagu.
34.	Nachpalli (near Kodmial)	: Ruined small Siva temple, Ruined small Vishnu temple.
35.	Bhushanraopet (Via Koratla)	: Small Siva temple, Small Venugopala temple
36.	Gambhirpur (via Koratla)	: Ruined Siva temple
37.	Elkaturthi	: Siva temple in the village, Single shrine temple on the rock near bus-stand, dilapidated Siva temple in Dhobiwada.
38.	Boinpalli	: Small Siva and Vishnu temples
39.	Ramajipet (near Sircilla)	: Ramalayam
40.	Maredupaka (via Peddapalli)	: Nagula Mallikarjuna temple
41.	Thakkalapalli (near Mallial)	: Vaishnava temple in the fields

42.	Challuru	: Venugopalaswamy temple
43.	Kamanpur (via Peddapalli)	: Venugopalaswamy temple
44.	Rajaram (near Jagtial)	: Sri Rama temple on the hill
45.	Gudem (via Sircilla)	: Venkateswara temple
46.	Avunuru (via Sircilla)	: Vaishnava temple
47.	Veenavanka	: Venkatesvara temple
48.	Kondagattu	: Anjaneya temple
49.	Stambampalli (near Vemulavada)	: Small Siva temple
50.	Metpalli	: Kesava temple in old gadi

Illustrations

1. Dhulikatta. Buddhist Stupa.

2. Dhulikatta. Ayaka slabs. Muchilinda Naga.

3. Dhulikatta. Figure of a woman.

4. Pashigoan. Ayaka slabs of Buddhist Stupa.

5. Adavi Somanapalli, Cave Temple I.

6. Adavi Somanapalli. Cave Temple I. Garbhagriha.

7. Adavi Somanapalli. Cave Temple III.

8. Vemulavada. Raja Rajesvara Temple. Door

9. Vemulavada. Raja Rajesvara Temple. Holy tank.

10. Vemulavada. Bhimesvara Temple. Wall.

11. Vemulavada. Bhimesvara Temple. Pillar.

12. Vemulavada. Bhimesvara Temple. Mahishasuramardini.

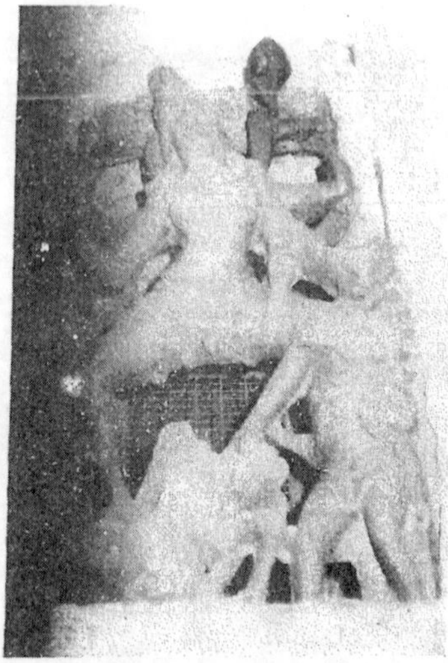

13. Vemulavada. Bhimesvara Temple. Jain Chaumukh.

14. Vemulavada. Bhimesvara Temple. Naga stone.

15. Vemulavada. Bhimesvara Temple. Surya.

16. Gangadhara. Bommalagutta. Jain Chakresvari.

17. Gangadhara. Bommalagutta. Adyanta Tirthankaras.

18. Dharmapuri. Ramalingesvara Temple. view from the South.

19. Dharmapuri. Holy tank.

20. Dharmapuri. Narasimha Temple. Mandapa.

21. Dharmapuri. Narasimha Temple. Brahma and Balarama.

22. Dharmapuri. Narasimha Temple. Dvarapala.

23. Choppadandi. Siva Temple.

24. Choppadandi. Siva Temple Wall.

25. Choppadandi. Devi. (Now placed in Karimnagar Museum).

26. Jammikunta. Siva Temple. Ganapati.

27. Sanigaram. Bhimesvara Temple.

28. Sanigaram. Mahalingesvara Temple. Ganapati.

29. Potlapalli. Jain image.

30. Potlapalli.Ganapati in archaic form.

31. Koratla. Mahadeva Temple. Parsvanatha.

32. Koratla. Mahadeva Temple. Prabha Mandali of Jain Image.

33. Polas. Pulastyesvara Temple.

34. Polas. Pulastyesvara Temple. Saptamatrikas.

35. Polas. Pulastyesvara Temple. Nagini with Mukuta.

36. Polas. Pulastyesvara Temple. Naginis.

37. Polas. Pulastyesvara Temple. Viragal.

38. Polas. Annapurna on Tank-bund.

39. Polas. Ganapati on Tank-bund.

40. Polas. Jain Image.

41. Polas. Venugopala Temple. Door jambs.

42. Nandi Mydaram. Nandi.

43. Nandi Mydaram. Amaresvara Temple. Naga Kanya.

44. Raikal. Trikuta. view from the South.

45. Raikal. Trikuta. Adhisthana. Detail.

46. Raikal. Trikuta. Pillar.

47. Raikal. Trikuta. Door.

48. Raikal. Trikuta. Kesava and Devi.

49. Raikal. Trikuta. Viragal.

50. Valgonda. Trikuta. view from the South-East.

51. Mallannapet. Mallanna Temple. view from the North-East.

52. Chilvakoduru. Trikuta. view from the North.

53. Chilvakoduru. Trikuta. Western Shrine.

54. Chilvakoduru. Trikuta. Dvarapala.

55. Chilvakoduru. Nandi Stambha.

56. Thotapalli. trikuta. Pillar.

57. Thotapalli. Trikuta. Door.

58. Thotapalli. Trikuta. Door jambs.

59. Bejjenki. Narasimha Temple. Pillar.

60. Bejjenki. Narasimha Temple. Base of the Pillar

61. Bejjenki. Narasimha Temple. Middle of the Shaft.

62. Bejjenki. Pillar. Capital Details.

63. Bejjenki. Pillar. Detail.

64. Bejjenki. Pillar. Churning of the Ocean.

65. Bejjenki. Pillar. Women with Play-sticks.

66. Bejjenki. Pillar. Drummer and Cymbal-beater.

67. Bejjenki. Pillar. Sculptures.

68. Bejjenki. Pillar. Sculptures.

69. Bejjenki. Pillar. Sculptures.

70. Bejjenki. Pillar. Sculptures.

71. Koheda. Mallanna Temple.

72. Kalesvaram. Main Temple.

73. Kalesvaram. Annapurna.

74. Kalesvaram. Ganapati.

75. Kalesvaram. Dvarapala.

76. Kalesvaram. Chaturmukha Linga.

77. Kalesvaram. Matsya-yantra.

78. Kalesvaram. Matsya.

79. Nagunuru. Main Trikuta. view from the North.

80. Nagunuru. Main Trikuta. Southern shrine.

81. Nagunuru. Main Trikuta. Upapitha. Detail.

82. Nagunuru. Main Trikuta. Wall. Detail.

83. Nagunuru. Main Trikuta. Panel below the door jambs.

84. Nagunuru. Garuda stambha.

85. Nagunuru. Temple beside the hill, view from the North-East.

86. Nagunuru. Temple beside the hill. Sikhara.

87. Nagunuru. Ganapati. (Now placed in Karimnagar Museum).

88. Nagunuru. Naga Stone.

89. Nagunuru. Siva Temple. Dvarapala panel.

90. Nagunuru. Siva Temple. Pillar sculpture.

91. Nāgunuru. Siva Temple. Pillar sculpture. Panchatantra tale.

92. Nagunuru. Trikuta beside P.W.D. Road.

93. Nagunuru. Small Temple near bus-stop.

94. Kothapalli. Trikuta. view from the South-West.

95. Kothapalli. Trikuta. view from the North.

96. Kothapalli. Trikuta. Wall. Detail.

97. Kothapalli. Trikuta. Door.

98. Jangoan. Main Trikuta. Partial view.

99. Jangoan. Main Trikuta. A section of the temple.

100. Jangoan. Main Trikuta. Bracket Figure.

101. Jangoan. Main Trikuta. Half pillars on the parapet.

102. Jangoan. Ruined Trikuta. Mandapa.

103. Manthani. Gautamesvara Temple. Wall.

104. Manthani. Gautamesvara Temple. A Ruined Section.

105. Chandravelli. Siva Temple. Wall.

106. Chandravelli. Siva Temple Adhisthana.

107. Chandravelli. Siva Temple. Door.

108. Chandravelli. Siva Temple. Ceiling sculpture.

109. Katkuru. Trikuta. view from the South.

110. Katkuru. Trikuta. Antarala Door.

111. Katkuru. Trikuta. A row of Miniature shrines.

112. Katkuru. Trikuta. Miniature shrines.

113. Godisala. Trikuta. Antarala Door.

114. Godisala. Trikuta. Sculptures below the door-jambs.

115. Godisala. Trikuta. Pillar.

116. Godisala. Trikuta. ceiling sculpture.

118. Godisala. Trikuta. Nandi.

119. Godisala. Trikuta. Bhairava.

120. Godisala. Single shrine Temples. Mandapas view from the East.

121. Mutharam. Trikuta. Southern shrine.

122. Mutharam. Trikuta. Antarala Door.

123. Mutharam. Trikuta. Upapitha. Detail.

124. Mutharam. Trikuta. Wall. Detail.

125. Mutharam. Trikuta. Wall. Detail.

126. Mutharam. Ganapati.

127. Thotapalli. (near Husunabad). Ganapati.

128. Rajaram (near Jagtial) Ganapati in Archaic form.

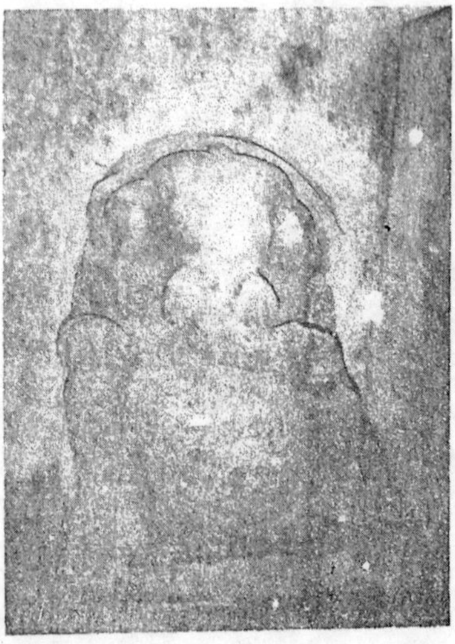

129. Gudimettapalle. Siva Temple. Antarala Door.

130. Gudimettapalle. Siva Temple. Pillar.

131. Vilasagar. Trikuta. Northern and Western shrines.

132. Vilasagar. Trikuta. Porch on the East.

133. Vilasagar. Trikuta. Wall.

134. Vilasagar. Hero stones.

135. Thimmapur. Trikuta. Extant Western Shrine.

136. Peddampet. Ruined pillar.

137. Peddampet. Figure of a woman. (Now placed in Karimnagar Museum)

138. Kasipet. Main Temple. Sikharas.

139. Kasipet. Pillar sculpture.

140. Ramagundam. Torana. From the East.

141. Ramagundam. Torana. From the West.

142. Neerakulla. Main Temple in river Maner.

143. Neerakulla. Miniature shrine.

144. Aravelli. Skanda. Vishnu. Nagini.

145. Karimnagar. Siva Temple. Doors.

146. Karimnagar. Siva Temple. Parsvanatha.

147. A model of Ganuvu (Oil-mill)

148. A model of Ratana (pulley device for lifting water)

Index